AMONG FRIENDS

CONTEMPORARY NORTH AMERICAN POETRY SERIES

Series Editors Alan Golding, Lynn Keller, and Adalaide Morris

Among Friends

Engendering the Social Site of Poetry

EDITED BY ANNE DEWEY AND LIBBIE RIFKIN

University of Iowa Press | Iowa City

University of Iowa Press, Iowa City 52242

www.uiowapress.org
Printed in the United States of America

Design by April Leidig

The University of Iowa Press is a member of Green Press Initiative and is committed to preserving natural resources.

Printed on acid-free paper

Library of Congress Cataloging-in-Publication Data
Among friends: engendering the social site of poetry /
edited by Anne Dewey and Libbie Rifkin.
pages cm. (Contemporary North American poetry series)
Includes bibliographical references and index.
ISBN: 978-1-60938-150-9, 1-60938-150-5 (pbk)
ISBN (invalid): 978-1-60938-171-4 (e-book),
1-60938-171-8 (e-book)
1. American poetry—20th century—History and criticism. 2. American poetry—21st century—History and criticism. 3. Poetry—Authorship—Social aspects. 4. Social networks—United States. 5. Mentoring of authors—United States. 6. Friendship. I. Dewey, Anne Day, editor of compilation. II. Rifkin, Libbie, editor of compilation.
PS323.5.A56 2013
811'.5409353—dc23 2012041961

CONTENTS

ACKNOWLEDGMENTS

SCHOLARSHIP RARELY HAPPENS in a vacuum, and we wish to thank the many people who have helped to make this book possible. First, we are grateful to the community of scholars whose work on gender, social poetics, or both has informed our own, including Rachel Blau DuPlessis, Andrew Epstein, Michael Davidson, Aldon Nielsen, Daniel Kane, Maggie Nelson, Bob Perelman, and the other scholars represented here. Two anonymous readers read the initial manuscript with generous attention and care. Their suggestions helped to strengthen the volume substantially. We are grateful to Lynn Keller, Adalaide Morris, and Alan Golding for their direction and encouragement as editors of the University of Iowa Press's Contemporary North American Poetry series, and for their example as scholars of contemporary poetry. A summer fellowship and sabbatical from Saint Louis University's Madrid Campus provided valuable time and resources to work on this project. Elisabeth Chretien of the University of Iowa Press, Sulma Farfán, and Adina Sandu were essential in preparing the manuscript. We thank them for their diligence and good cheer.

Second, we deeply appreciate the support of our friends who have inspired and enabled our work on friendship, particularly Randall and Lisa, to whom Anne dedicates this volume, and our families: our parents and Jane, Mario, and Gracian; Doug, Tess, and Joseph.

WE GRATEFULLY ACKNOWLEDGE permission to reprint the following published and unpublished material:

Daniel Kane's essay is an expanded version of "'Nor did I socialise with their people': Patti Smith, rock heroics and the poetics of sociability," by Daniel Kane in *Popular Music*, Volume 31, Issue 01 (January 2012), pp. 105–123. Copyright © 2012 Cambridge University Press. Reprinted with permission.

Lytle Shaw's essay is an edited version of "Non-Site Bolinas: Presence in the Poets' Polis," which appears as chapter 5 in his book *Fieldworks:*

From Place to Site in Postwar Poetry. Copyright © 2012 University of Alabama Press. Reprinted with permission.

Published poems by Robert Creeley: "As We Sit," "Bolinas and Me," and "Here" by permission of Penelope Creeley.

Unpublished material by Robert Duncan: Letter to Donald Allen, 13 March 1957, Donald Allen Collection, MSS 0003, Archive for New Poetry. Courtesy of Mandeville Special Collections Library. University of California, San Diego. Copyright © The Jess Collins Trust, used by permission.

Published work by Joanne Kyger: "Look the bird is making plans" and excerpts from *All This Every Day* by permission of the author.

Unpublished material by Joanne Kyger: by permission of the author and of the respective recipient or estate of the recipient, as follows: Unmailed letter from Joanne Kyger to Gary Snyder, 22 June 1959, courtesy of the Joanne Kyger Papers, Mandeville Special Collections Library, University of California, San Diego; Letter from Joanne Kyger to Gary Snyder, 5 March 1959, Letter from Joanne Kyger to Gary Snyder, 11 March 1959, Letter from Joanne Kyger to Gary Snyder, 5 May 1959, Letter from Joanne Kyger to Gary Snyder, 11 May 1959, and Letter from Joanne Kyger to Gary Snyder, 27 May 1959, all courtesy of the Gary Snyder Papers, Contemporary Literature Collection, Simon Fraser University, Vancouver, British Columbia.

Letter from Joanne Kyger to Philip Whalen, 19 January 1959, Letter from Joanne Kyger to Philip Whalen, 9 March 1960, Letter from Joanne Kyger to Philip Whalen, 23 June 1962, Letter from Joanne Kyger to Philip Whalen, 28 September 1962, Letter from Joanne Kyger to Philip Whalen, 23 January 1963, Letter from Joanne Kyger to Philip Whalen, 3 March 1963, and Letter from Joanne Kyger to Philip Whalen, 22 August 1963, all courtesy of the Philip Whalen Papers, Reed College, Portland, Oregon.

Letter from Joanne Kyger to Linda Russo, 20 March 2012 used by permission of Linda Russo.

Unpublished material by Sharon Mesmer: Telephone conversation between Sharon Mesmer and Maria Damon: 7 September 2010, used by permission of Sharon Mesmer.

Published poem by Jennifer Moxley: excerpt from "During this Revolution" used by permission of the author.

Published poems by Lorine Niedecker: "Consider," "Grampa's got his old age pension," and "T. E. Lawrence" used by permission of Bob Arnold, literary executor for the Estate of Lorine Niedecker, and University of California Press, © 2002.

Published poem by Patti Smith: excerpt from "female" used by permission of the author.

Unpublished material by Patti Smith: Letter from Patti Smith to Anne Waldman, n.d., used by permission of author and recipient and courtesy of Angel Hair Papers, Fales Special Collections Library, New York University.

Letter from Patti Smith to Anne Waldman, 24 May n.y., and Letter from Patti Smith to Anne Waldman and Michael Brownstein. n.d., used by permission of author, of the recipient, and of the Anne Waldman Papers, Special Collections Library, University of Michigan.

Unpublished material by Gary Snyder: Letter from Gary Snyder to Philip Whalen, 14 June 1959, and Letter from Gary Snyder to Philip Whalen, 5 July 1963, both from the Philip Whalen Papers, Reed College, Portland, Oregon, used by permission of the author.

Published poem by Gary Sullivan: "Fast-posting Flarfy" used by permission of the author.

Unpublished poem by Charles Vermont: "Vertical Portrait of Joanne Kyger" used by permission of the author.

Unpublished material by Anne Waldman: E-mail to Daniel Kane, 19 February 2012, used by permission of the author.

Published poetry by Lewis Warsh: "Definition of Great" and excerpts from *Part of My History*, used by permission of the author.

Unpublished material by Philip Whalen: Letter from Philip Whalen to Joanne Kyger, 12 March 1960, Letter from Philip Whalen to Joanne Kyger, 20 July 1962, Letter from Philip Whalen to Joanne Kyger, 1 November 1962, Letter from Philip Whalen to Joanne Kyger, 26 November 1962, Letter from Philip Whalen to Joanne Kyger, 12 December 1962, Letter from Philip Whalen to Joanne Kyger, 31 January 1963, Letter from Philip Whalen to Joanne Kyger, 8 March 1963, Letter from Philip Whalen to Joanne Kyger, 9 April 1963, Letter from Philip Whalen to Joanne Kyger, 25 May 1963, Letter from Philip Whalen to Joanne Kyger, 24 August 1963, and Letter from Philip Whalen to Joanne Kyger, 31 August 1963, all from the Joanne Kyger Papers, Mandeville Special Collections Library, University of California, San Diego, used by permission of Norman Fischer, copyright © The Whalen Estate and Joanne Kyger.

Published poems by Jonathan Williams: "John Chapman Pulls Off the Highway" and "Found Poem Number One" from *Jubilant Thicket: New & Selected Poems*, copyright © 2005 by Jonathan Williams, reprinted with the permission of the Permissions Company, Inc., on behalf of Copper Canyon Press, www.coppercanyonpress.org. "Onan's / Auto / Service" and "Found Poem Number One" granted by Thomas Meyer as literary executor of Jonathan Williams's estate.

AMONG FRIENDS

ANNE DEWEY AND LIBBIE RIFKIN

Introduction

Friendship would have to be not just "being liked." That one has to be likeable, accommodating. One would have to "like" also—i.e., like the other—and I think only by being oneself. Not accommodating.
—Leslie Scalapino, "Experience/'On' Sight"

LESLIE SCALAPINO'S portion of the piece that begins *Sight,* a long poem "written in pairs" with Lyn Hejinian, is an exercise in distinction. From the outset, Scalapino turns to face her coauthor in acts of differentiation central to her understanding of the collaborative work. Where Hejinian's statement stands as a more typical "introduction" to the project —what she describes as a "joint investigation into the working of experience"—Scalapino's offering responds to, performs, and preempts what her friend is saying to a degree that calls the "joint" status of the work into question. Hejinian states that "our emphasis was not on the thing seen but on the coming to see," a moment she calls "active and dialogic." Scalapino, for her part, describes and enacts the dialogue. Of the compositional process, she writes:

> Crossing "across" observation, "argument" which is a mode of extension—we tend to stay on our own "sides" in regard to the "subject" "experience." We attempt to draw each other across the sides of our "argument" or boundary, a form of pairs, and of friendship also.

Argument is everywhere in this internally contradictory passage. It is the live locus of exchange between the two sets of eyes engaged in acts of seeing and writing. It describes both a boundary and a meeting. If we follow the first sentence's appositional logic, argument becomes another word for observation, a sense of perception as always double—as Hejinian elsewhere puts it: "both thing and word . . . simultaneously immediate and mediate, in time and out of time" (*Poetry from Sojourner* 89, hereinafter *Sojourner*).[1]

Friendship is bound up in this complex sense of argument. It is enacted in extending out toward another person while maintaining one's own "side," the attempt to bring the other "across" to your experience, which, while necessarily failing, vitalizes the space between. "I want friendship that's real, because it occurs only," Scalapino says, capturing her sense of relationship as event. If being immersed in the present of shared "extension" is one of friendship's moments, realizing boundaries as the ground for self-articulation is another. Contentious, essaying, lived in writing, the friendship that Scalapino and Hejinian ultimately create in *Sight* is a form of what Hejinian would call the "language of inquiry," a "medium for experiencing experience" and, through the mediation of an other, recognizing that one is doing it (*The Language of Inquiry* 2–3).

Throughout the book-length prose poem, the two poets claim ownership of their interchanging segments by signing them with their initials. At the same time, they make liberal use of repetition, cycling words and phrases through the text to the point where authorial origins become unclear. As Scalapino insists in the passage we take as our epigraph, friendship hangs in this difficult balance between giving over and preserving "oneself." The seemingly simple possibility of "liking" another is contingent on sustaining a certain sense of singularity: "not accommodating." There is something of the cliché about loving yourself before you can love another in these lines, but with a keener sense of the distances traveled. "Being likeable" is not only a passive state, for Scalapino, it is a privative one, in the sense that "accommodating" entails fitting oneself to the other's dimensions. To achieve the capacity to actively "like" demands a resistance to what might in fact be the more comfortable condition of coming second, and arranging oneself accordingly. Instead, liking entails a hard-won discovery and maintenance of the limits of the self, in order to truly see and know the other in her difference. To like and be likeable, under the ever-changing conditions of experience, is the challenge friendship presents.

Historically, the positions of accommodating and not accommodating have mapped directly onto the gender/sex binary, and in most codified social relations it is still clear where one is meant to stand. A relatively unscripted relationship that we follow Scalapino in conceiving as uniquely inclusive of both positions, friendship presents transformative possibilities for women, and women poets in particular. We begin our introduction of this volume of essays on friendship, gender, and the social site of contemporary avant-garde and other movement-forging poetries with *Sight* both for its theory and practice of friendship and because of the fact that, begun by two poets affiliated with the Language school in 1993—a decade after the peak of its collective poetic production—the long poem enacts a feminist poetics explicitly outside the seemingly unified aesthetic agenda of the group. According to Hejinian, the potential "use" of a collaboration like *Sight* for a feminist poetics is the new kind of subject it can create: "The 'we' of collaborations is not the we of a gang;" she writes, "instead it can be the we of supervention, the we of surprise" (*Sojourner* 89). The essays collected here explore the ways in which friendships conducted inside poetic communities from the New American scenes through Language writing to Flarf and the African American writers' retreat, Cave Canem, both refract and seek alternatives to the varied features of the "we of a gang" that constrain the gendering of poetic voice, authority, and social positioning. In these intimate relations and the poetry that sustains them, we find spaces of contestatory, creative exchange, often more open to the surprises of difference and more revealing of the gendered conditions of poetic production.

The shared interest that launched this collection stems from our separate work on the way Denise Levertov's many and formative friendships with male poets illuminate the gender politics of her problematic position in the Black Mountain scene.[2] With a career that just manages to straddle the middle of the twentieth century and a fascinatingly ambivalent personal gender politics, Levertov's performance of and resistance to the female poetic roles historically available to her presents a complex subject of study. In her friendships with Robert Creeley, George Oppen, and, perhaps most notoriously, Robert Duncan, Levertov was notably *not* accommodating, in ways that proved pivotal in the careers of all of the individuals involved.[3] Like many of the friendships explored in this book, these relationships were conducted predominantly through letters, epistolary workshops set on the border between the public domains of political activism and the literary profession, and the more private spaces of poetic and personal self-fashioning. As a result, arguments between friends invite scrutiny on a range of levels: in terms of the psychodynamics of the poets individually and relationally, their developing poetic practices, and the large-scale social upheavals of the times that they shared.

Levertov's friendships with other poets reveal interesting fault lines in the often tacitly gender-blind allegiances of the postwar poetry community. For instance, her relationship with Creeley avoids the constraints of homosocial commitment that shaped his friendship with Charles Olson. Whereas loyalty to a common poetics and sense of identity structures Olson and Creeley's correspondence, Creeley and Levertov's is characterized by acknowledged differences in both poetic and personal conduct. This enables Levertov to be a critical sounding board for Creeley as he opens out from the tight lyrics he labored over with Olson to the looser poetics of his mid-career. While Levertov's friendships with Creeley, Duncan, and Oppen foreground gender or sexuality only occasionally, both issues become central as the friendships become unstable. As Levertov's political activity and changing poetics distance her from Duncan and Oppen, they react by feminizing her, illuminating the implicit homosociality of consensus and the volatility of gender as a stand-in for broader disruption during the intense questioning and change in gender roles of the 1960s. Duncan's poetry associates Levertov with a feminine otherness of public space characterized by heterosexual difference. Oppen's portrayal of Levertov as the embodiment of threatening, feminized revolutionary energy reveals the convergence of his association of women and their poetry with the domestic sphere, his anxiety about feminism's influence on political life and poetry, and his ambivalence about his own political position-taking. Not surprisingly, less scholarship has focused on the influence of these friendships on Levertov's own poetic development, but her numerous dedications and writing "toward" others configure dramatically different imaginative poetic forms.

The intriguing combativeness of friendships like Levertov's is certainly related to the personalities in the mix, but to read these dynamics in purely individual, biographical terms would be to miss the full range of their significance. As we discuss in what follows, friendships provide spaces for intersubjective becoming, through rivalry as much as through discovery of common ground. Desire for the friend is often bound up in the identity-forging dynamics of the relationship and—unchecked by conventions like married love or caught in institutional structures like mentorship—this charge can render them permanently unstable. Andrew Epstein's characterization of the highly collaborative, social poetics of the New York School poets as making "poetry . . . the continuation of friendship by other means," with its allusion to Clausewitz on war, captures the potential hostility in this creative negotiation between self and other (*Beautiful Enemies* 15). Friendship's extension across the boundary between public and private also enables us to read macrocosmic struggles—particularly the revolutions of gender and sexuality radiating out of the 1960s—in its intimate arguments. Friendships function not only as buffers against and wedges into poetic institutions whose exclusive gender politics would otherwise stifle women's poetic identity and practice, but also as microsites from which these institutions can be challenged and transformed. And, as in Scalapino and Hejinian's effort to share experience in *Sight*, friendships play out in writing, animating poetic language with distinctive intention, affect, and form.

Theorizing Friendship

This volume analyzes a variety of relations under the name of friendship. If this plurality of social affinities challenges the term's meaning, it also preserves an openness crucial to understanding friendship relative to other social and political relationships. We use the term "friendship" here to reflect voluntary intimate relationships—erotic or platonic, same sex and different, dyadic and nondyadic—often but not necessarily ones of affection or mutual support. Friendships form in the context of other social bonds (e.g., marriage or allegiance to a common cause) and may be shaped by them but differ from predominantly erotic, family, or patriotic ties. The intimacy friendship implies transcends the impersonality of such identity categories as race, class, or gender; unlike the "given" relations of family and political affiliation, friendships are chosen, opening a space of relative freedom in which to create new identities. As Michel de Montaigne writes, friendship "feeds on communication," having "no other model than itself" (139, 136).

Friendship's marginality compared to the more ideologically saturated roles of family member and citizen has led philosophers to consider its subversive or transformative function. John Stuart Mill and C. S. Lewis discuss friendship's potential to subvert patriarchal family roles and the collective identity of what Lewis calls "the herd."[4] Michel Foucault praises friendship (sexual or nonsexual) between men as capable of "inventing" new desires, pleasures, and relationships outside "the two readymade formulas of pure sexual encounters and the lovers' fusion of identity" ("Friendship" 136–37). Similarly, Adrienne Rich values friendships between women as nurturing "survival relationships" against her culture's idealization of romantic enthrallment as the most significant and defining relationship for women (56). Contemporary philosopher Marilyn Friedman analyzes friendship as a voluntary association that enables "communities of choice" to "reconstitute" seemingly natural identities of family or nationality, developing a fuller range of social nexes or constellations as potential sources of self-definition (287, 294, 301–02).

Insofar as these thinkers stress friendship's disruption of conventionally prescribed roles and the affective bonds and behaviors associated with them, they characterize friendship as *the* relation of difference. For two of the twentieth century's most powerful theorists of friendship, Hannah Arendt and Jacques Derrida, internal alterity is critical to the development of both individual and collective identity. Although both thinkers stress the capacity of friendship and its recognition of difference to transform other social bonds grounded in fictions of similarity or "fraternity," they differ in their understanding of the affect of friendship as well as its position with respect to larger social structures. For Arendt, friendship as local interaction is vital to "humanizing" the shared public world, whereas Derrida stresses friendship's power as extrapolitical relationship to rupture ties in the official body politic. They conceptualize how friendship can nourish the incorporation of difference into identity while sketching a spectrum of ways in which the emotional bonds of friendship can displace, negotiate, and transform civic allegiances.

Building on the Classical tradition of Aristotle and Cicero, Arendt views friendship as essentially public, "fundamental . . . for the well-being of the City" in its ability to transform our shared world (*Men in Dark Times* 24, hereinafter *Dark Times*). Arendt conceives of the "world" as that which "lies between people," an "interspace."[5] For her, identity emerges both from subjective expression of "who" one is through speech and action, and from the objective meaning assigned to those acts as reified by others. Whereas adhering blindly to ideology leads people to assign identity impersonally as "what" one is according to prefabricated categories and prescribes affective attachments to these identities through obfuscating and homogenizing sentimentality, friends recognize each other's uniqueness and have the capacity to develop a profoundly "humane" society (*Dark Times* 31). Only through friendship as "discourse," or "the constant interchange of talk," Arendt argues, do "the things of this world . . . become human for us" (24–25).

The "world" of friendship is both interpersonal and transpersonal, though inflected heavily toward the latter. As Michael Kaplan writes, "Arendt's 'friends' may be strongly committed to their own world, but this world does not seem to require . . . the participation of specific individuals." If, as Arendt stipulates, friends are loyal to the "interspace," "the individuals with whom this is comprised matter relatively less, except in a way mediated by the in-between" (Kaplan 33). "Sober and cool, rather than sentimental," individual participants in Arendtian friendships put aside private interests as well as ideological constructs to build a public realm shaped by all of its constituents (*Dark Times* 25).

Although she subordinates friendship to the *res publica*, Arendt would differentiate friendship from the figure of political fraternity through which it has been imagined, particularly since the eighteenth century. While recognizing the importance of unity among the oppressed or marginalized, she is wary of fraternity's exclusiveness, its inability to admit difference. Fraternity as an extension of the apparently universal or "natural" affect of compassion is clearly a necessity among "persecuted peoples," but it is "not transmissible" beyond the group (*Dark Times* 12, 13). Like Gotthold Lessing, to whom the lecture in which she theorizes friendship most fully is dedicated, Arendt values the "selective" nature of friendship over the "egalitarian" impulses of compassion and fraternity. Unlike fraternity, which can be a necessary escape but remains both mute and politically impotent, friendship "makes political demands" and "preserves reference to the world" (25).

Like Arendt, Derrida would distinguish friendship from "the economic, genealogical, ethnocentric, androcentric features of fraternity" that serve to unify the political state (237). Derrida focuses, however, on the rupture that this extrapolitical relationship produces in the public realm. Derrida's *The Politics of Friendship* builds on Friedrich Nietzsche's notion that the interchangeability of friend and enemy disrupts the "fraternization" of identity "as the symbolic bond alleging the repetition of a genetic tie" (99). Socializing with the friend becomes "a matter of thinking alterity," a mode of relationship free from "alleged universalism," or a conception of citizenry through "nationalisms, patriotism, or ethnocentrisms" (232, 236–37). Unencumbered by the "symbolic bond" that would produce the illusion of equality through the insistence on sameness, friendship concedes "the irreducible precedence of the other" (99, 63). Derrida's friend, like Nietzsche's, is "incommensurable" (62). Nietzschean "good friendship" comes with a "warning . . . not to give in to proximity or identification, to the fusion or permutation of you and me. But, rather to place, maintain or keep an infinite distance within [it]" (65). Unlike Arendt, whose friends yield their individual identities to the "interspace" produced between them, for Derrida, it matters a great deal that friends' "irreplaceable singularit[ies]" be preserved within the relationship (72). The maintenance of "distance within" friendship is here conceived as salutary, as it is in Hejinian and Scalapino's collaboration. As we will see in some of the relationships examined in this volume, however, the effort to resist "the fusion or permutation of you and me" can also lead to the end of friendship (65). Barrett Watten's discussion of various forms of belated separation from and individuation within the Language school's *The Grand Piano* project is one strong example.

The importance of "distance within" friendship situates Derrida, following Nietzsche, in a disjunctive tradition of conceiving a "community of those without community" developed by Georges Bataille, Maurice Blanchot, and Jean-Luc Nancy (Derrida 37). Nietzsche's "Among Friends," the epilogue to *Human, All Too Human,* imagines the book's reception by a group of friends in a pastoral setting outside time and history, united by a deep longing for the moment when "we reach the grave together" (Nietzsche, qtd. in Derrida 57). Their silent contract is a "tacit agreement" to come together without surrendering solitude (54). If Arendt's friendship is foundationally discursive, living and building a public realm on dialogue, Derrida's friends "ally themselves in silence within the necessity to keep silent," in order to maintain the relationship in the face of the truth of its instability—the fact that the other will never be wholly accessible to me (55). The social bond that friends share lies, according to Derrida, in this unspoken agreement to be alone together.

While not a direct citation, the title of our collection alludes to this Nietzschean notion of a bond forged in the affirmation of being "unbonded," a relationship in which difference, even disjunction, is fundamentally inscribed. Nietzsche's scene of reading, whether conceived in the most intimate dyadic terms or expanded into a broader concept of literary history, is another locus of the "incommensurable" friendships the essays in this volume explore. These are, after all, friendships "among" poets, and whether they are avidly reading and creating the conditions for each other's work—as Linda Russo argues for Joanne Kyger and Philip Whalen—or reaching out across catastrophic millennia, as Maria Damon claims Flarf poets and Dante Alighieri do, they build ties that disrupt the "fraternization" of tradition as well as contemporary literary community.

Among Friends mounts the argument that friendship is a promising site from which to trace the changing gender politics of post-1945 avant-garde and antiestablishment poetry. By studying how the intimate relationships that form the bedrock of community shape the poem as social site, these essays reveal tensions marginal and internal to the group as significant contexts of creativity and sources of change in poetry communities. This volume is designed to engender a more fine-grained understanding of the intersections of the literary and the social by examining poetic communities from the inside. As we conceive it above, friendship is a particularly rich space in which to analyze the fault lines in controlling ideologies of poetic institutions and practices, and to explore the intersections between the micropolitics of the literary community and the changes rocking the larger social and political landscape. Attention to the shape and tenor of both dyadic relations and looser, nondyadic networks of friends incites surprising new ways of thinking about the "we" of poetic subjectivity—compelling multilayered social understandings of poetic authorship and experience.

Gender and the Limits of Community

Friendship is a valuable site not only for understanding individual poets' enactment of gender relative to the social conventions of their time but also for rethinking recent literary history. As complement to the centrality of literary community in much criticism, it is particularly valuable in illuminating the redefinitions of poetic authority and association that have changed poetry as form and institution since Civil Rights, second wave feminism, gay rights, and other movements for racial, sexual, and gender equity. The poetics of community and organization of literary history around communities have been a productive focus for mapping literary history since the birth of the modernist avant-garde. As a crucial source of mutual support and promotion, group manifestos, alternate canons, little magazines, and anthologies have organized much post-1945 literary history. Communities have served, in Michael Davidson's terms, as "enabling fictions" to establish a countercultural poetics, as "not only a vehicle of personal expression but a complicated intertextual and dialogical field" (*The San Francisco Renaissance* xi, 17–22). Alan Golding's argument that such strategies alter poetic production and subsequently critical constructions of the canon (114–43) is borne out by critical treatments of the emergence of the New American Poetry, the Black Arts Movement, and the "Asian American avant-garde," which trace such growth from local scenes to national prominence and canonical category.[6]

Despite our efforts to compile a volume that would explore the intersection of friendship, gender, and poetic community across races and ethnicities, the relative absence of this kind of scholarship on the work of writers of color has led to a collection that analyzes predominantly white writers in communities whose self-definition stresses formal innovation rather than racial or ethnic identity. The lack of attention to race in criticism on white poets has limited the scholarship on the relationship between poetics and group dynamics whose evolution we trace below, while greater critical attention to race in poets of color has tended to focus interpretation of their poetry and social relations through the lens of identity. In analyzing the reception of innovative African American and Asian American poetry, Aldon Nielsen and Timothy Yu observe the tendency to study individual authors (rather than poetry communities) and key themes often derived from a "textual coalition" of identity traits.[7] Across the spectrum of criticism, the false but all too prevalent dichotomy between aesthetics and identity erases the contribution of minority writers to poetic innovation and obscures the sociopolitical dimension of white avant-garde movements (Nielsen 9–12, 39–41; Yu 49–50).[8] Poets and critics are beginning to break down these boundaries. The Black Took Collective, whose essay completes this volume, is a group of three younger poets who identify with a black avant-garde lineage even as they interrogate notions of blackness and avant-gardism. Founded in 1999 by Duriel E. Harris, Dawn Lundy Martin, and Ronaldo V. Wilson at Cave Canem, Black Took calls for "dissonance" within the African American writers workshop's entrenched traditions of lyric and narrative poetics, opening up formal spaces for hybrid performance art as well as social spaces for countering dominant constructions of race and sexuality.

Although many practices discussed in this introduction are characteristic of post-1945 poetry communities that profess race-based as well as race-blind poetics, it is with an awareness of the interpretive limits above that we outline the volume's contribution to the evolution of criticism on the New American Poetry and its successors. Within this critical tradition, understanding of the role of community in poetic production has become increasingly nuanced—from an initial homogenizing identification of "schools" to increasingly flexible models like the "nexus" and, most recently, analyses of how a community's social dynamics form its poetic subjects.[9] This last area of inquiry increases understanding of the poem as social site, the way the literary artifact both responds to and constructs the dense fabric of social interaction within which it is immersed. Daniel Kane characterizes the Lower East Side poetry community as a generative locus for a "poetics of sociability" that changes with the scene's fluid membership while it shapes the poets' work (*All Poets Welcome* 162, hereinafter *All Poets*). Lytle Shaw's "rhetoric of coterie" identifies a "mode of address and an actual context for that address" that constructs different communities or interlocutors and correspondingly different structures of self, challenging and exposing "historically inflected assumptions about community" and the limits of "universal" poetic voice (*Frank O'Hara* 4–7).

While a focus on community coincides, to a great extent, with the way poets represent themselves publicly, it has proven problematic for analyzing the role of women in poetic production. Avant-garde poetic communities reflect conventionally gendered Cold War constructions of cultural authority. Davidson's *Guys Like Us* traces how Cold War "heroic masculinity" and "compulsory homosociality" shaped a broad spectrum of the period's poetic subcultures (16–18). Libbie Rifkin's *Career Moves* argues that antiestablishment white male poets position themselves through an appeal to professionalism that reproduces constructions of masculine authority in Cold War culture.[10]

Much criticism replicates these authority structures. Highlighting men's roles as spokespeople, authors of key poetic statements, poetic genealogies, and editor-reviewers, it constructs men as the main agents of literary production and innovation. Canon formation and reception tended until recently to allocate one token woman to each school, often problematizing her right to a position within the group and failing to recognize women's agency in shaping poetic tradition. As early as 1989, Davidson reflects on the difficulty of placing women in *The San Francisco Renaissance*, "because the standard definition of the movement has no way of including them" (197). Women poets and the gender issues that emerge in critics' discussion of them are often granted separate chapters rather than integrated into analysis of the community itself. Conversely, the focus on community can obscure connections between women beyond the boundaries of poetic and critical communities. Laura Hinton and Cynthia Hogue observe that experimental women writers "are rarely found in conversation with one another because of aesthetic but also political, regional, and ethnic differences" (4).

Feminist critique has begun to identify the social and poetic conventions that have relegated women in the communities discussed in this volume and femininity to subordinate positions, or ignored them entirely. Kane's history of the Lower East Side poetry community in the early 1960s describes New York literary communities as largely "male enclaves" characterized by sexual and gender hierarchies in which men held the majority of power in the publishing and reviewing world, their gender masked by their poetic authority, and women, lacking such power, tended to be sexualized (*All Poets* 20). Kathleen Fraser writes about the absence of women experimental poet models, of "wait[ing] to be taken up by powerful male mentors," in scenes divided into male writers with one "token woman" (*Translating the Unspeakable* 29–31) in which men theorized and women were "sex objects who wrote poetry" (qtd. in Kinnahan 51). Maggie Nelson and Russo suggest that women's reluctance or indifference to writing manifestoes reflects their sense of disenfranchisement from or marginal status within a masculinist genealogy of tradition (Nelson 232–33; Russo, "Poetics of Adjacency" 148).[11] Feminist analyses of poetic form such as Rachel Blau DuPlessis's *The Pink Guitar* and *Blue Studios* and Linda Kinnahan's *Lyric Interventions* identify how profoundly gender hierarchies influence generic and formal conventions of lyric subjectivity, poetic inspiration, and the abstraction privileged in experimental poetics.

Although most critics recognize that significant changes have occurred in gender and sexual politics, the focus on community and its authority structures makes it difficult to identify other forms of agency and thus to evaluate how changes in gender roles and conceptions of sexuality have altered the Cold War structures of poetry communities that Davidson traced. Recent studies begin to map women's roles in shaping poetry communities and articulating innovative poetics. DuPlessis shows how second-generation New York and Beat women poets, especially Anne Waldman, redraw the gender line through leadership positions in publishing and teaching poetry ("Anne Waldman"). Ann Vickery's feminist genealogy of Language poetry identifies women-centered loci of poetic production. While the communal structures on which Vickery focuses—critical tradition, little presses and magazines, and discussion—are institutions that have characterized the avant-garde and writing about it, she explores how women use these structures to create support for and redefine experimentation with a feminist focus. Along similar lines, Elisabeth Frost traces women poets' need to establish a tradition of women's experimental writing to secure their belonging to the canon, and Holly Laird explores coauthorship between women.

While important in recognizing women's agency in avant-garde and antiestablishment poetry communities, studies of women in these communities tend to focus on how they inhabit structures of authority that mirror those of the masculinist avant-garde and may fail to recognize the emergence of new gender politics. Accession to such authority structures can of course reproduce as well as transform them.[12] Moving forward, we must also look outside these structures to identify new sites of women's poetic production. Some recent studies have begun this project, examining arenas of production beyond and within the traditional structures of community in order to rethink women's roles.[13] It will be important for such initiatives to critique the terms developed to interpret white women's experimental writing by recognizing the different contexts and agendas shaping the way white poets and poets of color reconceive authority and rewrite femininity and women's bodies.[14]

Yu argues that "after 1970, the question of race became central to the constitution of *any* American avant-garde" (1). From the vantage of individual friendships, this collection makes a similar argument about the role of gender, beginning as early as 1945. The essays in the first section of the volume explore how friendship reveals the gendering of poetic authority in a variety of institutions: readings, publishing, mentoring, the anthology and literary lineage, and the muse. The two women poets discussed by Russo and Kane craft epistolary and performance spaces in which to appropriate, challenge, and transform these institutions, simultaneously struggling with the politics of the gendered body implicit in them. Whereas Kyger writes herself out of masculinized forms of authority, Patti Smith uses male homosocial friendship to establish a masculinized "romantic" vatic presence that coexists in tension with the androgynous and feminine self-representations of her poetic peers in the second generation New York School. Using friendship as an optic, these essays expose gender hierarchies pervading a variety of institutions and the ways in which women begin to reconfigure these hierarchies as the postwar period extends into the 1960s and early 1970s.

The volume's second section contains essays that develop new perspectives on the gender dynamics of avant-garde communities by viewing these communities through the lens of the friendships that compose them, both dyadic friendships and friendships among members of a group. Shaw's essay on the hippie colony of Bolinas analyzes how the interpersonal relations framing poets' representations of the collective project reveal the gender tensions in their idealized visionary "present." Watten's, Peter Middleton's, and Damon's essays explore modes of collaboration that depart from the normative solidarity of the avant-garde community, from the early editorial struggles over *L=A=N=G=U=A=G=E*, to the highly structured long-term collaboration of a second phase of Language poetry in *The Grand Piano*, to the blog and email exchange among a cluster of friends that gives rise to the new coterie poetics of Flarf. Together, these essays show the individual negotiations within communities that fight, fracture, and queer the masculine and homosocial conventions that have characterized avant-garde authority since the early twentieth century. They thus begin to map new configurations of experimental poetry emerging in the post-feminist, digital age.

While the essays in section three focus, like those in the first section, on the role of dyadic friendship in poetic production, the third section explores the ways in which friendship shapes the poem as a social site whose space, voice, and form emerge through intersubjective exchange. Ross Hair's analysis of shared imagery in letters and poems by Lorine Niedecker and Jonathan Williams constructs an alternate poetics and lineage opposing those of the more public communities with which each poet was associated. Epstein examines the eruptions of sexual tension in Rae Armantrout and Ron Silliman's attempt at gender-bending collaboration. Vickery reveals the way Jennifer Moxley's friendship with Helena Bennett nurtures a new sense of self beyond relationships to family, poetry community, and tradition. All three essays show the possibilities that friendship offers for reimagining gender roles and their influence on poetic conventions.

The volume's concluding piece, "Black Took Collective: On Intimacy & Origin," performs these possibilities by investigating the relationship between origins and intimacy and how the body both resists and inhabits the gendered, raced, and sexualized projections of the American psyche. Through email discussion and shared writing, Harris, Martin, and Wilson reproduce the intimacy the Collective achieves in its staged performances, disrupting the idea of origin as a singular site as well as the notion of a stable, unfractured, identifiable self. In this epistolary essay and in the poetry and performances they produce, friendship offers a space of "fraught safety," where disagreement, annoyance, desire, and love make way for new forms of freedom—lived in language and on the body.

NOTES

1. Also published online as "Delirious Hem: A Tribute to Leslie Scalapino," by Ruth Lepson. lesliescalapinotribute.wikispaces.com/file/view/Ruth+Lepson4.pdf

2. Dewey, "Gendered Muses;" Rifkin, "'That We Can Somehow Add Each to Each Other?'" and "Reconsidering the Company of Love."

3. Levertov's relationship with Duncan has received the most attention, most comprehensively in Gelpi and Bertholf; Dewey, "Gendered Muses."

4. Mary Lyndon Shanley argues that the mutual respect of friendship is essential for breaking down what Mill sees as the "corruption of male-female relationship" in marriage (267–68); Lewis 39–47.

5. Whereas "On Men in Dark Times" focuses on the role of the "interspace" in the social fabric, *The Human Condition* views social interaction from the perspective of the human subject, describing this fusion of individual and collective as "inter-est," intersubjective being in which the potential for self-realization through meaning assigned by others lures engagement in the public world (182).

6. The "Asian American avant-garde" is Timothy Yu's phrase. Such studies include Howard Ramsby's and James Smethurst's analyses of the institutions and agents that generate the Black Arts Movement and Yu's of the establishment of "Asian American literature," all of which demonstrate the key role little magazines, editorial choices, and anthologies play in this process.

7. See Nielsen, 54. Yu builds on the work of Sau-ling Cynthia Wong to argue that mainstream reception of Asian American writers interprets a formally diverse body of writing through a "textual coalition" (Wong's term) of themes and tropes seen as representative of raced identity (Yu 101–04).

8. Several scholars bridge the divide. Smethurst shows that interracialism and the contribution of African American, Puerto Rican, and Asian American individuals and culture are "constitutive elements" of what is often termed the white bohemia of US Cold War culture (38–43, 55). Meanwhile, groups on both "sides" seek to evade the constraints of such categories. At the same time, significant

differences exist in the way that formal poetic claims and identity claims shape poetry communities. Kimberly Lamm criticizes Yu for eliding sociopolitical and aesthetic categories and not recognizing sufficiently the role of racism in constituting African American identity (831).

9. Early attempts to define "schools" or movements with a common poetics include, for example, studies of Black Mountain, New York School, and New American poetry by Ed Foster, Geoff Ward, and Ekbert Faas. More flexible approaches to community include Rachel Blau DuPlessis and Peter Quartermain's "nexus," conceptualized as a "genealogically," "situationally," "reception"-based association with some common definable aesthetic concerns, an organizing principle that can "embrace contradictions" as well as "bind, join, or connect" to "contribute to new ways of narrating literary history" (*The Objectivist Nexus* 2–3, 17–19), and Dewey's focus on Black Mountain poets' differing interpretations of a common poetics of "composition by field" in *Beyond Maximus*. Kane's *All Poets Welcome* develops the concept of a poetics of sociability.

10. Masculinist posturing in the group and in public statements may belie less conventional gender roles in one-on-one interaction. Women poets who critique the group's masculinist bias often express gratitude for the support of men poets in the same group.

11. Nelson cites Alice Notley's view that "the whole idea of a literary movement, the academy, the avant-garde, are all male forms" (qtd. in Nelson 133). Selective reception may also play a part in the perception of women as agents. Levertov's "Some Notes on Organic Form," for example, was much read and discussed but is rarely considered a representative manifesto.

12. See, for example, Rifkin's contrast of Waldman's and Bernadette Mayer's styles as workshop leaders in "'My Little World Goes on St. Mark's Place.'"

13. Lynn Keller's "Just one of / the girls" analyzes how, before the widespread publicizing of second wave feminism, women try to extricate themselves from the positions defined by the gender politics of these communities. Keller's *Thinking Poetry* develops new reading strategies based on innovative structures in experimental women poets' writing. Sara Lundquist demonstrates that collaboration between women establishes alternate social sites for artistic production to combat women's subordinate roles in poetry communities. Her study of Barbara Guest's collaborations with painters Grace Hartigan and Mary Abbott argues that collaboration freed both artists to explore their bodies, femininity, and imagination in a space more expansive than that which had previously characterized their work.

14. For example, bell hooks contrasts white feminists' tendency to polarize power relations between the sexes with black feminism's emergence in the solidarity between black men and women against common race oppression (70–71, 78–79). For hooks, white middle class women's embrace of liberal individualism stems from the chance to benefit from a "machinery of power" inaccessible to

black women (9–12, 62–63). Cheryl Clarke's *After Mecca* stresses revolutionary reconstruction of blackness as the primary context for feminist creativity in Black Arts poetry by women. Renée Curry summarizes structures of white privilege in women's poetry (e.g., invisibility of race, assumption of mastery or equality, ignorance of the other) in *White Women Writing White* (1–19).

PART ONE

Friendship and Women's Poetic Careers

ONE | LINDA RUSSO

How You Want to Be Styled

Philip Whalen in Correspondence with Joanne Kyger, 1959–1964

IN THE SAN FRANCISCO SPRING of 1959—just after "The San Francisco Scene" issue of the *Evergreen Review* shared editor Donald Allen's view of a new generation of writers and just before his anthology *The New American Poetry 1945–1960* would present a national portrait of the same—Joanne Kyger sat down to type a letter to Gary Snyder, then in Japan. Things, she informed him, were "quite hysterical with activity now with [Allen] Ginsberg and Don Allen here—Allen soliciting young boys and old poetry—everyone trying to get published."[1] Intentionally or not, this conflation of the two Allens portrays the male-centeredness of postwar poetic communities. It also hints at the contingency of literary communities and their self-constructed genealogies, and how these further extend to "trying to get published." Whether Ginsberg is retrospectively soliciting "old poetry" (from Whitman or Blake, for example) to elicit a filial connection in his own poems or whether either or both men are vying for the attention of "young boys," the suggestion is that poetic success(ion) and the male body work hand in hand.[2]

"Here," for Kyger—then a twenty-four-year-old poet who in time would publish over fifteen books of uniquely styled Buddhist-inspired poems with a social acuity and a keen interest in capturing the immediate, phenomenal world—revolved around Robert Duncan and Jack Spicer and a community of writers for whom poem and social environment were inextricably linked. The rhetoric and poetics of this time and place "synthesized matters of art, politics, and social theory into lifestyle" facilitating "alternative forms of community" both set apart from and critical of conservative contemporary mores, and thus the so-called Spicer Circle fulfilled a need for a sense of community in a homophobic society prior to gay liberation (Davidson, *The San Francisco*

Renaissance 29, 28, hereinafter *San Francisco*). In this social climate, membership was, arguably, *the* problematic for women writers; these alternate literary formations nonetheless maintained contemporary American society's gendered terms, taking shape as the "boy gang," that is, "the social organization most true to the artist," to use a phrase that came to Ginsberg (the story goes) in a dream (Johnson, 79, qtd. in *San Francisco* 176). In Duncan's preferred metaphor, the "boy gang" could make room for significant women: "We were the champions of the boys' team in poetry," he declares, allowing that "Joanne Kyger could play on the team, but she was a girl" (qtd. in *San Francisco* 175–76).[3] Even her nickname affectionately endowed to her by John Wieners, "Miss Kids" (Kyger referred to others as "kids" as a term of friendly affiliation), reveals her to be a female version of the (male) "kids" in the gang, but also an "outsider" whose presence helps reinforce the boundary that was necessary to define the "insiders." The intertwining of literary and (homo)sexual interests reinforced this boundary.

What's interesting here is not so much the acts of social boundary-making that facilitated a specific sense of community, but the fact that the chosen metaphors with their emphasis on contemporaneity belie the radical historical project of such alternative kinships. It is helpful to view these social formations against the "naturalized bonds of family" as Lytle Shaw does in his analysis of the "nominal family" implicit in the poems of Frank O'Hara (*Frank O'Hara* 29). He sees in O'Hara's naming of friends an attempt to "supplant" the biological family as site of the "transmission of culture" and to therefore present an alternative to "the filiative model" of the Great Tradition proposed by T. S. Eliot (*Frank O'Hara* 29).[4] In O'Hara's case, a fixed model of the family (parents and offspring) is unseated for a model based on the "local contingencies" of friendships and their shifting associations (*Frank O'Hara* 29). The articulation of gangs and teams of the San Francisco Renaissance similarly formed "nomimal families," and this casting of literary formation as purely social enables a reconfiguration of literary genealogy—the transmission of poetic "culture" from one to another—along strictly male lines of inheritance; self-defined concepts of family not only heighten but necessitate homosocial relations which may seem to form "naturally," just as boys "naturally" want to pal around with other boys. But these groupings are marked by ideologies that enforce the value of selected traits, such as maleness. Thus thinking through tradition becomes a way to stabilize categories of gender difference on which the exclusion of women poets relies.

The particularly exclusive tenor of this atmosphere is painfully obvious. How and why, then, did women persevere? Apparently, the depth of these entrenched exclusions was not immediately transparent to all involved. Kyger's own sense of poetry as "like marriage" exhibits the understanding that there *is* a "family" that a woman might join. Her comments reveal an understanding of joining and requiring the performance of membership not so much through participation in the contemporaneous formation, but through sharing its lineage: "Poetry is like marriage. [. . .] It's an attractive family with a long lineage which is as healing and [. . .] kvetchy as any family. [. . .] You have to be willing to be part of the *family history,* and I was really willing" (Kyger "Congratulatory Poetics" 112, hereinafter "Congratulatory," emphasis added). In retrospect, the distinction between this poetic community's synchronic and diachronic aspects seems clear enough. But what's fascinating about Kyger as a literary figure during the postwar period are her negotiations with her own developing understanding of this situation. For Kyger, the process of figuring out how to be a part of this community went hand in hand with parsing the significance of synchronic and diachronic connections.

While Kyger is often unquestionably swept up in the embrace of the "Beat generation," closer examination of this early period in her poetic career (1959–1964) lays bare some of the fissures in the "enabling fictions"[5] of poetry and gender during the San Francisco Renaissance. A closer look at the influence of these specific senses of community and genealogy on the development of her poetics allows for a more comprehensive sense of the ideologies underpinning the social sites of post–World War II avant-garde poetics. This is particularly significant during a period when the definition of poetics is being configured through male embodiment and sexuality, both homo- and hetero-, and the female body emerges repeatedly as a site whereupon homosocial values are reinscribed.[6] Davidson makes a compelling case for how women poets operating in the margins of the San Francisco Renaissance appropriate the "patriarchal ideology [that] pervaded the poems" (*San Francisco* 177) at that time, and indeed, the poems Kyger wrote in the early 1960s are particularly telling because they bear witness to a shift in her approach to her relationship to her mostly male community. Her social and literary relationships to several men inform this shift, but her long-distance friendship with friend and mentor Philip Whalen (they exchanged over fifty letters from 1959 to 1964) is particularly important. Whalen, who was ordained as a Buddhist monk in 1973, published five books during this period, establishing his poetic practice of tracking the ordinary mind experiencing its unfolding life. His letters served several functions, but most important, they provided an alternatively gendered social site that broke down the boy-gang barriers so that poetics, gender, identity, and genealogy could be enacted and discussed. In this way, they played a crucial role during the period that Kyger, from abroad (she lived in Japan from 1960 to 1964), came to terms with the limiting gender configurations of the social realm as she began to grapple with the larger genealogical project apparent in *The Tapestry and the Web* (Four Seasons Foundation, 1965).[7]

I Believe in a Group Poetry

Synchronic and diachronic aspects—"family" and "family history," to use Kyger's terms—are figured in the contrasting emphases of Spicer and Duncan, each tempered in different ways to the gender politics of this era's masculinist rhetoric. Spicer is well known for inducting members as kin through nightly social rituals in North Beach bars, and for effecting a group organization tinged with "cultishness" (Davidson, *San Francisco* 176) and insularity, "held together by pledges of loyalty and claims of territoriality" (Davidson, *San Francisco* 153).[8] A sense of insiderness was bolstered by claims against outsiderness, evident in his infamous localism and disdain of "squares" and the media-mugging Beats alike. As "teacher, critic, and goad," Spicer, on the one hand, maintained a "public forum in which poetry could be debated and argued into existence" and, on the other, fostered chaos and discord (Davidson, *San Francisco* 153, 29). He strongly supported "Blabbermouth Night" at The Place—a "kind of Dada free-for-all" (Ellingham and Killian 99) in which contestants, by spontaneously and nonsensically performing verbally, competed for prizes—because it helped reinforce the sense of community "essential for survival" among poets, according to Davidson.[9] Along with these synchronically stabilizing gestures, Duncan's esoteric approach to a poetic genealogy discovered through the body of the poem provided a sense of the "family history" as fluid, as an archive continually under construction. Their differences together articulated a set of practices central to the coherence of a poetic community whose values diverged from the then-dominant New Critical view.

Within this context, conflicting impressions of Kyger's status abounded: sometimes she was a muse, other times an emerging poet, a tenuous position that reflects the complementary frames presented by her mentors' poetics. Despite Kyger's willingness (and Duncan's approval), she was occasionally dismissed. Granted, it wasn't an easy group to belong to.[10] Younger poets sensed that "failure to attend the nightly bar scene was not far from treason and might result in ostracism"[11]; demands were high, with all-nighters resolving into a new day of banter, and Spicer's pugilistic approach, for better or worse, often set the tone. Kyger could be called on to play the part of "the dumb blonde" (Kyger, "A Conversation" 150), to flaunt the feminine masquerade; on at least one occasion the verbal banter emphasizing her sexual difference left her feeling "faceless" and "like a public institution which is a topic of conversation for everyone" (thoughts she would admit only to herself in an unmailed letter).[12] Thus contemporaneous performances secured poetics as a masculine, homosocial realm.[13] For someone who was only conditionally included, whose presence in the group might be invoked to mark out its *boundary*—as one who "could play on the team, but" only in some unspecified, but specifically gendered capacity—"membership" does not entail a definite position. She could not, like the men, acknowledge a lineage of forebears that confirmed poetry as a gender-appropriate activity. As a muse-figure, she has no genealogy; she is configured as an appendage to the male poet, a role Rachel Blau DuPlessis finds emblematized in Charles Olson's privileging of the syllable and more so in the incestuous union between "brother mind" and "sister ear" that produces it. Sister ear, collecting and translating messages for the brain, is a physiological mechanism only, "perch[ed] on the male mind of the male poet" (DuPlessis, "Manifests" 47). The (active) poet-mind/(passive) muse-ear binary manifests in the circular reasoning that a woman couldn't be a poet because she couldn't have a muse; according to the Cold War era's heteronormative terms, this would require "feminizing" a male for the purpose.[14] According to her own portrayal, Kyger had been playing the ear, one that whispers back to alleviate male poets' anxieties; her work took the form of "warm[ing] people up and pat[ting] them on the back and bring[ing] them messages, as some way of using [her] wits and questioning them" ("Congratulatory" 113). As an intellectual activity, this muse-like strategy seemed to work until she grew wary of being expected to "get into the dumb blonde routine" (Kyger, "A Conversation" 150).

It was an exchange one made, presumably, for the social benefits of belonging to a group. The Sunday Meetings, in particular, provided "two years of continuous poetry experience [that] served as the field of training for most of the Spicer / Duncan circle of young writers," including Kyger (Ellingham and Killian 152). Her own expression of her fears of being "groupless" attests to how powerful and necessary this connection was. Lamenting her plight with a tinge of self-parody, she wrote to Whalen, "all the White Rabbits are dead and gone and I don't belong to a GROUP any more and besides that everything is lovely."[15] Belonging to a "group"—in this case one that cohered around White Rabbit Press[16]—went beyond affiliation; the group was a dialogic site, a gathering of voices and arguments around shared ideas about poetry—an idea Kyger echoes in a 1974 interview: "In an ideal way I believe in a group poetry, a group of people writing in and out of the same thing, because that's the only way a voice gets strong" ("A Conversation" 151).

Willing to Be Part of the Family History

Participating in the social rituals of poetic synchronicity—learning the craft, giving readings and collaborating on performances, publishing in little magazines—reinforces a sense of currency, of belonging. It is how one realizes their "part" in a group. But entering into the lineage inducts one as a poet quite differently. The same gender boundaries and binaries worked in favor of men who could find their corollaries in the past and turn each other into poets. This is evident in the letters of Snyder, Lew Welch, and Whalen. Before they blew into San Francisco by 1958 carrying the seeds of Zen, they had for years been cocreating their lineage, with one reconfirming for another signs of their poetic parentage. Comparisons to Ezra Pound and William Carlos Williams reappear like pencil marks on a doorjamb to measure each other's progress. Williams, whom they had met as students at Reed College, served as a guide to new territory. Pound presented an unfinished map in his failure to understand the geography and culture of the western United States. That he "left something undone," Snyder wrote to Whalen in 1954, was "a great virtue" (qtd. in Gray 52). Welch spurred Snyder on: "Pound didn't get the point of those great big mountains, and you do. So make a language that talks about them better than his did" (qtd. in Gray 52).[17] As Timothy Gray points out, "if Anglo-American modernism could be rewritten to honor the particularities of the West Coast, Welch surmised, [Snyder] was certainly up to the task" (51). Despite the close friendships Kyger formed with these Northwest poets, this lineage, fitted to them like worn leather boots, seemed to raise blisters for Kyger. Having had no direct contact with important predecessors, she lacked a confirmation of her place. She felt like a "dumb failure" because she was too "coward" to write to Williams, as she reported to Whalen in 1962; her overinflated fear that Williams "will die before I ever write him" appears to have been realized.[18] That she felt she *had* to write to Williams—that this link to a past was a necessary gesture—is, in itself, telling. This relationship could elicit a feeling of intergenerational contact that poets around her often articulated as an intimate set of familial connections—from "papa" Pound to various "father" and "uncle" figures. In a gesture of inclusion, in one letter Whalen refers to Welch as Kyger's "Uncle Lew."[19] But this sort of connection must be confirmed at several points, like a web, and lacking the sort of social network through which connection is verbally conferred, Kyger was not yet "of" this lineage.

Such historical-social-poetic formations, as an alternative to New Critical poetry in the postwar period, are precisely what Allen was on the lookout for. His *The New American Poetry* anthology would unite the diachronic and synchronic dimensions of this alternative tradition, presenting current "families" of regionally affiliated poets (with some sense of genealogy suggested in presenting Olson as a figurehead) and extending a modernist lineage by positioning the anthology's contributors as "a strong third generation" following upon "the older generation" of early twentieth century poets (xi). Younger poets were conscious of Allen's project; Welch, for one, took steps to gain his attention.[20] Though Spicer likely recommended Kyger's work to Allen,[21] and while she may have been momentarily bolstered by this, she might not have expected to be included; by her own estimation, her poetry was still "looking for its proper direction, unique," as she wrote to Snyder—a feeling that was probably spurred on by the swiftness with which the scene was taking its textual shape.[22] To Snyder she wrote: "I start to get panicky and have to think over and over, be true to the poem be true to the poem so that I won't start writing things that people will like and that will be satisfying to everybody and understandable and publishable and in the end pure shit and not Joanne Elizabeth's poetry at all."[23]

Allen's solicitations heightened her concern about her status as a poet, and her determination, in response, to write "Joanne Elizabeth's poetry" suggests that she was less worried about social acceptance—that is, to the extent that writing "understandable and publishable" poetry would assure her status as part of a group—than she was about finding her place in the continuum of a poetic genealogy. A lineage is something one can join, given the proper attitude—an idea Bob Perelman reconfirms in his analysis of how poets position themselves toward the past to create a sense of poetic "generations." Perelman distinguishes "inheritance," which is "a matter of luck or grace" that "only happens to specific poets," from an "irreducibly democratic" kind of connection, which he calls poetic "influence" ("Fucking" 201). Duncan's sense of lineage has a built-in flexibility, calling on something not so loose as "influence," yet less happenstance than "inheritance" because hinging on the poet's willful surrender to the mysteries of the poem. Through writing poets made contact with their predecessors and discovered correspondences "in the sense of Yeats' discovering his cult of ancestral spirits in Swift and Blake" as Duncan put it, and the poem itself reveals the continuation of tradition (Duncan, "Introduction" 88). Kyger's call to "be true to the poem" suggests inheritance is less a matter of luck and grace, and more a matter of being present to the writing of the poem. But however much Duncan's nuanced understanding of poetic continuity was gender-inclusive, and however much his "feminization of tradition" (Davidson, *San Francisco* 130) provided an alternative to the masculinist imperatives through which modernism was propagated into contemporary poetics, and however much Duncan's sense of lineage *could* accommodate Kyger's emergence as a poet, synchronic social dynamics called for gender performances that conspired against it.[24]

If the issue for Kyger is finding a context in which she could "respond to the demands of immediacy" (Davidson, *San Francisco* 127) and thus write "Joanne Elizabeth's poetry," the fact that she was preparing at this time to join Snyder in Japan is significant. The trip might promise, at least, a removal from the gender-contrariness she confronted, and spending time with Snyder, a figure on the fringes of the San Francisco Renaissance, might suggest an escape from its centrifugal energies. Indeed, in his own specificity as a Buddhist, philosophically inclined, nomadic mountain-climbing poet he was plainly different. In the months before her departure, in letters in which they both worried over how she would fare in the socially arid climate his situation offered, Kyger professed to Snyder that she was ready to leave her coterie lifestyle behind: "I don't care about there being no boheme [*sic*] bars or parties [in Kyoto]—they never really meant much to me and function hardly at all in my life—only a means to escape in the past and I have no desire to run away now."[25] On the contrary, these social sites can be overwhelming, and her removal to Japan could be seen as granting an opportunity to shift from maintaining her position in social performances to figuring out why it required so much maintenance. Yet my sense is that though the move alleviated certain social tensions, Kyger merely exchanged one set of expectations for another—the Spicer clan's for those of her husband-to-be, Snyder—and that her concerns were reformulated around this new role.[26] In the end, however, her new situation would present a liberating social distance from her poetic community, a distance that also facilitated her correspondence with Whalen, where she could air her concerns and reconfigure her relation to the social realm of poetry and its problematic ideologies.

Do You Suppose Joanne Kyger Will Go Screaming Mad with Boredom & Nobody but Me to Talk to?[27]

"Running away" into a busy social life would not be a temptation in Kyoto, as suggested by these words Snyder wrote to Whalen prior to Kyger's arrival, which subtly jest at her love of the social aspect of poetry. Yet the wariness he expresses was not unfounded. Not because it anticipates that Kyger would often be bored and lonely as the wife of a dedicated Buddhist acolyte who arose in the morning dark to attend to studies and temple duties and spent his evenings meditating—these she was—but because they accurately portend the difficulties she would encounter as a poet isolated from her community. Travelling to Japan presented complications: a language barrier, an unfamiliar, relatively unmodernized city and its alienating culture, and a temple setting unwelcoming to her own efforts at zazen.[28] In all, her new domestic situation was physically and psychically trying. The usual difficulties of relocating one's life must have compounded the sense of dislocation from community. Visits from American poets were infrequent. The socially conservative Ruth Fuller Sasaki, who, as director of the First Zen Institute of America, had hired Snyder, hosted occasional dinner parties, but there was, simply, no social network that Kyger could fall into. She seemed wary, expressing to Snyder prior to her departure doubts about having adequate support: "It will perhaps be more than you will be able to give or spare w/your attention to zen studies [. . .]. I know that I need warmth and reassurance and probably much when I first arrive."[29]

Whalen's letters from across the Pacific provided some of this attention, but they more importantly maintained a sense of connection to the community she left behind. Gossip provided a conduit to her poetic home; their exchanges extended its literary conversations and energies. Whalen inveighed her to "stop fussing about and correcting your verses [and] WRITE MORE POEMS."[30] He acted as agent, placing her poems in the hands of editors of a few of the little magazines that were an important facet of emerging alternative poetic communities in the postwar period—occasional and regular publications that, along with poetry readings, workshops, and other gatherings that serve as sites of information exchange between mentors and friends, manifest the web of associations that provide a sense of contemporaneous family for poets.

In the absence of a shared geographic place and its daily interactions, little magazines played a significant role as textual manifestations of connection, and for Kyger this seems to have been intensified not only by her distance from her community, but by her uncertain place, as a female, within it. This is evident in the events that shook out after Kyger's first publication from abroad. When several poems appeared in *Foot*, edited by Richard Duerden, in 1963, not only were dates she considered an important aspect of the poems missing, but the poems were attributed to "Joanne Snyder" in the table of contents, with "(née Kyger)" appended under the text of the poems. (Kyger and Snyder had wed in Japan soon after she arrived; this appellation was to make the poems identifiable to her friends, Whalen later explained.)[31] This gesture of retrieval was not adequate; she had wanted to be known by her so-called maiden name. While she doesn't explain her dissatisfaction, "Snyder" in effect replaced *her* name, the one under which she had previously given readings and published, the one under which she is a poet and not a wife of a poet, and this editorial assumption offered a window onto how others—Whalen included—saw her. But naming, and the married name as it signifies a shift in identity, is only part of the issue. Through this San Francisco magazine, as a representation of a social space within which her poems "performed" her identity, she could maintain continuity with her "past" self as a constituent of the community she had left behind. This misnaming disrupts this performance. Whalen responds by exhibiting care, asking her "how you want to be styled" for future reference.[32]

Whalen does what he can to stave off her uncertainties more generally. His letters avidly encourage her writing, and he seems to have solely sustained her appearance in print. They provided a compassionate chorus, with comments like "Donald Allen was much impressed with your stuff, don't kid yourself,"[33] and "All the world is delighted with your poems."[34] He confirms that she has garnered Duncan's continued interest, who, Whalen writes, "says he really ought to write to you & how to begin? [. . .] I told Duncan to write to you all about poetry, that you'd enjoy that."[35] Yet while he was helping her stay connected, he was also prompting a shift in her poetic affiliation away from the

Spicer Circle.[36] He bluntly reported their reception of her appearance in *Change*: "Stanley said they were very unimpressed with your poems. Of course all they're impressed by is each other, or by Jack Spicer. It is a closed world."[37] Tellingly, it was not the kind of news she'd hoped for[38]—though her published poems, Whalen assured her, "shine."[39] His always unconditional support contrasts starkly with the reports he sends. For instance, several unflattering portraits highlight the tactics that spring up in Spicer's version of the polis. He "simply continues his old habit of writing lampoons & manifestoes & tacking them up in the gentlemen's room at various bars in North Beach," Whalen writes.[40] This caricature seems designed to encourage Kyger to recognize the gender exclusivity of this "closed world." More so, he details the "Horrible idiot squeals & grimaces" that result from Spicer's agitations amidst a generally boisterous scene with "Everybody mad at everybody else and enjoying every minute & squeak of it"[41]—words that might promote a new perspective on the coterie she had left behind.[42] At the same time Whalen nudged her away from a "not too inerrsting [*sic*]" Spicerian cosmology: "I still think a lot of that particular section [. . .] sounds like Spicer. [. . .] Take away the hell stuff," he advised of one poem, "& I'd like hit [*sic*] better."[43]

And If I Get Noisy G. Will Get Mad

Her response to the misnaming episode in *Foot* passed with just a little spilled ink, but it suggests a shift in her concerns away from securing her place in a literary family (being part of a group) and toward understanding her place in a *literal* family that threatened to affect her social role. Here Kyger's concerns about her agency and identity are palpable, and in her letters we get a glimpse of an attempt to resolve the domestic identity she'd been plunged into with the poetic identity she was trying to nurture.[44] She writes querying about the wife of another famous poet: "What was Dorothy Pound's problem anyhow, why didn't she ever *say* anything [. . .] She certainly doesn't seem to show any initiative."[45] This question poses Shakespear as a representative of a particularly female problem in the literary field: silence. Whalen wagers she "was just a continuous Inspiration or something"—that is, Pound's muse—but Kyger requests "a better evaluation" of "Mrs. Pound" who was "silent all the time."[46] Married to a self-proclaimed son of Pound, Kyger is perhaps trying to unearth the "literary" roots of ideas about how she *should* sound: how will her shift in social status affect her reception when she returns to San Francisco as the wife of a famous poet? Thinking about their projected trip to San Francisco (it never occurred), Kyger complains in a letter to Whalen that "nobody will pay any attention to me because I'm a wife and if I get noisy G[ary] will get mad."[47] The right kind of attention has been difficult to achieve; Kyger often expresses frustrations over feeling a loss of this in the company of men. Her comment in a letter to Whalen from India, where the couple had met up with Ginsberg in 1962, confides that she didn't get along with him in part because "He wouldn't pay any attention to what I sd."[48]

Her sense of the relationship between gender, noise, silence, and literary and social identities is particularly significant if she's unearthing something of a literary tradition of wifely silence. In the very least, the new "Joanne Snyder," she seems to feel, in the tradition of the literary Mrs., can't make the sort of "noise"—a term that reverberates with the capers of Spicerian "Blabbermouth Nights"—that the old "Joanne Elizabeth" had. While her prior social identity is problematic, silence isn't the solution. She needs to create an independent position, one that is clearly readable, to avoid the danger of being eclipsed by the traditional but still actively constructed sense of the female role as wife and muse. Kyger's identity conflict could be resolved, she felt, through the poem: "If I wrote some good poems," she comments in a letter to Whalen, "I wouldn't need any attention."[49] Text, in other words (the published poem that presents a poet to a community and vice versa), can stand in for the dislocated social self by garnering sought-after "attention," literary and social, that can be taken as a sign of belonging. And publishing a "good" poem means, to Kyger, claiming her place as a poet within her community, thus alleviating the need to call attention to her social self by "getting noisy."[50]

I Live Every Day for the Mail[51]

Whalen's letters created a venue for discussing her poetics (apparently the only venue available to Kyger) and thus filled in for her absent San Francisco mentors. One letter details his theories, offering an alternative to Duncan's and Spicer's senses of the poem as originating "outside" the poet: poems are "examples of modes of being," he writes; they are what "exists in my own mind"—i.e., they exteriorize this, as graphs of a mind moving, to use Whalen's well-known phrase.[52] In this regard, Whalen is Kyger's closest poetic peer; her practice of capturing consecutive phenomena owes much to this sense of the poem, particularly because he conceptualized the poem not as an end in itself but a means to "self"-realization. As he wrote in a 1960 letter to Ginsberg, Whalen was eager to "make new stories, poems, metaphors" which make it possible to "get started on the way to figuring out for yourself what you are" (qtd. in Falk 104). Stressing the "what" rather than the "who" not only undoes the stable definition of self at the heart of Western metaphysics—an undoing prompted by an exploration of Eastern philosophy for many poets of the Beat generation—it also unhinges poetry from gender as a category of difference: "Poetry is what we do."[53] This inclusive phrasing dissolves troubling binaries: she is not only wife or muse to the poet but is herself also a locus of activities, intellectual, creative, and domestic.[54]

Whalen's conceptualization of poetics—as wrought through multiple acts of being that constitute one as such, as a form of self-realization—emerges as a kind of gender critique of the social aspect of poetry in the hands of Kyger in "Look the bird is making plans." Whalen found this poem "strange but exciting,"[55] and it is clearly taking steps in a new direction. The poem presents the activity of a hybrid bird / woman figure transcending gender-segregated spheres, the "upstairs" rooms where men (poets, presumably) talk, the kitchens where women idle: "Look the bird is making plans / talking to men in the room upstairs / poking at crumbs in the kitchen" (Kyger, *About Now* 83). The title echoes a snide comment one might make to others regarding "the" woman in their midst, thus portraying women's status from a male perspective (she might be dubbed a "bird" or a "chick," and he, the predatory "cat"). One imagines also the catty japes stitched through an evening with Spicer at The Place. This poem was included in her letter to Whalen worrying about "getting noisy" and soliciting his opinion of Dorothy Shakespear, and it replays gender ideologies that commonly define marriage in this period: the diminutive female in the figure of the bird, selflessly attending to domestic duties: "& whose rights do I worry about / Keep the house." Mid-poem, the gesture of apostrophe grammatically (con)fuses the "I" of the poem and the bird:

> I'll
> go bird you keep this place
> at the very farthest wall
> pushing & scratching to get out (Kyger, *About Now* 83)

A confusion in subject-verb combination, typical of Kyger's early poems, dually identifies the agent of the "pushing & scratching" as both the I and the bird, yet a distinction between these two figures is necessary if the I is to escape entrapment.[56] The confusion is resolved in the final line, where the I refuses this scenario: "I'm going"—i.e., leaving her bird-self behind. Within the larger autobiographical frame of *The Tapestry and the Web,* this declaration resonates with her own "heroic" return to San Francisco and her divorce from Snyder. But this poem also suggests how, with Whalen's urgings and through situations from her immediate social context, Kyger creates some subjective distance from then-prevalent ideas about women's roles. In this poem a new self emerges to navigate the social sites of poetry with a sense of control over her circumstance and thus her identity. Writing herself *into* the role of the poet by separating herself from the domestic "bird," in other words, Kyger reinscribes her role in the social realm.

Kyger had expressed a desire for her poems "to do something fantastik [*sic*] and original," and, apparently, here it was.[57] Whalen responds with irrepressible praise—he is "totally overwhelmed" by these "real live poems"; they are "superb," "something," "beautiful work"; "I never saw such ones."[58] But by the time she received his reply, she had already written to say that "the poems aren't any good I realize now."[59] Why? Because, apparently, they are the product of a female mind: "I feel now you can only be a good poet if you['ve] got a good controlled strong honest mind," she writes, whereas "women's writing and minds tend to be more elusive, sloppy and vague then [*sic*] men's—more trying to articulate an emotional life which seems to be of primary importance [. . .], to women only. It's not very interesting reading is it."[60] Retrospectively we can speculate whether Snyder's gender-essentialism may have been playing a part in prompting such insecurity.[61] Apparently responding to the misogyny echoing throughout her comments and assuming the deprecating notions of the Spicer Circle to be their source, he counters with: "I still don't think that Stanley Persky and Jack Spicer are in total control of poetry. Their ideas about it have been expressed long ago [. . . they are] bankrupt European poopoo [*sic*]. Don't you believe it."[62] Once again Whalen attempts to derail Kyger's reliance on Spicer. His letters offer a particular view of her San Francisco community, but more importantly she was not pressured into a particular performance, as muse or wife or as that figure of slightly lesser stature, the "female poet." They provided an enabling, because alternatively gendered, space in which Kyger could process the gender-loaded experiences as reflected in "Look the bird is making plans" and to imagine anew her relationship to contemporary social sites.

One of Two "Male-Females"

Whalen had, in the time they spent together in San Francisco, taken part in her transition away from the raucous social scene around the Spicer Circle (they both roomed at the East-West House, a residence centered on Buddhist practice, in 1959); it's clear that he cared deeply about her, and it's hard to say how intentionally unsettling he meant his communiqués to be. But he seems to have used their correspondence as an opportunity to complicate his own gender identity. Responding again to Kyger's worries about her "female lineage," so to speak, as constituted through perceived limitations of the female mind, he presents himself as a gender-bender, flatly challenging prohibitive gender binaries with an effete self-portrait that undercuts the performative swagger of Spicer's public goading: "I feel horribly distracted & don't want to do anything except lie down & read Gertrude Stein or set here & write a novel about spiders & cotton strings, buttermilk & nasturtiums. I must also wash clothes, & how shall I find the strength to walk down to the Laundromat."[63] Sounding like a beleaguered housewife himself, he shows sympathy toward the challenges of the domestic sphere—although he deftly reverses the usual paradigm. It's not housework that leaves him too tired to write, but the other way around. He offers himself as a model of bigendered subjectivity, able to tackle intellectual debates even while beset by housekeeping chores; his letters alternately deliver disputations on poetic form and stir-fry recipes. By presenting himself as a figure in which the literary and nonliterary coexist; by presenting their correspondence as an alternatively gendered site—a space that neutralized the gender ideologies that dictated many of her own insecurities about her status—their friendship escapes the pitfalls of the era's sexual politics. In this regard, the news and performances Whalen's letters bring may serve as a palliative, deflating the import of the (masculine) public sphere prevalent in contemporary poetry.

As a gender-bender himself, perhaps he is more open to viewing her as his gender-bending equal. One comment he makes is compelling in this regard: "So anyway you now have a giant underground reputation in the avant-garde as being really way far out and up there, leading the muses, just as you ought to be doing and I am very pleased indeed."[64] These words seem to be designed to flatter her muse sensibility, even as they acknowledge how "far out" people consider her as a poet.[65] That is, Whalen, as a representative of her poetic community, holds a space for her there, as both muse (her old social role) and poet (her new social role). Facilitating is, in fact, the role Alice Notley conceived for Whalen in her fantastical genealogy of American poetic innovation, *Dr. Williams' Heiresses*. She dubs him one of two "male-females" of his generation and thus in a position to usher women poets into existence.[66] In Kyger's case, this seems to be due to how he created a textual space—in their correspondence and through his work as an agent—for Kyger to develop her poetics, to "real"-ize her "self" as poet despite the masculinist poetic context of post–World War II American poetry.

NOTES

1. Joanne Kyger, letter to Gary Snyder, 5 March 1959, Gary Snyder Papers. Henceforth letters in this collection are denoted as "Kyger to Snyder" with date.

2. What Bob Perelman dubs the "esoteric poetic inheritance" of Ginsberg's "Whispered Transmission" is a good example: this refers to the sexual relations that connected Ginsberg with Whitman through a succession of men who had slept with someone who slept with Whitman, in which, Perelman writes, "physical contact [. . .] in its underlying logic is actually re-embodiment" ("Fucking" 201).

3. He includes other women on his San Francisco team (Helen Adam was "godmother," Fran Herndon "head poster-maker").

4. Eliot: "the primary vehicle for the transmission of culture is the family." *Notes Towards the Definition of Culture* (qtd. in Shaw, *Frank O'Hara* 29).

5. This phrase is used by Davidson (*San Francisco* ix) to refer to myths about origins that blend seamlessly with literary history and that, when presented as a narrative of unified events and figures, may be taken *for* history. In the case of the San Francisco Renaissance, Davidson argues, these fictions obscure the role of opposition as a constituent feature, and in this regard the reductive characterizations of this period as dominated by Beat literature (and related in merely anecdotal histories) are particularly problematic, because Beat is in turn dismissed as a lifestyle rather than a set of valid and historically significant literary practices. This reductive gesture, I would argue, extends to the misappropriation of Kyger as a "Beat" poet when she is rather a genealogically syncretic poet whose poetics and identity are informed by oppositions in the larger literary field.

6. One instance of this is Spicer's notorious attack on Denise Levertov, delivered in the public reading of his poem "For Joe" in January 1958 while she was making a guest appearance at San Francisco State University's Poetry Center. "For Joe" offers to explain how select people won't understand "why men don't like women" and exclaims that "The female genital organ is / hideous." Also according to Ellingham and Killian, "all present felt implicated in Spicer's misogyny" (124).

7. There is more to be said about this project than can be put forth here. For a start, see "Dealing in Parts and Particulars: Joanne Kyger's Early Epic Poetics" (Russo, 2002) for a treatment of *The Tapestry and the Web* as enacting a genealogical project.

8. These ideas have a history of their own in the Berkeley Renaissance coterie Duncan, Spicer, and Robin Blaser had created to nurture their work in the late 1940s, where "gayness, poetry and community [were] of a piece" (Damon, *The Dark End of the Street* 160). Their medieval sense of kinship can be seen as prefiguring the San Francisco Renaissance as a larger poetic movement that instilled a sense of community. See Damon 153 ff., and Davidson, *San Francisco* 28ff.

9. Davidson elaborates: "The creation of a literary avant garde depends on complicated forms of bonding and self-definition that establish authority within the group. To the outside, such bonding may seem exclusive and narrow, but to the initiates it is essential for survival. Literary infighting and warfare [. . .] are important components in strengthening resolve and developing a strong platform. If this creates insularity, it also forges important types of opposition since by controlling who is 'in,' the community may also legislate who is 'out'" (*San Francisco* 28).

10. This is clear when one reads the literary-critical portraits of Spicer by Davidson ("Compulsory Homosociality"), Damon (*Dark End*), and Ellingham and Killian.

11. Dora Geissler interview, quoted in Ellingham and Killian (146).

12. Kyger, unmailed letter to Snyder, 22 June 1959, Joanne Kyger Papers, Mandeville Special Collections Library, University of California, San Diego.

13. Davidson provides a compelling analysis of models of performance and action marked by gender that constructed poetics as a male performance in this period. Spicer in particular, he argues, favors a poetics of masculinized action over feminized "reflection" and, further, forecloses the role of the feminine (and by extension women), reclaiming discourse as a "heroic," masculine social form ("Compulsory Homosociality" 201, hereinafter "Compulsory").

14. Kyger recalls encountering this ideology through Snyder, who "told [her] that a woman couldn't be a poet because she couldn't have a muse" ("Congratulatory" 113). And the fact that even within a context that already challenged gender norms (such as the Duncan-Spicer circle) a woman couldn't "feminize" another serves as further proof of how this alternative community maintained the sense of poetry as "man's work."

15. Joanne Kyger, letter to Philip Whalen, 19 January 1959, Philip Whalen Papers. Henceforth letters in this collection are denoted as "Kyger to Whalen" with date.

16. Joe Dunn and Graham Mackintosh's White Rabbit Press grew out of Spicer's Magic Workshop (February to May of 1957)and published books by Duncan, Spicer, Olson, and Sunday Meeting attendees Harold Dull, George Stanley, and Ebbe Borregaard—people she gathered with several times a week. The Sunday Meetings were sometimes given over to press business. See Ellingham and Killian, 112–15.

17. Timothy Gray explains that though Whalen and Snyder would "continue to respect Pound and Williams for their literary daring, and especially for their Asian-inflected poetics, they found themselves edging closer to a rugged West Coast style grounded in local landscapes and the oral literatures of indigenous cultures" (51).

18. Kyger to Whalen, 28 September 1962.

19. Philip Whalen, letter to Joanne Kyger, 12 March 1960. Joanne Kyger Papers. Henceforth letters in this collection are denoted as "Whalen to Kyger" with date.

20. Welch wrote thanking Whalen for "softening up Don Allen," to whom he had sent "neat copies of a generous sampling for consideration" (Welch 140), suggesting that by this date Whalen was assured a place in the anthology. That Whalen and Snyder had already impressed Duncan as "having Pound" was significant to Allen's decision as well (Duncan, letter to Donald Allen, 13 March 1957, Donald Allen Collection).

21. Kyger wrote to Snyder on 11 May 1959: "Evidently Spicer and others have been talking to [Donald Allen] about my stuff and so now I get included in the general hauling away of San Francisco material."

22. Kyger had also experienced recent throes of anxiety elicited by her first public poetry reading, which put her "on the verge of complete nervous idiocy," as she further wrote to Snyder, because she "had discovered that no one poem was fit to

read"; she had been "convinced [. . .] that the reading was going to be a complete Failure" (Kyger to Snyder, 11 March 1959).

23. Kyger to Snyder, 5 May 1959.

24. For instance, Duncan cited, in his introduction to his reading at the Poetry Center in 1956, Stein, Moore, and H.D. as among personal influences and "great inventive Masters of our day" (Bertholf 80), and while Duncan's influence is reflected in Allen's introduction to the anthology, the final gender ratio of *The New American Poetry 1945–1960* presents a different reality in that four out of the forty-four poets included were women (Helen Adam, Madeline Gleason, Barbara Guest, and Denise Levertov).

25. Kyger to Snyder, 27 May 1959.

26. A letter to Whalen provides some details about the circumstance of their marriage (which happened very soon after she arrived in Japan): "I [. . .] feel very trapped and you can't imagine what ideas that boy has about marriage and what a wife should be" (9 March 1960). These early letters are laced with hyperbole, but it seems safe to say that Snyder had clarified certain expectations.

27. Snyder to Whalen, 14 June 1959, Philip Whalen Papers.

28. The Daitoku-ji temple where Snyder studied provided a separate temple where women could sit zazen (meditate), but the same Buddhist training that men received was not available to women.

29. Kyger to Snyder, 27 May 1959.

30. Whalen to Kyger, 31 January 1963.

31. Whalen to Kyger, 31 January 1963. This makes little sense, since Kyger's friends would know she was by then married to Snyder (the marriage was publicized in Bay Area newspapers). In another attempt to appease her, Whalen admits that he had become accustomed to addressing letters to "Joanne Snyder," which seemed to be her preferred name. The reasons for this editorial decision seem to be unclear even to Whalen.

32. Whalen to Kyger, 8 March 1963.

33. Whalen to Kyger, 12 December 1962.

34. Whalen to Kyger, 9 April 1963.

35. Whalen to Kyger, 26 November 1962.

36. Whalen placed her poems in *Foot* (ed. Richard Duerden) and *Change* (ed. Ron Loewinsohn), and not magazines associated with the Spicer Circle (*J* and *Open Space*).

37. Reference to either George Stanley or Stan Persky, both members of Spicer's circle who edited magazines (*J* and *Open Space* respectively) in which Kyger's poems appeared. The letter from Snyder cited in the next footnote suggests it was Persky. Whalen to Kyger, 25 May 1963.

38. As a consequent report from Snyder informed Whalen, "Joanne was terribly cast down by that pipsqueak Persky's criticisms of her recently published poems.

The style of his letter was rather pretentious etc. but she shdnt [*sic*] be so vulnerable" (Snyder to Whalen, 5 July 1963).

39. Whalen to Kyger, 25 May 1963.

40. Whalen to Kyger, 1 November 1962.

41. Whalen to Kyger, 26 November 1962. This was likely in reference to Spicer's *The Heads of the Town up to the Aether* (Auerhahn Society, 1962).

42. It's true, too, that Kyger had begun to reposition herself vis-à-vis Spicer before she departed for Japan through the parodic "Dharma Committee" she initiated; its jabs at Spicer, while thoroughly Spicerian, could also be taken as a separating gesture. See Ellingham and Killian, 144–55.

43. Whalen to Kyger, 31 January 1963.

44. She'd shared her take on their marriage in a letter complaining that when they went to the consulate to sign some forms that Snyder dismissed as "registering," he nonetheless directed her to "put down Snyder instead of Kyger." She felt that signing her name thus "made it legal," as though she got "TRICKED into getting married" (Kyger to Whalen, 9 March 1960). It's unclear whether this is playful hyperbole on her part, though it's clear that their marriage—a union required by Ruth Fuller Sasaki—was something she gave into not entirely freely.

45. Kyger to Whalen, 23 January 1963.

46. Kyger to Whalen, 3 March 1963.

47. Kyger to Whalen, 3 March 1963.

48. Kyger to Whalen, 23 June 1962.

49. Kyger to Whalen, 3 March 1963.

50. It's interesting to speculate whether her physical (social) absence even augmented her attempts at a textual (genealogical) presence. Not in the sense that her absence spurred curiosity about her work (perhaps it did), but in that it was a helpful circumstance given the period's gender dynamics.

51. The sentence quoted in full: "I live every day for the mail, things will get better won't they, thank you for telling me to work on my book perhaps I won't be so snively [*sic*] if I can do that" (Kyger to Whalen, 9 March 1960).

52. Whalen to Kyger, 20 July 1962.

53. Whalen to Kyger, 20 July 1962.

54. In this way, both Kyger and Whalen cultivated a poetry capacious enough to accommodate a broad sense of self.

55. Whalen to Kyger, 24 August 1963.

56. Just how this grammatical ambiguity reflects gender inequity becomes clearer when the circumstances of the poem are taken into consideration. "The bird" is an allusion to a housekeeper of sorts, an educated and divorced woman originally from Tokyo, who had resided in the house prior to Kyger and Snyder's arrival. It was not an unusual situation. Kyger elaborates: "The house was very tiny, two little rooms and a tiny kitchen, with an attached wood burning bath, and

a 'benjo' [toilet] attached on another side. There was a little room up some stairs which comprised a second floor. We shared the toilet, the bath, and the miniscule kitchen with her. Whenever she had to go to the toilet, she passed through our 'big' room which we slept in at night. She was very quiet and polite, but always close by and 'there.' There was never any sense of 'privacy'" (Letter to the author, 20 March 2012). Kyger knew, however, that the woman, Mrs. Hosaka, had no other place to go, and, ironically or not, she serves as a figure for limited female mobility at a time when Kyger is "making plans" to leave Kyoto.

57. Kyger to Whalen, 23 June 1962.

58. Whalen to Kyger, 8 March 1963.

59. Kyger to Whalen, 22 August 1963.

60. Kyger to Whalen, 22 August 1963.

61. See for instance Snyder's poem "Praise for Sick Women" (*Riprap and Cold Mountain Poems*). Invoking menstruation, it conveys reverence for female fertility but also asserts a Cartesian dualism to relegate women to corporeal experience. Women are confused by (intellectual) "discipline"; they have a "difficult dance to do, but not in mind" (Snyder, *Riprap* 4).

62. Whalen to Kyger, 31 August 1963.

63. Whalen to Kyger, 24 August 1963.

64. Whalen to Kyger, 9 April 1963.

65. This line is preceded by Whalen's testimony that Ron Loewinsohn found her poems "so good it scares him & all who get a look at them" (Whalen to Kyger, 9 April 1963).

66. Notley refers explicitly to women who emerged in the 1970s—herself, Bernadette Mayer, Anne Waldman—but likely she would include Kyger in this time frame, if only because she asserts that no females were born in the postwar generation that gave rise to the "male-females."

TWO | DANIEL KANE

I Just Got Different Theories

Patti Smith and the Poetry Project at St. Mark's Church

FROM HER TIME AS a young performance poet in New York in the late 1960s to her current position as punk rock's *éminence grise,* Patti Smith has foregrounded the image of the poet as privileged seer. Simultaneously, Smith's emphatic rejection of stereotypically "feminine" personae in favor of an at-times masculine performative stance has placed her outside normative gender categories. I want to read Smith's romantic impulses alongside her willingness to stir up gender trouble within the context of Smith's activity in the Poetry Project at St. Mark's Church, the preeminent public face of the Lower East Side poetry scene of the 1960s and 1970s in which second generation New York School poets (among them Anne Waldman, Lewis Warsh, Bernadette Mayer, Michael Brownstein, and Gerard Malanga) held sway.

The Poetry Project, after all, is where Smith gave her first (and now practically mythological) poetry performance with Lenny Kaye on 10 February 1971, introduced by poet and Poetry Project Director Anne Waldman. And yet, as I will discuss shortly, the site for Smith's coming out party—a site she has returned to repeatedly[1]—was and is in many ways temperamentally opposed to the heroizing discourse Smith insisted on. Particularly given *Just Kids,* Smith's recently published memoir looking back on her relationship with the photographer Robert Mapplethorpe, I want to look at how Smith's friendships with and evocation of male artists played alongside her critique of the female. I believe there is a connection between Smith's negotiation of male and female performative roles and her repeated insistence on the Poet as divinely inspired. It is that connection that I want to read together with what I call a poetics of sociability typical of the Poetry Project scene at the time. Ultimately, this essay will show how Smith's gendered play between male and female, vatic authority and sociable lighthearted writing, proved crucial in informing her own brand of proto-punk rock.

The Poetry Project was not just the place that Smith first made a public name for herself. It was a site where she negotiated friendship literally and metaphorically as a way to establish herself in New York's downtown scene, from which she launched herself into the overground world of corporate record labels and rock 'n' roll concert arenas. Smith's negotiating friendship with Project-affiliated poets was equal parts target-based ingratiation and strategic distantiation verging at times into overt disrespect. This distantiation, performed fairly consistently in interviews during the early 1970s and reinvoked (if in a much tempered version) in *Just Kids*, successfully kept Smith from becoming fully absorbed into the Poetry Project scene.

Why this "both / and" approach to becoming friends with Project-affiliated poets? Friendship, as the editors of this collection rightly insist, can for women poets prove a site for "intersubjective becoming" that serves as a buffer against and wedge into masculinist avant-garde poetic communities (*Among Friends*, Introduction). Friendship can also be used in wholly opposite terms. Smith's aching toward and achieving stardom was predicated partly on an invocation of the authority of poetry to further burnish her spectacular aura, an aura gained in part by being associated with the coolest downtown poets around. Intuiting the cultural capital to be gained from an alignment with avant-garde poetic communities fairly oozing with street cred, Smith engaged with the Poetry Project scene in part to wedge herself not into a localized, collaborative poetics community, but into the then hypermasculine world of rock 'n' roll. Smith danced a complicated dance, simultaneously pantomiming *and becoming* that heroic, markedly male divinity whose authority she consistently celebrated both on and off the page prior to and during her big break out.

Making a Mark at St. Mark's

Smith moved to New York City in the late 1960s not to be a musician but to be a poet. She soon began frequenting the vibrant literary scene based at the Poetry Project at St. Mark's Church in New York's East Village. Smith cultivated friendships with writers including Waldman

(Director of the Poetry Project from 1966 to 1976), Brownstein, and Mayer, as well as Beat figures committed to the Project including Allen Ginsberg and Gregory Corso. Her 10 February 1971 reading found her sharing a bill at the Poetry Project with Malanga. And yet, in recollecting this early performance, Smith discloses what seem to be her ambivalent feelings about being absorbed into the coterie:

> Gerard generously agreed to let me open for him. The Poetry Project, shepherded by Anne Waldman, was a desirable forum for even the most accomplished poets. Everyone from Robert Creeley to Allen Ginsberg to Ted Berrigan had read there. If I was ever going to perform my poems, this was the place to do it. My goal was not simply to do well, or hold my own. It was to make a mark at St. Mark's. I did it for Poetry. I did it for Rimbaud, and I did it for Gregory. I wanted to infuse the written word with the immediacy and frontal attack of rock and roll. (*Just Kids* 180)

While Smith acknowledges here that the Poetry Project was *the* place for exciting poetry during this period, I want to pause on that word *even*. "Even" as it is written here connotes improbability, a kind of latent "can you believe it!" that subtly but firmly positions anything resembling a group effort (as embodied in words like "Project" and "forum") as secondary to individual accomplishment. That Smith then goes on to assert her desire to "make a mark at St. Mark's" emphasizes her desire to in effect transcend absorption into community by metaphorically scoring or wounding the very edifice that houses the "Project"—to make one's mark on a place, after all, is to alter it, not fit into it. Smith is reading at the Poetry Project not to further ingratiate herself into a material and highly active literary grouping that was pushing conceptual and collaborative writing to its limits through publications including Vito Acconci and Bernadette Mayer's *0 to 9* or Larry Fagin's *Adventures in Poetry*. Rather, Smith is in effect getting ready to stage a reactionary, romantically inflected intervention in a dominant postmodern institution whose members would in all probability question anyone using the word poetry with a capital "P."

Smith's efforts were in real contrast to writers running the show at the Poetry Project. The impulse toward community there, far from being predicated on the kind of heroizing gestures favored by Smith, were instead based on more casual effects. We might look to the lines "Don't be horrible sourpuss/Moon! Have a drink!/Have an entire issue!" included in Ted Berrigan and Ron Padgett's collaboratively produced poem "Waterloo Sunset" as a kind of metaphor for the overall ambiance of Project-related poetry—lines like these point to the way in which the agency for the creation of meaning and pleasure in the text is offered metaphorically to the potentially cranky and overly serious Moon/reader, as opposed to being linked materially to a site of privileged authorship. Poetry Project-affiliated writers deflated seriousness in an effort to enact an especially diffuse and amenable mood.[2]

Smith, on the other hand, worked aggressively to reinstate uniqueness in the figure of the poet. We see this through her isolation of two male literary figures—Arthur Rimbaud, Corso—whom she will "do" her reading for. Poets who are read consistently as agitating if not outright repudiating affiliation with a collective, Rimbaud and Corso are famous as much (if not more than) for their outlaw auras as they are for their poetry. Rimbaud's dramatic departure from the poetic sphere for a life of trading and gunrunning in the Horn of Africa has become the stuff of legend. Corso's reputation as the bad boy of the Beat generation, replete with endless retellings of his heckling poets at the Poetry Project, his womanizing, his thieving, and drug use, are similarly well known and often overshadow the merits of much of his poetry.[3] All this is by way of saying that Smith—even within the context of nostalgic retrospection as we find it in *Just Kids*—emphasizes her affiliation not with the group but with solitary outlaws.

Smith, as Waldman sees it,

> was not coming out of the New American Poetry as so many of the other poets who were around the Project, and allied with the NY School or Black Mountain or Robert Duncan or the Beats in those days. Or inspired through the Modernists particularly—Pound, Stein, Williams, Stevens . . . But her poems were iconic and she took on icons as subject matter. Every poet has their particular Rimbaud, and hers was the renegade *maudit*. Her themes often had to do with trials and redemption which I found interesting. She wore a cross around her

> neck. The poems were tough, working class, romantic, aspirational. Very different from the experimental work of Bernadette Mayer, Alice Notley who were more complicated on the page. (Waldman, email)

The kind of position-taking that Waldman describes would ultimately serve Smith well in the mid-1970s as Smith retooled her work for an audience accustomed to the heroic stance typical of the late 1960s male rock star (a Hendrix, a Morrison).

I emphasize the distinctions between Smith and the scene at the Poetry Project particularly because I am struck by the way in which Smith in the *Just Kids* excerpt above has essentially domesticated Waldman by portraying her as a shepherd. Waldman is rarely mentioned in *Just Kids* as an interesting and important poet in her own right. Rather, she is the tender of the flock. While "shepherd" is not necessarily gendered male or female here, we can at the very least think about the traditional hierarchies of genre that place the pastoral at the bottom of the three-rung ladder made up of, respectively, pastoral, georgic, and epic (Weller 143). Smith, aligning herself with male figures for whom poetry was always uttered with a capital "P," draws the line here between a poetics of sociability typical of the Poetry Project scene and her own favored world populated by literary outlaw deities.

To further illustrate Smith's gendering stardom, we can look to the manner in which Smith framed the time around the reading in *Just Kids*. This was a period when Smith was having an affair with the playwright Sam Shepard, using a room Shepard rented at the Chelsea Hotel as the location for their trysts. Descriptions of their romance find Smith highlighting those aspects of the relationship that follow a notably homosocial trajectory. "Sometimes we just sat on the bed and read," Smith explains. "I was reading about Crazy Horse and he was reading Samuel Beckett." It was a boy's life, really—in fact, as Shepard was often gone, he let Smith "stay in his room by [herself] with remnants of him: his Indian blanket, typewriter, and a bottle of Ron del Barrilito three-star rum" (*Just Kids* 180). Highlighting the male-inscribed nature of what at times sounds like a deliciously inappropriate relationship between a scoutmaster and a scout, Smith embraced Shepard's permission and used that time to develop a sense of herself as a youthful outlaw. "I was writing a poem for Sam, an homage to his obsession with stock cars. It was a poem called 'Ballad of a Bad Boy.' I pulled it out of the typewriter, pacing the room, reading it aloud. It worked. It had the energy and the rhythm I was looking for" (*Just Kids* 180). Looking to another buddy to see whether the poem was any good or not, Smith "knocked on Robert [Mapplethorpe]'s door [at the Chelsea]. 'Want to hear something?'" she said (*Just Kids* 180). That Smith's ideal "energy" and "rhythm" emanated out of discourse circulating around stock cars and bad boys, rum drunk in secret chambers, and an overall emphasis on male camaraderie is telling in the context of Smith's debut reading at St. Mark's.

Smith used the occasion of her debut reading to distance herself resolutely from ideations of community. Enacting the outlaw "Crazy Horse" style in both attitude and dress (Smith describes how she wore "a pair of black snakeskin boots" [*Just Kids* 180] to the event), Smith approached the reading with a wonderfully bratty bravado. After describing the makeup of the audience—the crème de la crème of New York's downtown scene including Andy Warhol, Lou Reed, Joe Brainard, and Mayer—Smith explains how she dedicated the evening to criminals from Cain to Jean Genet.

> I chose poems like "Oath," which began, "Christ died for somebody's sins / But not mine" [. . .] We finished with "Ballad of a Bad Boy" accompanied by Lenny's strong rhythmic chords and electric feedback. It was the first time an electric guitar had been played in St. Mark's Church, provoking cheers and jeers. As this was hallowed ground for poetry, some objected, but Gregory was jubilant. [. . .] The reception had its thundering moments. [. . .] But afterward I was so filled with adrenaline that I behaved like a young cock. I failed to thank Robert and Gerard. Nor did I socialize with their people. I just high-tailed it out with Sam [Shepard] and we had a couple of tequilas and lobster. (*Just Kids* 182)

This kind of youthful arrogance, gendered male via the phrase "young cock," very much set the pattern for Smith's yoking an essentialized masculinity onto her own androgynous body to set herself apart from the poetry pack. Rejecting collaborative community in favor of reaching toward stardom, Smith figured early on that conventional femininity might not be the best way to be her generation's Mick Jagger. Smith thus acted like a cock in an effort to keep from being herded into the Poetry Project by shepherdesses like Waldman.

In fact, a recording of the reading confirms that Smith approached the evening with real nervous aggression. Following her version of Brecht's "Mack the Knife," Smith went on with her "Dedication" described above. This part found a young snarling Smith insisting on aligning herself with an almost entirely male pantheon:

> This reading is dedicated to *crime*, all that is criminal. [. . .] To the rhythms of prison! The great escapes from Devil's Island. The petty thief. The whores of Mexico. To Anne Powell the only woman Genet could love. [. . .] The pool hall hustler, the pirate saint, the crimes of passion, the dance of the boxing ring. The masters of Russian roulette [. . .] Johnny Ace, Jackson Pollock, James Dean, Mayakovski, the 38 of the Cowboy, Gene Krupa, Mary Magdalene, the only woman who could make our savior weep. And to Christ himself, Christ! The great escape artist! Greater than Houdini. And the finest faggot in history having 12 men to lick his feet. The radio, the movie camera, Blaise Cendrars, the electric guitar, and Sam Shepard. (*Patti Smith at the Poetry Project*)

Most poets at the Poetry Project begin their sets by thanking the organizers. Not so Smith. Her brusque entry suggests she was already beginning to carve out a performance aesthetic for herself as rocking iconoclast aligned generally with male nonconformists. Women that make it into this picture are, for the most part, prostitutes, muses, and lovers of famous men.

Despite her behavior, or perhaps *because* of it, Smith soon established herself as a significant figure in the downtown scene affiliated with the often interrelated communities attached to the Poetry Project and the Warhol-dominated Max's Kansas City. Perhaps this is so in part because poets at the Project were sympathetic to collaboration and read Smith's work in a band as resonating with that particular ethos. As Waldman recalls it, "Patti's debut reading at the Project was exciting, original, performative. Lenny Kaye was in sync with her ethos. He was clearly the principle collaborator in her work, from the start. A 'band' is a collaboration" (Waldman, email). All that said, Smith, excepting a single appearance in the Project-affiliated journal *The World* and a later appearance in the 1971 anthology *Another World: A Second Anthology of Works from the St. Mark's Poetry Project*, did not publish in the journals affiliated with St. Mark's. Instead, her poems and music reviews ended up being published in nationally distributed magazines including *Creem* and *Rolling Stone*.

Smith recognized that community could in fact be limiting to an artist eager to assert herself within a privileged lineage of literary heroes. By January 1973, Smith had grown out of the very social milieu that played such a large role in establishing her public persona. Of a New Year's Day event at the Poetry Project, Smith recalled, "Later that evening I sat on the floor of St. Mark's for the annual marathon reading. It benefited the church and went on from early afternoon to well into the night, with everyone contributing to the perpetuation of the Poetry Project. I sat through much of it sizing up the poets. I wanted to be a poet but I knew I would never fit into their incestuous community. The last thing I wanted was to negotiate the social politics of another scene" (*Just Kids* 214). By 1975, the year she released her now-legendary album *Horses*, Smith had very much managed to be part of the Poetry Project while maintaining her distance from it. Where did her aggressive iconoclasm come from, why did she continue to participate in poetry events at the church (as she does to this day) in spite of her hostile posture, and what, in the end, can this teach us about the way friendship is used in part to negotiate the journey from communitarian poetry scene to deific, male-inscribed rock 'n' roll stardom?

I Pretty Well Hate Most of the Stuff You Guys Do

Even during the early period of her tenure in New York in the late 1960s, Smith was grappling with the fact that the aesthetic at St. Mark's conflicted with her own sense of what was important in poetry. An undated letter from Smith to Waldman (here excerpted), written when Smith had recently arrived in New York, shows Smith consciously setting herself apart from the surface cool she associates with Frank O'Hara and the St. Mark's poets who followed in his wake:

Dear Anne,
I'm sending you the book you wanted, I'll also read it myself. Right now I'm reading Flaubert. not Madame Bovary but his Tales. He's really neat cause he really knows sound. O shit maybe the guy who Translated him does.

Anyway it's great to find music in unsuspected places. listen to this part, it's like a Dylan song (John Wesley Hardin type) (I'm quoting from memory but I'm sure it's pretty close) He came to her. He said he was sorry how he behaved. She wanted to run off but straightway he began talking of the crops. Shit I think he's great.

I'm Telling you this to sort of introduce you to my feeling of poetry. I believe it's quite different then most of you guys. I love Frank O'Hara but I also love Vachel Linsey (who is shoddily Treated in Frank's personalism essay). It may be arbitrary To love Them both but it's just that I take my *music personally.*

I pretty well hate most of the stuff you guys do cause it seems you not only violate sound but disregard it completely. I also love you guys cause you keep poetry alive. I think it's real neat what you're doing, I just got different theories. I was raised on Little Anthony + The Imperials and Dylan Thomas + what I do is sort of an intentional combinations.

Right now The stuff THE BAND does, Dylan + Flaubert is my most loved stuff. I must say I read you guys avidly. I'll Tell you I like That one you writ called Late Mescaline Sonnet. Especially The last couple of lines.

Maybe it's kinda presumptuous of me to say this stuff but I don't give a shit. I'm Taking The Time off to write you cause I Think you're a real neat girl. Oh I like the red haired guys[4] poems too. (qtd. in Kane, "Nor Did I Socialize," 111–12)

This letter is, in essence, a performance where Smith juggles a variety of literary and social modes. She positions herself as amenable to the Poetry Project, while simultaneously distinguishing herself from it through self-consciously unfashionable references to writers frozen out of respectable avant-garde circles. To begin with, Smith's reference to Lindsay knowingly refers to O'Hara's essay "Personism," in which O'Hara asserted cheekily, "Now, come on. I don't believe in god, so I don't have to make elaborately sounded structures. I hate Vachel Lindsay, always have; I don't even like rhythm, assonance, all that stuff" (*Collected Poems* 498). While out of fashion at the time Smith was writing this letter, Lindsay was perhaps best known for what he called his "singing poetry." Lindsay was, at the turn of the twentieth century, absolutely invested in the history of the medieval troubadour (and was in fact referred to during his lifetime as the "Prairie Troubadour"). Lindsay essentially wanted to reinvigorate that intimate link between a populist audience and performer, travelling by foot throughout the United States declaiming his verse.

One might argue that Smith's isolating Lindsay as distinct from what "you guys" (Waldman and, one might assume, related figures including Warsh and Mayer) were doing in the 1960s was in fact unfair given the fact that the Poetry Project was itself a site for the public performance of poetry. The Project, featuring at least three public readings per week, certainly maintained a space for poetry as a primarily performative act. Yet we need to make a distinction in terms of the *audience* associated with a troubadour like Lindsay versus the Poetry Project community. In fact, I want to step back a bit from the very word "community" as it is associated with the Project and suggest, following Lytle Shaw's work on O'Hara, that "coterie" might be a more appropriate framework through which to read the difference between the oral poetics culture championed by Lindsay in the 1910s and the preponderance of poetry readings taking place at St. Mark's during the 1960s. Like Shaw, who traces coterie back to its medieval roots in peasant collectives agitating against their landlords, I also want to insist that I don't necessarily see any elitist, pejorative associations attached to "coterie" (*Frank O'Hara* 21).[5] Rather, I see "coterie" as having much more in common with the possibilities of a dissident microcommunity. Particularly given the collaborative nature of readings and publications at the Project, "coterie" resonates with the preponderance of actual communes in the late 1960s and early 1970s, social formations defined as much by who is excluded as by who is included, and which are established in opposition to a wider consensus culture.

In light of Shaw's recuperation of the collective, even latently transgressive, elements of the word "coterie," I would like to propose that the Poetry Project in the early 1970s be understood not as a privileged group of *littérateurs* but rather as an association of like-minded dissenters carving out temporary autonomous zones of collective production and dissemination in the face of a dominant poetics and attendant politics which insist on a construction of the Poet as privileged, Muse-inspired genius.[6]

Now, this is a very different approach to the oral transmission of a poem compared to the one that Smith takes on through her privileging of Lindsay and Dylan Thomas. John Brinnin's recollections of a typical Thomas reading—in this case, one of Thomas's performances in New York's YM-YWHA—illustrates how Thomas's orality was very much in the service of extending his practically shamanistic persona:

> at the appointed time he walked on to the stage, shoulders straight, chest out in his staunch and pouter-pigeon advance, and proceeded to give the first of those performances which were to bring to America a whole new conception of poetry reading. [. . .] When he concluded the evening with a selection of his own works—encompassing both tenderly lyrical and oratorical passages with absolute authority, it was difficult to know which gave the greater pleasure, the music or the meaning. Some of his listeners were moved by the almost sacred sense of his approach to language; some by the bravado of a modern poet whose themes dealt directly and unapologetically with birth and death and the presence of God; some were entertained merely by the plangent virtuosity of an actor with a great voice. In every case the response was one of delight. Ovations greeting him as he came on and as he went off were tremendous, but the sweat on his brow flowed no less copiously either time. It was my first full and striking knowledge of the fact that Dylan was alone, that he had been born into a loneliness beyond the comprehension of those of us who feel we live in loneliness, and that those recognitions of success or failure by which we can survive meant nothing to him. (Brinnin 18)

This is in essence a familiar vision of the Poet as isolated seer, a figure summoning ecstatic social response and union while maintaining a shamanistic separation from community. While some poets who read there played the part of shaman, with its mass readings, its political poetry-reading benefits, its call-and-response ethos, nothing could be further from the values developing at the Poetry Project through the 1960s than the aura built up around Thomas in the 1950s.

These kinds of qualities affiliated with Thomas and Lindsay were, if not entirely discredited at the Poetry Project, nevertheless not part of the overall culture there. This resistance to romantic wildness can in many ways be seen as an inheritance from the first generation New York School of poets. O'Hara, for one, had identified the assertion of a privileged self enacted through performance as, well, embarrassing. "I can't stand all that Welsh spit" is what O'Hara had to say about Thomas (qtd. in Schuyler 286). It was this radical rejection of the mechanisms of stardom in favor of a poetics of sociability within the poetry community in New York that Smith was to find so dispiriting. Even as she recognized the Poetry Project was "the place to do it," she determined she should transcend it. In a remarkably candid interview with Victor Bockris published in 1972, Smith laid out her goals as they related in part to her negotiation with the Poetry Project at St. Mark's:

> v. you're a writer in the middle of a literary scene and you're totally ignoring the literary scene around you. how long can you keep going on your own?
>
> p. I can keep going because I'm constantly stimulated by earth's glitter. I'm constantly stimulated. I'm not at any loss for material. (Smith and Bockris 11)

As we see here, Bockris was somewhat agog at Smith's choice to remain aloof despite her all-access pass to a desirable coterie ("in the middle of a literary scene"). After all, it is not the writers who are "totally ignoring" Smith. Rather, it's Smith who's "totally ignoring" them. Bockris continued pressing Smith on this question by asking her point-blank about whether she could actually learn anything from the downtown poets:

> v. does the fact that you don't find any younger writers you learn from depress you?

p. their life styles don't attract me. I think I'm ballsier, a better performer. I think they can learn from me.
v. so you feel the people you can learn from are the rock and roll scene?
p. yeah in the sixties it was jim morrison, bob dylan, now its still the rolling stones. there was smokey robinson. I can still get excited about humphrey bogart. I like people who're bigger than me. I'm not interested in meeting poets or a bunch of writers who I don't think are bigger than life. I'm a hero worshipper, I'm not a fame fucker, but I am a hero worshipper. (12–13)[7]

Smith's candor here is refreshing, if pretty reactionary when viewed in the context of the neo-Dada collaborative scene then ruling the day at St. Mark's. Not for her the collating parties, the group readings, the self-published small-circulation anonymous and pseudonymous publications. Rather, rock 'n' roll as a model for performance poetry helps Smith reestablish and celebrate the divide between privileged stage and underwhelming page. Rock 'n' roll, particularly by the late 1960s and early 1970s, had essentially become a vehicle for deification rather than a celebration of the quotidian, when the small-scale clubs, halls, and streets made way for the Roman-imperial grandeur of the amphitheater and festival. Rock in the late 60s and 70s celebrated mass-market values attendant to the seduction and economic exploitation of huge crowds. (Woodstock, after all, was an economic catastrophe not by design but because of the organizational failures of its backers.) While much can be said for Smith's starting her music career in tiny clubs like CBGB's, we should not forget that the end goal was to play—as the Patti Smith Group did, eventually—in large arenas in the United States and Europe. That Smith wanted to essentially imbue poetry with the bigger than life theatrics of the rock 'n' roll stage show suggests a real intervention into and critique of the avant-garde poetics and attendant ethics of the period.

Bockris went on to question Smith on her own terms. Employing the kind of terminology we associate with rock 'n' roll, Bockris asked Smith which poets she would like to "tour" with:

v. if I was to offer you a reading tour with three other poets who would you choose as the three other poets?
p. jim carrol, bernadette mayer, and muhammed ali.
v. why?
p. because they're all good performers. ali's a good performer. he's got great rhythms. [. . .] he's entertaining. bernadette mayer because I like what she does conceptually. she's a real speed driven poet sometimes I don't like her because she's overly political and too influenced by st marks, but she's also a good performer. jim carrol because I think he's one of the best poets in america. [. . .] it kills me he's 23 he wrote all his best poems the same year of his life as rimbaud did. he had the same intellectual quality and bravado as rimbaud. he's a junkie. he's bisexual. he's been fucked by every male and female genius in America he's been fucked over by all those people. he lives all over. he lives a disgusting life. sometimes you have to pull him out of a gutter. he's been in prison. he's a total fuck up. but what great poet wasn't. I think the st marks poets are so namby pamby they're frauds they write about today at 9:15 I shot speed with brigid sitting in the such and such they're real cute about putting it in a poem but if jim carrol comes into the church stoned and throws up that's not a poem to them that's not cool. if you could play with it in your poetry that's okay but if you're really with it that's something else. they don't want to face it. (15–16)

Performance, as far as Smith is concerned, takes precedence over poetry. Very little of Smith's response relates in any serious way to what actually goes into the poetry of Ali and Carroll. When Smith does acknowledge Mayer's actual writing (as opposed to her lifestyle), it is framed almost entirely as critique. Mayer is problematic because she's overtly political. Mayer is maybe not so great because she doesn't stand out from the St. Mark's crowd enough. And what's the problem with the St. Mark's poets? They are "namby pamby," and for two interesting reasons. One is because they all have a group style predicated on the "I do this, I do that" mode popularized by O'Hara. Two is because they are frauds—Smith accuses the St. Mark's crowd of pretending to be dissolute, speed-shooting *poètes maudits* when in fact they can't handle a real drug-addicted, vomit spewing writer like Jim Carroll.

It seems here that Smith looked to poetry not so much for what the art had to offer her as a model for her songwriting, but for what the *discourse* of poetry could provide her with in terms of thinking about how to make actual lifestyle and performance choices. In a related interview with Bockris, for example, Smith acknowledges why she was initially drawn to French poetry and fiction. In response to Bockris's question, "Why are your influences mostly European: Rimbaud, Cendrars, Celine, Michaux?," Smith replied, "It's because of biographies. I was mostly attracted to lifestyles, and there just wasn't any [*sic*] great biographies of genius American lifestyles except the cowboys." Smith went on to explain that she was writing a "poetry of performance" because

> of Victorian England, how they crucified Oscar Wilde. Poets became simps, sensitive young men in attics. But it wasn't always like that. It used to be that the poet was a performer and I think the energy of Frank O'Hara started to re-inspire that. I mean in the Sixties there was all that happening stuff. Then Frank O'Hara died and it sort of petered out, and then Dylan and Allen Ginsberg revitalized it. (Bockris 42)

FUCK YOU JESUS!

Poetry as lifestyle played a very real role in Smith's self-fashioning. In her numerous articles on literary figures from William Blake to Rimbaud to Corso, Smith was as likely to stress these writers' outrageous antics as she was to refer to their actual poetry. In her foreword to Corso's *An Accidental Autobiography*, for example, Smith opens with an anecdote that illustrates and celebrates Corso's antiestablishment gestures:

> I first encountered Gregory long ago in front of the Chelsea Hotel. He lifted his overcoat and dropped his trousers, spewing Latin expletives. Seeing my astonished face, he laughed and said, "I'm not mooning you sweetheart, I'm mooning the world." I remember thinking, how fortunate for the world to be privy to the exposed rump of a true poet. (xi)

Interestingly, Smith continues in her foreword to align herself materially with Corso: "My living space was akin to his—piles of papers, books, old shoes, piss in cups—mortal disarray" (xi). This raggedy bohemia, in evidence most ideally in the rebellious figure of a poet-outlaw like Corso, would be absorbed and redirected by Smith into what would soon be called punk rock.

Despite Smith's ambivalent and at-times openly hostile attitude toward the St. Mark's scene, she nevertheless chose to work within the loose institutional structures related to the Poetry Project. Crucially, Smith's first poetry book *Seventh Heaven* (1972) was published through the Telegraph Books imprint, edited by Bockris and for the most part committed to publishing figures affiliated with the second generation New York School and the related Warhol scene. By 1972 Telegraph Books had published books including Berrigan, Padgett, and Tom Clark's collaborative book *Back in Boston Again*, Bockris's *Face*, Malanga's *Poetry on Film*, Brigid Polk's *Scars*, Tom Raworth's *Heavy Light*, Aram Saroyan's *The Rest*, Tom Weatherly's *Thumbprint*, and Andrew Wylie's *Tenderloin*. Most of these little books emanated affection for a loosely defined experimentalism characterized by sociability.

Even something as odd as Polk's *Scars* resonated with the collaborative turn in poetry. *Scars* is composed "from a selection of Warhol superstar Polk's collection of ink prints she made of celebrities and her friends' scars with accompanying explanations of the wounds by those who'd been scarred" (Cooper). Thus, like the Berrigan / Padgett / Clark work, the idea of this book as something related to a stable subject named "Brigid Polk" is compromised as the reader scans through a number of personages' scars including Peter Fonda's foreskin scar; Jonas Mekas's thumb scar resulting from a "cut," as Mekas explained, made "deeply with an axe at age ten" (qtd. in Polk n.p.); Genevieve Waite's burn scar; Malanga's testicular scar ("undescended testicle / until age 13 / operation successful") (qtd. in Polk n.p.); and so on. Most interestingly in the context of this particular essay, Smith is also included in this all-star roster.

Her contribution really sticks out—not because of the nature of her scar, but because of the tone and diction of her submission: "Scar Left side. patti smith. On april 26 1967 / I bore my first baby / and ripped up the / left side of my belly / FUCK YOU JESUS" (qtd. in Polk n.p.).[8] The heretical petulance of FUCK YOU JESUS alongside the oddly outdated phrase "bore my baby" agitated very strongly against the otherwise faux-naive, gentle, and generally whimsical contributions of the other featured figures. Even here, Smith is visible as both in and outside of the in crowd. Smith's inclusion in a book studded with "superstars" (to use Warhol's semi-ironic term) is a testament to her place among the glitterati of New York's cultural undergrounds. And yet, her decision to use a somewhat archaic diction alongside a punk posture that anticipates her cover version of Van Morrison's "Gloria" (beginning with Smith's line "Jesus died for somebody's sins but not mine") marks Smith's refusal to become fully absorbed into the group sign of the book. Smith doesn't want to "fit in" too well, as such acceptance runs the risk of erasing the heroic, individualist persona Smith was so committed to developing. And yet, rubbing metaphorical shoulders with figures like Polk, Malanga, Warhol, and Mekas certainly adds counterculture sheen to Smith's name. This "both / and" approach to rejecting and participating in a wider artistic community was to characterize Smith's negotiations of the literary and musical spheres for a number of years.

The primary way Smith defined herself outside the potentially limiting circles of the downtown avant-garde was to embrace heroic representations of rock 'n' roll stars and project them via the purportedly "high-art" form of the poem. In a letter to Brownstein and Waldman written in the early 1970s, for example, we find Smith declaiming: "MUSIC another Smith fight for musical poetry speech. I don't consider my stuff songs I'LL rebel god dammit I'll call them poems even if they get on the top ten AM radio. I want to get music back like YEATS YEATS DYLAN THOMAS ELDER EDDA JESSE JAMES sunny and the sunglows. I'll fix you guys" (qtd. in Kane, "Nor Did I Socialize," 117–18). "I'll fix you guys," addressed as it is to Waldman and Brownstein, a poet and then Waldman's partner, clearly works to set Smith up as the voice of authenticity and poetic rebellion looking to enlighten the implicitly staid world at St. Mark's. This is not to say that downtown poets affiliated with St. Mark's weren't themselves challenging the distinctions between high and low art. The emphasis on orality and performance underscoring the scene at the Poetry Project, the collaborative and communal ethos feeding into the production of poems, the rejection of literary value in favor of coterie affiliation as a standard for publication, the extension of the allusive field of poetry to include celebratory references to contemporary rock musicians including the Rolling Stones, the Kinks, and Neil Young[9], all worked to effect a serious if temporary challenge to the hierarchies that would situate poetry as a primarily high art form. Innovative poets of the preceding generation, particularly Ginsberg, had also been vocal about their appreciation for rock 'n' roll.[10] But for all the demotic chatter around avant-garde poetry in the late 1960s and early 1970s, no poet affiliated with the scene approached the synthesis of rock 'n' roll with poetry with the single-mindedness of Smith.

Opposed to Smith's efforts to imbue a vatic romanticism back into poetry was, as has been suggested already, the problematic of femininity. What Smith had to do, in the end, was to challenge what she perceived to be an inherently feminized aesthetics of (to borrow from Hélène Cixous and Catherine Clement)[11] diffusion and effervescence, an aesthetics that urges us to write outside self, outside center—in other words, an aesthetics that Smith understood to be at the core of the cutesy poetics affiliated with and promoted by the St. Mark's scene. Indeed, *Seventh Heaven* shows Smith employing straightforward narrative, a monologic speaker, and a general tendency to associate creative power with an idealized masculinity. Ultimately, as she put it in the opening stanzas of her poem "female," Smith was committed to "boy rythums [*sic*]." The second stanza of the poem continues in a complicated way to idealize creativity (here analogized with "barbarity") as male gendered:

> I ran around with a pack of wolves. I puked on every
> pinafore. Growing breasts was a nightmare. In anger
> I cut off all my hair and knelt glassy eyed before
> god. I begged him to place me in my own barbaric race.
> The male race. The race of my choice. (Smith, *Seventh Heaven* 44)

"Work your ass off to change the language," Mayer famously advised her students, adding, "and don't ever get famous" (80). Smith flouted Mayer's rules. Far from working her ass off to change the language, Smith, as we see in "female" and related poems including "mustang sally," "fantasy (for allen lanier)," and "death by water" (Smith's paeon to Jim Morrison), adhered to some fairly conventional literary practices in the service of both idealizing a pantheon of star-touched men and (for the most part) relegating the female, when she did appear, to the status of abject embarrassment, muse, or doomed beauty. And as so many of her idealized figures were men, part of Smith's process was working out how to align her own femininity with a value system that, as she wrote "female," privileged the "male race."

"female" anticipates Smith's later transformation into the gorgeous, boyish figure gracing Mapplethorpe's stunning cover for Smith's 1975 album *Horses.* Shirt, suspenders, and jacket strategically covering Smith's large breasts, the outline of a slight mustache visible on her upper lip, a vaguely confrontational expression on her face, and her "narrow hipped" figure accentuated by her tight pants, Smith's self as it is enacted here embodies the pose practiced initially within the pages of Smith's poetry.

Smith insisted, "I aint no women's lib chick. so I cant write about a man because I'm under his thumb but a woman I can be male with. I can use her as my muse. I use women" (Smith and Bockris 9). As contemporary reviews of Smith's poetry performances in the early 1970s attest, such attitudes informed Smith's own masculinist public style. "Looking like a female version of Keith Richards [. . .] Patti Smith is the poet as macho woman—hip, tough, sexy, raging" (McCarthy 42). Even then, though, fans of Smith the performer recognized that the poetry was in the service of performance, and that performance would ultimately be realized most ideally as song. "Still, Patti Smith is better heard than read. So see her if you get the chance. And hope that someday soon an adventuresome record company will sign her up and really give her a chance to wail" (McCarthy 42). Beginning her life as a performer in the context of a sprawling, community-oriented poetry scene "shepherded" by a woman, Smith worked hard to define herself apart from it even as she used its stages to promote her developing style.

I'm Gonna Be a Big Star

What resulted from her efforts, of course, was *Horses,* a record that can be defined without fear of histrionics as a major and often lyrically profound musical achievement. Readers, however, have probably detected a critical tenor to this essay. Where is that critique coming from? Smith insisted that anyone who dared call himself a poet should be, ideally, an outlaw, a seer, and a visionary. "I'm gonna be somebody, I'm gonna get on that train, go to New York City, / I'm gonna be so bad I'm gonna be a big star and I will never return," Smith exulted in "Piss Factory," featured on Side B of her debut single. And that's what she did. Is there an unavoidably problematic element to such self-fashioning, predicated as it is on the mechanics of stardom and the reification of hierarchies that always and forever raise the performer—materially and ideologically—above the audience? Maybe it is partly due to these performative stances that Smith's influence can be detected more within male "arty" circles of post-punk and indie music (Sonic Youth's Thurston Moore as Parnassian poetry-penning guitar god; R.E.M.'s Michael Stipe as poetic tortured soul) than in the ideologically driven, punk-inflected and avowedly feminist "riot grrrl" phenomenon of the late 1980s and 1990s, a scene indebted more to the style of British punk bands like the Slits and the Raincoats than it was to Smith's comparatively baroque efforts.

Perhaps, then, the critical tone implicit in this article is based on the disappointment one feels when faced, yet again, with how easily efforts to create a community that at least attempts to resist a star system—whether it is in poetry or in punk—are compromised. I suggest this even despite the fact that Smith's music affected me deeply and wonderfully from the instant I heard Smith sing out "Suddenly! Johnny! Was surrounded by! Horses . . . horses . . . horses . . . horses . . ." I am also not quite so naive as to think that poets affiliated with the St Mark's scene didn't have their own forbidding mechanisms determining status. And yet, at least the St Mark's crew provided a model of sociability that questioned inherited values regarding seriousness generally speaking, the status of poetry as an autonomous art form, and the "visionary" as a necessary part of what defines an authentic "artist." The narrative of Smith's rise to stardom was, as I have argued, predicated on the initial engagement with and ultimate rejection of a poetics of sociability that determined one didn't have to be an inspired visionary to engage with poetry. One didn't even have to be a "self," as it were, as poetry could be made in groups, could be part of the fabric of a local, ever-shifting, autonomous community / coterie. Smith pushed back on all that. She pushed back hard.

NOTES

1. As of this writing, Smith's most recent appearance at the Poetry Project was on 9 February 2011—an anniversary celebration of her first performance at the Project. Smith was again introduced by Waldman and accompanied by Kaye.

2. See Kane, "*Angel Hair* Magazine" 345–46.

3. As Smith herself notes, Corso often heckled poets in the downtown scene: "Gregory took me to the St. Mark's Poetry Project, which was a poets' collective at the historic church on East Tenth Street. When we went to listen to the poets read, Gregory would heckle them, punctuating the mundane with cries of *Shit! Shit! No blood! Get a transfusion!* In watching his reaction, I made a mental note to make certain I was never boring if I read my own poems one day" (*Just Kids* 138).

4. The "red haired guy" was in all probability poet and post-punk troubadour Jim Carroll, whom Smith was soon to become romantically involved with.

5. As Shaw argues rhetorically, "Who would want to defend the idea of coterie? In everyday speech, literary communities are good, coteries are bad: the latter term seems to mark a threshold at which some ethical breach can be registered. But by whom, how?" ("On Coterie").

6. For more, see Kane, *All Poets Welcome*.

7. Smith would repeat variations on the "hero" theme in a number of her interviews. "I've always been hero-oriented," Smith insisted to Penny Green in a 1973 interview published in Warhol and Malanga's *Interview* magazine. "I started doing art not because I had creative instincts but because I fell in love with artists. I didn't come to this city to become an artist, but to become an artist's mistress. Art in the beginning for me was never a vehicle for self-expression, it was a way to ally myself with heroes, 'cause I couldn't make contact with God" (Green 25).

8. A PDF scan of Smith's contribution to Polk's book is available to view on Dennis Cooper's blog, http://denniscooper-theweaklings.blogspot.com/search?q=brigid+polk. See *Just Kids* for Smith's recollections of her first child, whom she had as a teenager and gave up for adoption.

9. There are multiple references to rock 'n' roll throughout the poetry of St. Mark's affiliated figures. For a sampling, see Warsh and Tom Clark's collaborative series "Chicago"; Ted Berrigan's poem "Bean Spasms"; Berrigan and Padgett's collaborative poem "Waterloo Sunset" (named after the Kinks' song), and Clark's "From 'Neil Young'", a series of poems that relineate Neil Young lyrics verbatim.

10. "Ginsberg above all [. . . regarded] that [1960s] generation of songwriters as supremely important. In 1981 he praised the 'evolution of rhythm and blues into rock 'n' roll into high art form, as evidenced by the Beatles, Bob Dylan, and other popular musicians influenced in the late 1950s and '60s by beat generation poets' and writers' works'" (Coupe 8).

11. Cixous and Clement famously argue for an understanding of women's erotic pleasure and power as emanating out of the biologically determined decenteredness inherent in women's libidinal and procreative abilities (90–91).

PART TWO

Community 2.0

THREE | LYTLE SHAW

Presence in the Poets' Polis

Hippie Phenomenology in Bolinas

[. . .] I address Bolinas
as if it were a condition
to be occupied
as if it Arose
not after Frisco that monsoon of lights
but rather the unclaimed silt beach of
phonepoles, bridges, houses, shoes—a last outpost takes
out here, and the rest of the world a wake
of minor shocks not for a moment
to be received as
history
—John Thorpe (*The Cargo Cult* n.p.)

THE WORD BOLINAS produces a knowing look in poets who lived through the 1960s. But like the writing we associate with the town whose road sign on Highway One has long been a tradition for residents to remove, the look seems to indicate a state of unrecoverable experience, a "condition / to be occupied" and thus a spatio-temporal engagement in a here-and-now that by definition cannot be communicated. As such, Bolinas might be considered, within poetry history, a kind of synecdoche for the utopian 1960s, the 1960s of hippies, communes, consciousness—a set of aspirations that often seem to disqualify themselves, to fall into caricature, before they open up for analysis. Considering the uneven reception of 1960s and 70s countercultures, artist Mike Kelley puts his finger directly on this problem.

> How does the relationship of the French Situationists to their culture compare to the Yippies' relationship to American culture? What's

> the difference between Malcolm McLaren's hip capitalism and Frank Zappa's "selling out" jokes? How does the Clash's role as a "political" band compare to that of the MC5? You'll never know. Because all the Americans I've just mentioned are categorized as hippies, not artists. (145)

But rather than clear the Bolinas poets from the charge that they were hippies, I want instead to take seriously the implications both of their individual artistic practices and of their larger social aspirations, especially the proposition that Bolinas itself might take on a new, exemplary function as the poets' polis, the one town in the United States explicitly organized around the possibilities of poetry as a collectively pursued enterprise, with poet-citizens not as a marginal subculture, but as dominant public figures—school board representatives, press, lawmakers. This possibility gets registered frequently in the poetry of the period, as, for instance, in Philip Whalen's 1971 poem: "Too busy to see anybody in New York / A few French paintings, shoeshine / New tweed English pants two pounds real Camembert cheese / Who is there to see in New York anyway / Everybody's moved to Bolinas" (*Scenes of a Life at the Capital* 9). One measure of this poet population shift was the 1971 *On the Mesa: An Anthology of Bolinas Writing*, published by City Lights. Robert Creeley, Joanne Kyger, Lewis Warsh, Ebbe Borregaard, Bill Berkson, David Meltzer, and Tom Clark (along with nine poets less remembered by literary history) all appear in the anthology.[1] We also know from poems and memoirs that many other poets arrived, passed through, and sometimes remained within Bolinas, including Joe Brainard, Ted Berrigan, Alice Notley, Philip Whalen, Andrei Codrescu, and later Robert Grenier. From the beginning of their migration, poets were prominent and visible in the town—population approximately 500—and often played an active role in town politics. And we should hear the still unsettled possibility of a poets' town in the many references to Bolinas in late 1960s and early 1970s American poetry: would it be just another backdrop for poet superstars (now under the rubric of the guru), or would it actually achieve a more horizontal, democratic social organization? Could the negated real neighbors of Williams's and Olson's largely imaginary polises—the Marcia Nardis and Vincent

Ferrinis—finally make contact with the more established poets sifting through the cultural residue of their towns, or was keeping them at arm's length the sacrifice necessary to demonstrate that one did not accept the contingent as the utopian, the person next door as the ideal addressee?

Poetry of this period charges the word Bolinas with a broad array of meanings. Still, we see repeated ambitions and fantasy structures: escape from the "unlivable" cities; connection with non-Western knowledge and daily life; establishment of local political autonomy; total involvement in non-deferred pleasure among a closely knit group of friends—in an infinitely absorbing "now" that offers itself as a kind of hippie phenomenology. Despite the obvious differences between the functions of poetry in the social formation of Bolinas and its functions for Gary Snyder in Kitkitdizze or Amiri Baraka in Newark, Bolinas is part of the same transformation of the poetics of place: from the atomistic, future-oriented practices of William Carlos Williams and Charles Olson, to the collective attempts to live place undertaken by 1960s poets—to merge a literal space with the kinds of social formation that remained merely potential in Williams and Olson. This often entailed a move from center to periphery, with periphery conceived both culturally (San Francisco to Bolinas) and economically or racially (New York to Newark). In these new remote locations, poets sought to ground their new roles in communities they themselves helped to create.

We tend to think of modernity's large-scale movements and tensions between center and periphery as colonial dramas that necessarily play themselves out on an international scale. To analyze such tensions within the smaller scale of the single nation is usually, by contrast, to address questions of regionalism. But even if one considers critical (and not merely symptomatic) models of regionalism, the writing that took place in Bolinas in the late 1960s and early 1970s is difficult to understand in these terms. The "meaning" of the place, and its challenge to the centers of San Francisco and New York, is not passed down, for instance, through divergent and particularized speech practices or local traditions, but constructed primarily in the present by those who have chosen to converge there. Nor is this meaning (for many of the Bolinas writers at least) containable and representable strictly by the enumeration of a series of *descriptive features*. In fact the attempt to be fully *inside* Bolinas, both geographically and socially—a concern for many of the poets—produces a crisis in representation wherein deictic references to "here" and "now" create a kind of incantatory mantra that, paradoxically, only signals presence as a greater and ultimately unmasterable concern. Phenomenological being gets undermined in Bolinas by an acid-tinged linguistic turn. So too the poem as the self-evident unit of composition and experience gets displaced—at least in the practices of Creeley, Kyger, and Warsh—by the ongoing serial temporality of the book as frame. As such, this writing participates in a wider shift that occurs throughout American experimental poetry in the 1960s—especially in the work of George Oppen and Jack Spicer—from the poem to the book as unit of composition.

Creeley's 1974 book *Thirty Things* provides an instance of this kind of serial composition; but the book's organization is not merely a "formal" feature. Rather, seriality here takes on a social dimension: individual poems lose their autonomy as they get recast within the larger social space of the book. These are poems that have friends. And these friends, meanwhile, are organized within the discrete space of Bolinas. The book references its production in Bolinas by dedications,[2] by the inclusion of monoprints made by Bobbie Creeley (now Bobbie Louise Hawkins), which are often based on photos of the poems' dedicatees, and by reference to the geographical and social world of Bolinas. All of this works to ground an otherwise extremely abstract short poem like "Here," which reads in its entirety: "Here is / where there / is" (Creeley, *Thirty Things* 31).[3] Being occurs in a proximate relation to a subject, a relationship that can only be marked by an iterable spatial marker, "here." At the same time, to articulate this "position" on being is also to indicate its *relational* status, so that "there / is" suggests at once occurrence and also the possibility of recognizing here's opposite, there, for another subject who would be removed from the focal point of any subjectively oriented "here."

Elsewhere in Creeley's work this absorption is figured as a kind of eternal recurrence that takes off from the specific geographical features of the Bolinas beach and channel, as in Creeley's poem "As we sit," where a kind of phenomenological now, running for four three-line stanzas, concludes in a single line stanza—"as we sit"—that restates the title and therefore casts the reader back to the beginning, and thus into an endless circuit of this sitting.[4]

As We Sit

There is a long
stretch of sky
before us. The road

goes out to the channel
of the water. Birds
fly in the faintly

white sky. A sound
shuffles over
and over, shifting

sand and
water. A wind
blows steadily

as we sit. (Creeley, *As We Sit* 27)

While the lure of this absorption is, for most Bolinas poets, positioned *against* the rush (and the perceived violence) of urban life, its positive content remains for Creeley, as Charles Bernstein says, "to audit [. . .] not the things of a life but its conditions" . . . "Here / there, self / other are, in Creeley's poetics, projected fissures rather than lived durations" ("Hearing 'Here'" 293, 296). Bernstein is right; and yet Creeley's choice is not so much to choose fissures *instead* of durations. Rather, he seems to go out in search of durations, like a good member of the Bolinas community, only again and again to discover these fissures.

Other Bolinas writers were less attentive to the linguistic and philosophical problems inherent in mapping an immersive, collective now. Most of the poems in *On the Mesa*, for instance, are thematically organized around countercultural concerns: antiurbanism, ecological activism, sustainable and organic agriculture, group sex, alternative medicine, drug use, non-Western religion, and Native American knowledge and history. As a whole, *On the Mesa* overlays these thematic concerns within a larger synthesis of some of the main elements of Donald Allen's hugely influential 1960 anthology, *The New American Poetry*.[5]

> Like those Rabelasian characters who took to the mountaintops during plague and caroused and told stories completely unharmed [. . .] while the plague went on below them, like those in Noah's boat who took to high ground during the flood [. . .] so these poets have taken to the Bolinas Mesa, high ground, while the world goes awash around them, practicing a little "Black Mountainery," a little "New York Schoolery," and a little Tom Foolery. (Daniel Moore, epigraph to Weishaus n.p.)

Michael Bond's poem "The Moon on Black Cherries" may be taken as typical of this antiurban retreat to high ground.

> everything that I can learn, that man with his mind
> can learn, must first have been unlearned
> once before, in the journey from the prairie
> to the city
> the most advanced of minds
> is only best
> at doing with a machine the tasks
> the heart was once at home with (Bond 9)

The poem continues by suggesting the city not only as a literal trap, but as a persistent category of thought, even among the rural utopians: "not only the prisoners of 2nd Avenue / but also we who bring our city minds / to the grassland" (Bond 10), where the speaker rediscovers the Native American past: "our dead, grandfathers, our / ancestors, have feet of grass, / bones of air // skin of clear stream water / with their sharp eyes they watch me" (Bond 12).[6] Similarly, in his "Songs of David Dog the Lion," David Meltzer pictures ravaged cities from which sensible humans must flee—"Each step a snapshot of hell on earth"—and proposes the poem itself as evidence of the poet's transformation into a new, shamanistic role of seer who produces such songs under his new, Native American inflected name (15). Moreover, both poems celebrate these projects—the renunciation of the urban and the reconnection with a rural model of place, including a vertical or transhistorical link to Native American culture—by bringing them into contact with an almost infinitely expansive "now," whose frequent restatement, as I mentioned, becomes itself within many Bolinas poems an insistent thematic, even a kind of transcendental content.

Associated with a forcible self-abstraction from decaying urbanism and the administered consciousness of national politics, American history with a capital "H", consumerism, and Vietnam, Bolinas is not simply an alternative locale, but rather—like many communes developed during the same period—a deprogramming center, now run by poets, that might allow for the phenomenological bracketing necessary to return consciousness to itself.[7] But not surprisingly, few could agree on precisely what course this de-instrumentalization should take, what role poetry would play in the process, and what kind of a "now" could be built as a result. While most of the *On the Mesa* poets fill this now with countercultural themes and depiction of lived durations, Creeley, by contrast, tends to project it as an unresolvable gap that constitutes both the linguistic depiction of temporality and the larger social formation that would share it. And yet Creeley's position is not simply one of demystifying or ironizing Bolinas's elapsing present. Rather, he goes to work daily, in real time, at once embracing the "intimate and approving community" of Bolinas and charting the temporal and linguistic gaps that emerge when he tries to frame its now in words (Creeley, *Tales Out of School* 101). And yet this, too, is conceived as a negation of instrumentality: "It's almost as if I've given so much to that idiot war I'm damned if I'm going to give it my experience of words" (Creeley, *Contexts of Poetry* 194).

If Creeley's attempt to foreground this now was perhaps the most self-reflexive, other poets did make similar attempts without lapsing into pure thematic writing. In some ways Warsh's 1972 book *Part of My History* parallels Creeley's *A Day Book*: both quotidian and serial books collapse distinctions between poem and notebook or journal and move around a variety of late 1960s countercultural locations before winding up, entranced, in the thick present of Bolinas. Warsh's title presents a central paradox inasmuch as the book (which is largely unconcerned with the past) will only *become* part of a history once its emphatic emphasis on fully occupying the present has receded into the past. He writes in "Definition of Great," included in *On the Mesa,*

Momentarily

the language of description is lost

what you see with your eyes is enough, for you, anyway

but how to get that sense of what you saw across

to another person

it's possible

through the spirit in your voice

when you say

"it was great!"

(Warsh, in Weishaus 125)

The claim of the poem is that the language of description is not so much lost here as transcended when the power of seeing gets transmitted by spoken tonality. And yet the statement (very much like the knowing looks with which I began this essay) does, ultimately, rely on a model of interior experience—so that it remains part of someone else's past, *Part of My History,* the enthusiastic report of an offscreen activity.

Compare this to Creeley's "Bolinas and Me . . ." which begins with an absorbing image of sunset among a circle of oaks, only to circle the poem back to a dilemma about how such absorption can be conveyed in language.

Holy place we stand in,
these changes—Thanksgiving,

in the circle of oaks,
the sun going west, a glowing

white yellow through the woods.
To the west all the distance.

> Things move.   You've come to here
> by one thing after another, and are here.
>
> Flat thoughts in recalling
> something after.   Nostalgic twist
>
> of everything so thought—a
> period of thought here. (Creeley, in Weishaus 31)

"Flat thoughts in recalling / something after" suggests a loss of complexity when one later tries to recall a rich, immersive moment.[8] But these thoughts are also, more fascinatingly, a threat in the present itself: either recalling intrudes and produces something secondary, "something after," or the very attempt to bring to mind, to recall, a possible futurity, a state that would follow from the saturated present, itself produces the flatness. To think in such a way, to occupy the present with such singular insistence, is to anticipate nostalgia, and this makes such thinking part of an inevitably finite "period of thought here." After forty years, one might also hear these lines in the broader context of literary history. Unlike Berkson, Kyger, Grenier, and others, Bolinas would in fact be a short "period of thought" in Creeley's career. And yet in part because that career has been more closely studied than those of other writers associated with Bolinas, it becomes easier to relate the smaller scale linguistic concerns of Creeley's Bolinas writing to the larger transformation in literary history with which his writing is often associated.

What comes to a head in Bolinas for Creeley is not so much a new understanding of language's relation to terms of space and time that would emerge in discrete poems, but rather a new concept of seriality that would obliterate the discrete poem as a category, inscribing it in a simultaneously denser intertextuality and looser concept of organization based on the book as unit. Creeley's "period of thought" in Bolinas represents not just one among equally significant periods in Creeley's career, but rather the culmination in *A Day Book* (1972) and *Thirty Things* (1974) of the drive toward a serial, quotidian poetics that had begun most noticeably in *Pieces* (1968), though this trajectory obviously begins before Creeley's move to California. Still, Bolinas, as a project of place and community, becomes a way for him to focus and acknowledge a shift in his own writing—a shift that, by addressing place directly, also liquidates most of the practices historically involved in its depiction.

For other Bolinas writers, like Joanne Kyger, reflexivity about place takes on a more explicitly social cast. Kyger, too, might be understood to develop a kind of serial, book-based writing that culminates, especially in her 1975 book *All This Every Day,* in a quotidian account of Bolinas.[9] But for Kyger, distraction from a gripping "here" is framed less in terms of the constitutive relations between language and thought than in terms of those between a subject and her social context.[10] That is, much in the way that a poet like Alice Notley will later reinterpret a New York School poetics of distraction from the point of view of a mother's *forced* distractions, so Kyger analyzes the gendered world from which various West Coast Zen poets are or are not quite able to abstract themselves into ambient cocoons—and the extent to which their doing so becomes a kind of public performance.[11] Seven years before her move to Bolinas, on a trip through Japan and India with her then husband Gary Snyder, and, for a time, Allen Ginsberg, Kyger was already taking note of the social implications of poetic and spiritual authority. Here, for instance, is her account of the three poets' meeting with the Dalai Lama.

> The Dal is 27 and lounged on a velvet couch like a gawky adolescent in red robes. I was trying to say witty things to him through the interpreter, but Allen Ginsberg kept hogging the conversation by describing his experiments on drugs and asking the Dalai Lama if he would like to take some magic mushroom pills and were his drug experiences of a religious nature until Gary said really Allen the inside of your mind is just as boring and just the same as everyone else's is it necessary to go on; and that little trauma was eased over by Gary and the Dalai talking guru to guru like about which positions to take when doing meditation and how to breathe and what to do with your hands, yes yes that's right says the Dalai Lama. (*Strange Big Moon* 194)

What should be emphasized here is not merely that Ginsberg saddled the Dalai Lama with tedious accounts of his hallucinations, but that Kyger approached the encounter less as an acolyte than as a courtier, and that Ginsberg's disruptive behavior got squelched not by a move toward humorless prostration before the master, but rather by Snyder's surgical remark, followed by his ascension to parallel guru status. Even or especially in these elevated surroundings, Kyger was capable of what Anne Waldman calls her "campiest wit" (Foreword viii). "The thing is, I am sounding rather bitter because it's been years since I've been able to get any wild martini attention. All I do is stand around in this black drip dry dress in India" (Kyger, *Strange Big Moon* 195). At times, Kyger can sound very much like Edie Sedgwick trapped in an ashram.

Like Philip Whalen's, Kyger's work often occupies a space between absorption and distraction, between a successful Zen experience and the petty social world. The difference is that the antagonist in Whalen tends to be his own ego; however, in Kyger it tends to be the egos of others—especially the other rock-starish male poets with whom she was in close contact: Snyder, Ginsberg, and then in Bolinas, Creeley and briefly Ted Berrigan. We see this dynamic at work, for instance, in the first poem of *All This Every Day*, a book title that, like many of the poems I have addressed so far, uses an empty shifter, "this," to point to Bolinas as a site of repeated and expansive awe.

> He is in the mountains and in the streams, the fields.
> Call upon the Lord Ganesha and he
> will appear
> immediately
> as saviour of grace and belief in the seen.
> (Kyger, *All This Every Day* 11, hereinafter *All This*)

Here a Hindu deity becomes the genius loci of a landscape that could be Californian, or at least is in most of the other—also largely serial—poems in the book. Whatever the source of this immanent emergence from the landscape, a belief in such possibility quickly and playfully qualifies itself, the register of religious awe and piety becoming that of quotidian exclamation: "Birthless, Deathless / Oh Man, what a High I was having" (*All This* 11). Moreover, the need to tell of epiphanic spiritual experience ultimately seems to turn it into a kind of dogma that props up the speaker's would-be guru status.

This teaching is known as the secret
of VEDANTA
Ponder over it and treasure it and all success
will come to you,
becoming the friend of all.

Soooo Serious
Soooo Gentle
Soooo full of wisdom
One nods out, gently faints upon the revelation
of the first thought or so
into this (Kyger, *All This* 11–12)

Throughout Kyger's writing intimations of revelation, rather than delivering the immanent joy they suggest, instead seem to bring about a division (either in the speaking subject or among people): the desire to cash in on revelation, to construct oneself as a guru, becomes a temptation from which the poem or one of its speakers turns away: "I don't believe in any / of your gods or powers / It's all Bullshit // I don't even believe / In My powers or gods // Her dying words were / Keep the house clean" (*All This* 69).[12] Far from dismissing introspection or the cultivation of non-Western epistemology, however, Kyger demonstrates a desire instead to puncture claims toward authority ("Soooo Serious / Soooo Gentle / Soooo full of wisdom" [*All This* 12]) by running deictic references to immersive interiority up against hippie objects ("some flutes / from Peru" [*All This* 53]), debutant exclamations[13] ("Drinking some Coffee—I wonder what / my social calendar is for today" [*All This* 24]), and Benzedrine lists and associations ("Often I try so hard with stimulants / which only graze the surface / like I wish to become surface" [*All This* 55]).

Her poem "October 29, Wednesday" begins, "In a crowd of people I am suddenly elevated. No matter that / the crowd follows Ginsberg and Snyder, out on a quick / demonstration march thru the halls of a tall building out / into the gardens, their faces among the trees as little / Chinese sages grained into the wood" (*All This* 22). Again, immersive and rewarding experiences seem to overlap with an analysis of the parceling and disseminating of poetic authority. The poem continues:

from a
cross legged position, I rise slowly off the ground in a
crowd of people, easy as can be.   ELEVATED!   Mr. Ginsberg
and Mr. Snyder frown, not so much?   As they are on their busy
way, as groups of people pour their respect and devotion to-
wards them.   Pour, pour—they're busy drinking it up all day
in teacups.   Do you think we've sent these young ladies and
gentlemen in the right direction?   That is to say, haven't
we sent them in the right direction though.
With my back against a stone wall
in a courtyard, I am closing my eyes and—Now if you will
just observe me, I will move up off the ground, hopefully
as much as a foot, two feet, grind.   In my Tibetan bathrobe.
Silence. (*All This* 22)

Here it's not enough to be elevated; one must also be *taken* as elevated —and thus the risk of the masters' negative judgments. Throughout this poem—as throughout most of *All This Every Day*—Kyger links the social dynamics of her poetry circle to a guru system of eastern spiritual education. Since she, Snyder, Ginsberg, and other New American poets had traveled to India and Japan and studied the countries' literature and religion, the link is more than a distant analogy. What is perhaps surprising, though, is that transPacific contact here bestows not so much liberation from a Western worldview as a new set of figures for a system of hierarchical prestige—a kind of caste system of poets.

Tracing this doctrine's concrete effects in the behavior of younger poets, the last part of the poem provides an ironic rejoinder to the two older poets' self-satisfied conversation about the good of their teaching: "Well then, on the greens in front of the / Mansion are walking Tom Clark and Ted Berrigan, what chums! / Do you think I could possibly fall in step, as they turn same / to far flung university on horizon, gleaming. You bet your / life not. The trouble, says Ted, with you Joanne, is that / you're not intelligent enough" (*All This* 22). This, then, is one sense in which Kyger anatomizes the Bolinas scene: showing meditative consciousness not as pure interiority, but rather as a kind of social currency that can give rise to different forms of authority.

It's important to stress, though, that Kyger's inclusion of such details is not merely a matter of sour grapes. First, Kyger was herself by this point a highly respected poet—the only woman accepted (however grudgingly) into the Spicer Circle. And by the time she had come to live in Bolinas, she was established as a poetry luminary on close to equal footing with the men. We might hear her objections, then, not so much as about her own particular status as about the extent to which the Bolinas experiment would be dominated by gurus. One indication of this is offered by a short poem, written by Charlie Vermont, in the first issue of *Big Sky*. The poem, "Vertical Portrait of Joanne Kyger," was hand scrawled in the magazine:

form
id
able (Vermont)

Of it, Vermont writes: "Bolinas was to poetry much as Key West might have been to literature when Hemingway was there. Except it happened to be Robert Creeley. At that time, there were not a lot of women who stood in their own right, not as there are now. So Joanne was one of the many pioneers. Bolinas was mecca." Speaking of how Kyger, "made [her] choices more believable" than those of other people, Vermont continues: "She was not in awe of the great ego-maniacs abounding during those 'expansive times'" (Vermont n.p.).

But whereas the self-acknowledged "failure" of Creeley's version of phenomenology seems to emerge from the infinitely recursive relationships between quotidian events and the language that would fix or give witness to them, for Kyger this failure occurs because of the continual puncturing of the brackets with which phenomenology holds back exterior historical explanation in order to study perception in its "pure" state.[14] It is not that Kyger wants to, but cannot quite, arrive at phenomenological consciousness, but rather that she insists on seeing such consciousness in relation to the very brackets that would enable it:[15] "Communication, I said, is not the word, you are after. That/assumes separation to begin with./Hear how people have a focus, a guide, go back inside—/Is outside! Dead heart, alive" (*All This* 33). This double vision, moreover, plays itself out geographically within the multiple poetic affiliations to different branches of the New American Poetry implied by the Bolinas anthology. Framed this way we could say that Kyger's oscillation between a West Coast meditative poetics and an East Coast cultivation of dailiness is not so much a synthesis as it is a revelatory way of running one against the other—so that disembodied flights keep touching down into the gendered bodies and social contexts that make them possible.[16] Or, as Joe Brainard notes in his 1971 *Bolinas Journal*: "One Joanne contradiction occurred to me this morning. That of being so down-to-earth, and so romantic too" (n.p.).

Brainard's journal, with which I will conclude, reads like an ethnographic report on Bolinas by a participant observer newly arrived from the opposite coast.[17] Brainard, who would spend only a short time in Bolinas, responds with characteristic deflation to the possibilities of the new space: "it's always nice to know you can take a loud shit without feeling self-conscious about it." Still, this freedom does not seem to open up new aesthetic possibilities: "Sitting here only a few feet away from the ocean it's hard to think of anything to say (except 'ocean') so I guess I'll stop." After noting an inability to match the compellingness of place to any acceptable aesthetic register, Brainard turns to what he sees as the central terms of the community—ones that will go on to have a frightening afterlife within suburbia: "A lot of being inside your head here. A lot of talk about it. And a lot of talk about other people's heads too. And a lot of talk about houses." For a community obsessed with consciousness, heads and houses get foregrounded as its necessary sites, the physical and architectural frames in which experiments in reinventing consciousness must take place. Brainard's tendency throughout is to literalize the terms of the Bolinas experiment by attending to its letter more than its spirit. Not surprisingly, then, drug experiences present not only a realization of consciousness grounded in place, but a bummer-like sorting or anatomization of the hazards of the current social formation: "Today is the longest day of the year and so a lot of us are going to take acid. Possible Bolinas acid dangers: too many people, poison oak, sunburn, and *me*." And yet Brainard does ultimately have an acid experience that focuses what many of the Bolinas writers are constantly gesturing toward: "So amazing to be 'in' everything so much. So very way back deep in there, 'being' with it all. Breathing with it all. So busy, the bugs, and each blade of grass. And those chills that run up and down your spine with the wind." As open as Brainard is to this kind of experience that embodies what many in Bolinas were after, in the end he reacts negatively to the Bolinas poets' insistence on presenting such a state as a life goal, a continuous and absolute present: "It seems to me that there is a lot to be said for 'finding' yourself in your head, as opposed to 'being' there."

For Brainard then, unlike Kyger, self-proposed pragmatic goals, rather than externally imposed social conflicts, puncture pure consciousness, re-grounding the meditative self in the here-and-now. And yet Brainard's reading of the politics of authority in Bolinas blurs this very distinction, suggesting that, whether or not this pressure comes from Kyger herself, Brainard is asked to decide upon a pecking order between Kyger and Bobbie Creeley. "Why do I find it a bit awkward being with Joanne and Bobbie together? Like I have to somehow avoid playing favorites. [. . . They] appear to be very good friends but, I don't know. I get funny vibrations between them sometimes." While Creeley can understand the Bolinas scene as essentially "intimate and approving," Brainard, like Kyger, suggests that these very gestures of intimacy and approval also convey another set of meanings, especially palpable to those who find themselves in the scale of power somewhere between Bolinas's sage gurus or levitating gods and the Marcia Nardis and Vincent Ferrinis who serve them respectful tea, and seem eternally barred from integrating themselves into the community as absolute peers.

My point here is not to present Brainard as the dystopian observer of the Bolinas utopia. Nor is it to give an easily cynical view of the supposedly inevitable contradictions and failures of the stupid hippies so important to conservative revisions of the 1960s. Rather, it is to suggest something of the collective nature of the assumptions about place Brainard encounters among those poets—like Creeley, Warsh, Kyger, and their less-remembered colleagues—who have sought refuge from the fallen cities on the Bolinas mesa. Whereas Williams and Olson used the category of place to bring the past to bear on the future, Bolinas writers used it to focus a kind of expansive present—be it saturated with countercultural sound bites, or purged of all but deictics to highlight the problems coming to be known as the metaphysics of presence and the sociology of literature.

At roughly the moment of Olson's death in 1970, his coterie correspondent Creeley, in a sense Olson's primary figure of virtual collectivity, gravitated toward the center of a new kind of polis that radically shifted the aims of Maximus's labors in Gloucester: if the vertical, historical axis of place still figured into Bolinas writing by a far less researched evocation of Native Americans in Marin, these references worked not to open up an array of historical and cultural materials that might be collaged into new alternative genealogies. Instead, the turn to a kind of timeless place was undertaken paradoxically to authorize consciousness in its total negations both of the vertical axis of diachronic thought and of the horizontal axis of the kinds of synchronic thought (patriotism, familial consciousness, etc.) that situated one as a docile subject of The Man, who himself took on increasingly urban features. This turn to place was thus in a sense an emptying of the category of what are usually its constitutive features.

And yet this paradoxical cultivation of place as a negation was hippie phenomenology with a purpose: consciousness here was not the privileged neutral term that might arise by the careful bracketing of the two primary nonphilosophical machines of explanation—external history and internal psychology. Rather, as the word itself becomes a mantra, consciousness was that fragile antidote to the forms that symptomatic history then took, both in time and across it: militaristic nationalism, reactionary racism, intentional and unconscious sexism, rampant consumerism. If the classic phenomenologist negated history (and psychology) in total in order to study the *form* of consciousness, the hippie phenomenologist negated symptomatic history in order to *live* consciousness as a present (and also at times anticipatory) refuge—in this context the capacious "now" of Bolinas that organized so much poetry from the period. And yet the most powerful poets also negated something of their horizontal social circle in order both to zoom in on this moment and to establish the poetic authority to be seen as one whose consciousness-at-work-zooming-in was worthy of sustained attention.

While the familiar hippies stockpiled this "now" with inventories of countercultural stances, others treated its tenuous existence as the problem, not the solution, of their poetry: in Kyger's case the lure of selfless absorption running up against both the instrumental function such absorption could have among authorized poets and the gendered distractions that pull some thinkers out of it; in Creeley's case the ongoing mismatches between perceptual states and the linguistic markers that would render them accessible to others. But it is not simply that Creeley, Kyger, and the other more reflexive poets undermine naive hippie dreams of self-presence-in-consciousness as resistance. However different the results, experimental poetry's turn toward a vanishing, ineffable, or continually punctured now was part of the same large-scale social negation, the refusal of monumental temporalities, that characterized the counterculture of the late 1960s and early 1970s. To affirm this now was not simply to locate its presence in authentic nonurban spaces like Bolinas, where it might organize exemplary microcommunities. One affirmed it, instead, by locating now's continual recession as the constitutive feature of such a community.

NOTES

1. Gordon Baldwin, John Doss, Keith Lampe, Bill Brown, John Thorpe, Lawrence Kearney, Michael Bond, Max Crosley, and the editor Joel Weishaus.

2. The increasingly intersocial aspect of Creeley's poetry can be registered in the number of dedications we find in *Thirty Things*, including ones to Robert Grenier, Tom Clark, Joanne Kyger, Ted Berrigan, Ebbe Borregaard, and Stan Brakhage.

3. The book begins with an epigraph from Williams's *The Descent of Winter*: "It is. It is the thing where it is."

4. A similar version of this stasis occurs in Creeley's poem "Still" (*Thirty Things*), which plays on the dual sense of the title word as both the lack of movement and an uninterrupted temporal continuum: "Still the same/day?/Tomorrow" (*Thirty Things* 57).

5. Donald Allen was himself living in Bolinas at the time of the new anthology. Weishaus describes the collection as "a gathering of poets & writers & artists living on or around the mesa in Bolinas, California. Not so much a school of poets as a meeting of those who happen to be at this geographical location at this point in wobbly time." He goes on to explain that "several divergent movements in American poetry of the past 20 years (Black Mountain, San Francisco Beat, 'New York School' of poets) have come together with new Western and mystic elements at the unpaved crossroads of Bolinas" (*On the Mesa* back cover).

6. "I left New York one month ago," writes Andrei Codrescu—one of those who would soon visit Bolinas—"because the ugly tensions on the street took hallucinatory forms" (Kane, *All Poets Welcome* 180).

7. Even when Bolinas poetry evinces a rare interest in what lies "over the hill" (as the totality of land outside Bolinas was called), this world tends to get folded into the quotidian pace of Bolinas life, as in the following passage from Lewis Warsh's *Part of My History:* "Walk to Peppers and realize how warm it is *outside.* (M's cabin behind the Gibson House is best in mid-afternoon light.) Buy a copy of the San Francisco Chronicle. Bobby Seale manacled to chair in Chicago courtroom. Coffee, rice krispies with raisins, some cinnamon crackers" (n.pag.). Even Joe Brainard, who visits briefly, uses the term: "Went over the hill today to do some shopping with Bob and Bobbie" (n.pag.).

8. This interest in place as a matter of partiality and partialness can be traced all the way back to his poem "The Innocence" of 1951, included in Donald Allen's *The New American Poetry,* which concludes a short analysis of perception, distinguishing the edge of the ocean, with: "What I come to do / is partial, partially kept" where the act of recording the scene in the present is "partial" (both interested and incomplete) and partially kept (both partly recorded and partly remembered) (77).

9. The last poem in her 1970 *Places to Go,* "Descartes and the Splendors Of," is a kind of meditation on sense-certainty that provides a self-consciously humorous "grounding" in the history of philosophy for the kind of work being taken by many people in Bolinas.

10. Michael Davidson sees this as a failure of focus: "too often the poems seem to indulge distractedness for its own sake" (*The San Francisco Renaissance* 188).

11. For this account of Notley, see chapter one of my *Frank O'Hara: The Poetics of Coterie.*

12. Or, alternately: "I always say OM / that interrupts the silk mantle in which she is clothed / out of gentility and hides you too / which out of deference to a past you ignore" (Kyger, *All This* 20).

13. Related interjections include: "I could use a little rest too / I only slept 11 hours last night" (Kyger, *All This* 21) and "I hate what I cannot see" (*All This* 15).

14. There is considerable difference between Edmund Husserl's and Maurice Merleau-Ponty's versions of this bracketing; the latter understands it in a more porous, less absolute sense: "The philosopher, in so far as he is a philosopher, ought not to think like the external man, the psychophysical subject who is *in* time, *in* space, *in* society, as an object is in a container. From the mere fact that he desires not only to exist but to exist with an understanding of what he does, it follows that he must suspend the affirmations which are implied in the given facts of his life. But to suspend them is not to deny them and even less to deny the link which binds us to the physical, social, and cultural world. It is on the contrary to *see* the link, to become conscious of it. It is 'the phenomenological reduction' alone which

reveals this ceaseless and implicit affirmation, this 'setting of the world' which is presupposed in every moment of our thought" (Merleau-Ponty 49).

15. Kyger's interest in these questions can be gauged by the title of her 1989 book, *Phenomenological.*

16. Ron Silliman calls Kyger "the poet who really links the Beats, the Spicer Circle, the Bolinas poets, the NY School and the language poets, and the only poet who can be said to do all of the above" (email to Linda Russo, 28 April 1998, posted on the *EPC*: http://epc.buffalo.edu/authors/kyger/silliman.html).

17. Of the social scene, Brainard writes, for instance: "News that Ted Berrigan is coming out here totally zaps my mind. (Help). One of the nicest things about being here is not having a past to live up to. Or down to. I love Ted, but—" (n.pag.).

FOUR | PETER MIDDLETON

When L=A

Language, Authorship, and Equality in *L=A=N=G=U=A=G=E* Magazine

L=A=N=G=U=A=G=E (1978–1981) is one of the most distinctive American poetry magazines of the second half of the last century. More zine than magazine, more etics than poetics, industrial in its unadorned appearance: the first and many subsequent issues of the first three volumes of *L=A=N=G=U=A=G=E* magazine, edited by Charles Bernstein and Bruce Andrews, present an assertively utilitarian ethos that belies its radical innovations.[1] You would hesitate to call this ethos an aesthetic and would certainly want to add that all-purpose adjective minimalist. Its white folded stapled foolscap sheets and IBM courier typescript do not invite visual excitement, and only the masthead word L=A=N=G=U=A=G=E in a heavy black sans serif commands special attention. Both then and now the magazine invited questions about itself, about everything from its design to its aims as a poetry journal. Are its linking bars echoing the kitsch neon titling and naming used in popular culture, or is this an equals sign, a reminder that all signs are fungible, any hint of gematrical powers thoroughly extirpated? Ron Silliman appeared to assume the latter when he wrote in *L=A=N=G=U=A=G=E* No. 6 that "if A=B and B=C, then A=C, etc." it follows from such logic that "identity begets substitution, exchange, reproduction" (Silliman, "Benjamin Obscura"). What sort of magazine is it that has no table of contents, no pagination, and as in the first issue presents you with a series of short pieces of prose about poetry, language, and authorship, whose authors are identified only by name at the end? What relation do the contributors have to the editors? Almost all the contributions are very short and many bear traces of considerable cutting, making some appear more like excerpts that allude rather than stand alone. A striking feature of the magazine is its use of recycled material from elsewhere. The second issue of April 1978 begins with an italicized extract from Roland Barthes's *Writing Degree Zero*, one of a significant number of similar short passages in this and later issues that have been lifted from existing publications and then integrated with the rest of the discussion by the magazine's contributors and correspondents, so that actual quotations, essays, reviews, poetic prose, and even letters to the editor, all jostle together. The more you look the stronger the editorial control appears, to the point where the editors can seem to be speaking through the choice of words and passages in these carefully framed contributions, as if those contributions were quotations in an editorial argument.

My aim in this article is to discuss that unusual editorial policy as an experiment in distributed or collaborative authorship, on the basis of a loose analogy with the forms of authorship found increasingly in the sciences, and inherent in cinema, although my focus will be on the consequences, intended and unintended, on the emergent identity politics of the period, primarily on feminism. I need therefore to make a methodological point. A full history of the magazine would certainly draw on a wide range of sources and contexts, including poems and other essays by the many contributors, reviews and scholarly studies that allude to the magazine and its New York milieu, published and (mostly) unpublished correspondence, new interviews with the protagonists, histories of literary journals, and above all a full discussion of the complex politics of gender, ethnicity, class, and cross-cultural connections that was in force. My assumption here is that any such research would still need to start with the recognition of the interpretive consequences of the magazine's unusual form. This requires a reading of its assembled internal decoherences and cross-referencings, its juxtapositions and its ascriptions, that collectively create the potential for a new kind of text. I want to approach the magazine ethnographically, as it were, and try to prize it loose from preconceptions about poetry magazines and literary history, by treating the magazine as if it itself were a literary work whose authorship remains to be described.[2] One of my main contentions will be that an unexpected consequence of this distributed authorship is a fractalization of identity, especially gendered identity, because the identity ascribed to a named "author" frequently has to be shared across a range of other "authors," including the editors and other participants in the discussion (whose status varies from intended contributor, to the outsider status of a writer of a "letter to the editors," to a co-opted author such as Roland Barthes or Fredric Jameson).

Readers of *L=A=N=G=U=A=G=E* at the time were themselves not always sure what was going on. In the second issue, in what is titled "Letter to the Editor" (and we might wonder what makes this contribution a "Letter to the Editor" in a manner that some similar contributions are not so described), John Taggart complains in response to the first issue that the reviewers "feel an obligation to turn the review into a performance as near an 'original work' as possible," with the result that the work under review becomes merely an occasion for the reviewer to produce "their own performance" in its place. A sting in the tail: "& if you say after all everyone knows everybody else, well I ask you!" Is Taggart identifying a coterie, an in group of friends so inward with each other that they don't need to give attention to a work they are reviewing because everyone writing for the magazine already knows? Another "Letter to the Editor" is more sympathetic to the aims of the magazine, though the writer also detects efforts to represent, or perhaps instaurate, a community. In this letter, John Perlman says: "the serendipity of relationship I take as key—and that, however manipulated the *purpose*, it remains arrogation to wear credit for the connections *mind* affixes, skims." Is the magazine an assemblage that represents a serendipity or random yet fortuitous collection of contributions? Perlman notices editorial manipulation, too, and perceptively speculates about the implications of this editorial "arrogation," or as my dictionary glosses it, "claiming as one's own," by the editors. Are the editors claiming the work of the writers for the magazine for their own in a dissolution of authorship in the editorial process? Or are they helping a community to speak to itself?

The editors were evidently aware that readers would be wondering what sort of magazine they were reading, and from time to time reflexively address such questions. In an interview published in Supplement No. 3 of *L=A=N=G=U=A=G=E* in 1981, Andrews offers the most explicit answer. This magazine is an extension of friendly exchange amongst poets: "it has to do with writing as an exploration and a presentation of the possibilities of language [. . .] It's something a number of poets around the country and in Europe now talk about but most of that discussion has taken place privately in correspondence, people's journal writing, etc. We've all been engaged in that project in the mail and in conversation for years and are trying in a small way by doing the magazine to get some of that discourse out into a more public realm" (Howe, "The Pacifica Interview").[3] Friendship between poets made public as they talk about language: is this what the magazine offers, a representation of the new form of poetic friendship?[4] This answer only raises more questions. Why are poets talking about the possibilities of "language" rather than poetry, and about the pressing new politics of gender, "race," and class with which many of the contributors were engaged? What are the editorial strategies, ideologies, social practices of writing and reading, and modes of authorship at work, and how do they inflect the emerging poetics of this network of writers? Is friendship as a practice of assumed equality a model equal to the task the journal set itself?

I want to explore what might be required to answer these questions, especially the last. Similar questions could of course be addressed to many poetry magazines, but in most of them these issues tend to be muted. *L=A=N=G=U=A=G=E* magazine foregrounded these questions both explicitly and in its highly unusual editorial composition, to the degree that it invites the kind of close reading we give to a poetic text. It did so for two reasons. First, it emerged at an unusual historical moment, when the very medium of poetry appeared to have been annexed to a new quasi-scientific theory of language that dismissed authorial agency and imagination as variously essentialism, humanist illusion, ideological effect, or other pathologies of the signifier, and when the radical politics that had united the earlier generation of the New American poets was fracturing along ethnic and gender fault lines that were seemingly inherent in the person. Language theory and identity politics appeared to have all the authority. Second, an anthologizing editorial policy emerges as a result of the constraint of producing a cheaply printed and relatively small magazine while aiming to squeeze in as many contributions from poets as possible, and moreover attempting to further stimulate intensive debate by adding pertinent extracts lifted from other publications and by authors outside the magazine's own network of readers and elective contributors. The editors cut contributions freely to fit them into the short slots available, and they looked around for passages from authors that spoke to the magazine's concerns and spliced these in as well. The phenomenology of this magazine therefore differs quite radically from the norm and destabilizes existing textual conventions around authorship. In doing so, it creates a forum for many of the concerns that its contributors felt at the time, about their position as poets in relation to the new dogmas of language and about their own gender or ethnic identity.

Although the magazine is called *L=A=N=G=U=A=G=E* and the majority of its contributions mention language, often pervasively, authorship is at least as important a theme. Poets, readers, critics, and others all talk about what it means to write poetry, either for themselves or for others, and they worry away at many different aspects of what for them is a problem. They know that influential literary theorists have argued that the author is dead, and the author's functions have been distributed amongst various legatees: language, readers, primary process, identity politics, power. Although the contributors publish their poems elsewhere, and the great majority are singular productions, not collectively authored, the magazine enables its contributors to locate their work in a shared "conceptual workplace" and to reveal partially at least the long chain of agency by which their poetic texts become publications, a chain that extends beyond the moment when a specific sapient body places words on a screen or paper. The result could be described as an experiment in collective authorship. We need to proceed cautiously here, however. What happens to identity, to whiteness or gender, when we talk of collective authorship? Is this a way of evading identity, or might this be a way of reperforming gender identity, restaging the necessarily complex infrastructures that make the feminine and the masculine something quite different to a homogeneous set of criteria, features, or actions? Does the magazine offer glimpses of a poetics that would make possible new types of reconciliation that acknowledge the oppressions against which gender and ethnic activists were striving, or are such differences treated as irreconcilable and ignored? Might there be some sort of fractal gender at work?

The kind of challenge we are faced with in considering this question is evident in the first issue. Rae Armantrout's essay, "Why Don't Women Do Language-Oriented Writing?," is placed at the back. Does this mean that this is an issue at the bottom of the agenda? Because there are no page numbers, no structuring of sections of the magazine, placement of a contribution at the start, the middle, or the end of one of the issues of this magazine does not function in the normal manner as a marker of its relative status that depends on proximity to the front cover. Perhaps we can read Armantrout's essay's position at the end of the magazine as a strong conclusion to the preceding arguments, a resolution that carries with it the authoritative endorsement of the editors who have chosen and positioned the essay, and also read it as drawing together strands from earlier contributions by other authors. Its position at the back does, however, leave it exposed to a doubt: has it been relegated here because the editors think of this as an unimportant women's concern? We readers are given few explicit cues to decide these questions. What we can say is that these uncertainties frame the essay with another implicit question: is it important to discuss "Why Don't Women Do Language-Oriented Writing?" and what are the consequences of deciding either way? In this manner, Armantrout's leading question is editorially made to resonate with the entire project of the magazine even while as readers we might wonder what sort of dialogue is possible.

To grasp how the essay resonates requires closer examination. Armantrout starts with what to her is the obvious answer to her title, the observation that anger impels some women poets to "describe the conditions of their lives," a project which "entails representation," and so they do not want to "participate in the analytical tendencies of modernist or 'postmodernist' art." Behind this statement would be a troubling question for *L=A=N=G=U=A=G=E* magazine: is it just a forum where poets engage in postmodernist analysis? Armantrout ironizes her own title by pointing out that there is a mirror question that should be asked—"Why don't more men do language-oriented writing?"—and the failure to ask it suggests that the question of her title conceals a masculine sense of superiority, since if the question was asked in a gender-neutral manner, the answer would be unlikely to be framed in the sort of gender-specific terms that the title question tendentiously insists upon. Armantrout concludes her essay with a concern about the conceptual implications of the idea of "language-oriented" because it seems to her that "to believe non-referentiality is possible is to believe language can be divorced from thought, words from their histories." Poststructuralist dogma argued that language was thought and that thought could not take place in the absence of language, but it had little to say about history, a concept that it regarded with suspicion as being another idealization like subjectivity, experience, and feeling. Armantrout distances herself from such dogma because she values truthfulness: "The writers I like are surprising, revelatory. They bring the underlying structures of language / thought into consciousness. They spurn the facile. Though they generally don't believe in the Truth they are scrupulously honest about the way word relates to word, sentence to sentence. Some of them are men and some of them are women." Inquiry and experiment with language are not enough on their own; they should be guided by what Bernard Williams, who also doesn't believe in absolute Truth, and instead endorses truthfulness, calls the virtues of truthfulness, by accuracy and sincerity.

Armantrout's essay is impressive in its clarity about the issues at a time when the authority of both poststructuralist theory of language and identity politics were at their height. She shares the editors' commitment to inclusiveness, but she is wary of basing that inclusiveness on any sort of commitment to an epistemology or methodology allegedly entailed by the new theories of language and the new politics. She is definitely testing the limits of what is possible for the magazine, but publication in this first issue, even in the uncertain position at the back, gives these ideas legitimacy within the discourse that Andrews describes. At the same time many tensions are evident. Can non–language-oriented writers participate, especially those women poets who are too angry to be postmodernists because they must represent their lives? What will the magazine have to say about the values of truth and objectivity? How will the magazine represent political differences around gender, "race," or other divisions? Her essay is set out in an interrogative mode, and the magazine intensifies it.

Central to the understanding of these questions is the treatment of authorship in everything that *L=A=N=G=U=A=G=E* does—and fails to do. The years when *L=A=N=G=U=A=G=E* was appearing were also the moment when theoretical debate about the phenomenon of authorship hit the headlines. The most famous modern essay on authorship, Roland Barthes's "The Death of the Author," appeared first in French in 1968, but it was its appearance in 1977 in *Image-Music-Text* that gave it prominence. Two years later in 1979, Michel Foucault's almost equally famous and probably more influential essay "What Is an Author?" appeared in an English translation in Josué V. Harari's collection of essays, *Textual Strategies.* These essays are now so embedded in literary pedagogy and theory, treated as instructions for textual analysis, that the actual conceptual strategies and their performative rhetoric (Barthes's deliberately camp style full of the spirit of the impending "Mai") are overlooked. Yes, we agree with Barthes and Mallarmé, "language speaks" not the author, and poets like Mallarmé strive "to reach that point where only language acts, 'performs,' and not 'me'" without recalling that what was meant in the 1970s by "language" is not quite the same as today (Barthes 143). We hear the suggestion that the writer of a text is simply its "scriptor" and crucially, "is in no way equipped with a being preceding or exceeding the writing" filtered through decades of feminist and queer theory, new historicism, postcolonial theory, and the new theories of affect (Barthes 145). Yet if we look back through the impasto of literary theoretical refinements to what Barthes and Foucault were heard to say by poets in the 1970s, we can still be surprised. Barthes is keen to emphasize that the death of the author is not a literary pose; new knowledge in both linguistics and philosophy underwrites his demand for a new scholarly understanding of literary composition. The poet is "an empty process" (Barthes 145).

The empty poets writing for *L=A=N=G=U=A=G=E* were asking themselves what then is a text if it is not the laborious work of expressive invention? Barthes might be describing *L=A=N=G=U=A=G=E* magazine's assemblage of quotations, extracts from letters, and edited statements when he calls it "a multi-dimensional space in which a variety of writings, none of them original, blend and clash [. . .] a tissue of quotations drawn from the innumerable centres of culture" (Barthes 146). This certainly finds favor with Andrews who reviews *Image-Music-Text* in *L=A=N=G=U=A=G=E* 6 in his distinctive weave of paraphrase, quotation, and commentary, strongly endorsing Barthes's account of how "the subject loses authority, disappears, is unmade into a network of relationships, stretching indefinitely. Subject is deconstructed, lost, 'diminishing like a figurine at the far end of the literary stage'; deconstituted as writing ranges over the surface" (Andrews, "Code Words"). And Andrews notices the anarchic political gestures that lead Barthes to talk of the disappearance of the author as "truly revolutionary since to refuse to fix meaning is, in the end, to refuse God and his hypostases —reason, science, law" (Barthes 147). We should, I think, be shocked at this claim that reason, science, and law are all guaranteed by the authority of a transcendental God, and not for instance by the pragmatism or "scrupulous honesty" that Armantrout appeals to. Andrews, however, believes that this authorless writing has revolutionary potential: "Writing must look toward a radically transformed society that would provide the code (and the ideal communication system and counter-communication system) needed to *fully comprehend* it" ("Code Words", emphasis in original). Here is a role for the poet as author.

Foucault's essay goes over similar ground in a more engineered style. Modernist writing creates "a space into which the writing subject constantly disappears," and the author doesn't so much disappear as become a "function," the guarantor of a mode of discourse (Foucault, "What Is an Author?" 142, hereinafter "Author"). From this point he makes a strange prediction that could have been a description of a project like *L=A=N=G=U=A=G=E* magazine: "I think that as our society changes, at the very moment when it is in the process of changing, the author-function will disappear" and "all discourses, whatever their status, form, value, and whatever the treatment to which they will be subjected, would then develop in the anonymity of a murmur. We would no longer hear the questions that have been rehashed for so long: 'Who really spoke? Is it really he and not someone else?' [. . .] And behind all these questions, we would hear hardly anything but the stirring of an indifference: 'What difference does it make who is speaking?'" (Foucault, "Author" 160). This was a question that *L=A=N=G=U=A=G=E* magazine recurred to again and again, though the answers are not always as Foucault expected. It turns out that this collaborative authorship does have room for subjects to relocate themselves, but only within certain limits. It can still matter very much who is speaking, because identity matters. White, masculine, scientist, poet, Protestant: these are hegemonic identities that invisibly inflect authorship as much as the identities whose difference was becoming so visibly politicized in the 1970s.

Even riding the tide of intellectual fashion for continental thought, essays on authorship would not have had the impact they did if not for other cultural shifts, and I think it is important to grasp that what was happening in *L=A=N=G=U=A=G=E* magazine had counterparts in a wide range of other seemingly distant cultural practices. After all, much of what Barthes and Foucault were saying had already been rehearsed by Anglo-American critics from I. A. Richards and Cleanth Brooks to Frank Kermode and E. D. Hirsch. What happened in the 1970s was that authorship became an increasingly unstable legal, scientific, and cultural category. Sometimes authorship was extended. The confessional personal lyric had become the dominant model of poetry in the leading magazines and anthologies, the type of poem singled out for literary awards. Confessional authenticities exclusive to the author's own inner life were markers of authorship: memories, personal information, and other contingent particulars that signified the expressivity of the writer named as the originator of the poem. This was an author who, to paraphrase Barthes, did indeed exist before the poem, think, suffer, live for it, and was in the "same relation of antecedence to his work as a father to his child," a relation all too often literalized in these poems.[5]

Copyright law was also undergoing change. The Romantic idea of the originating genius, on which confessional poetry ultimately rested, had provided a poetics of authorship that had become the basis of modern copyright law, as Mario Bagioli explains: "in the case of copyright, an author obtains rights in the material inscription of his or her originality precisely because it is produced by something—personal expression—that is his or hers to begin with" (254). Many developments were challenging these norms. New scientific authorships were growing in size to the point where it was hard to know even what sort of intentionality, knowledge, and consciousness could be attributed to the collective authorship; this foundational model was questionable. As Peter Galison explains, the "we" inscribed in the scientific paper appears to function as the "collaboration-as-experimenter" or the "collaboration-as-author" (329). What, he asks, is "the constitution of the collective self" that authors these papers? And we might add, what new poetics of authorship might correspond to these changes in scientific copyright? The team effort is not composed of a set of individuals who all take full responsibility for the entire project; "it is entirely possible, even likely, that no one individual (much less a group of individuals) is entirely in control over the full spectrum of justificatory arguments that feed all the way down into the guts" of the experimental setup (329). Could we read *L=A=N=G=U=A=G=E* magazine as the work of a similar collective self?

Film theorists were also proposing new models of authorship. By the late 1970s, American auteur theory had been long established in film discourse as a means of attributing the aggregate authorship of all those involved in the facture under a single vision, and was being challenged by those like Constance Penley and Janet Bergstrom who argued that "the crucial question in determining the relationship of the spectator to the filmic discourse, how he or she is placed and thereby understands it, becomes: who 'speaks' beneath the deceptively neutral and objective voice of the 'third person' narration" (125). Indeed another contributor to the same issue was prepared to go even further. Stephen Heath argues in the Autumn 1978 issue of *Screen* that "in the last resort any discourse which fails to take account of the problem of sexual difference in its enunciation and address will be within a patriarchal order, precisely indifferent, a reflection of male domination" (53).

The editors show considerable awareness of these issues, and one way to consider the entire project of the magazine might be as a dialogue between the two editors about two differing models of how authorship is constructed within the sociality of language: Andrews, as we have seen, is comfortable with poststructuralism and writing as a "perpetual signifier, modelled on a permanent revolution" (Andrews, "Code Words"); Bernstein has a more pragmatist understanding, closer to that implied by Armantrout. He is dismissive of Derrida, preferring instead Stanley Cavell's Wittgensteinian ideas of language, even reprinting extracts from the forthcoming opus *The Claim of Reason*: "In philosophizing, I have to bring my own language and life into imagination. What I require is a convening of my culture's criteria, in order to confront them with my words and life as I pursue them and may imagine them."[6] In the same spirit Bernstein argues in a preceding note that "poetry, with written language as its medium, is, in fact, the exploration and realization of the human common ground, of 'us,' in which we are" (Bernstein, "The Conspiracy of 'Us'"). Andrews represents language as a medium or field of latent energies; Bernstein conceives it as an ensemble of social interactions. When Bernstein says that poetry's engagement with language can be "the exploration and realization of the human common ground, of 'us,' in which we are" he is going to the heart of the challenge that Armantrout raised in the first issue. Is there common ground, and can it be represented by a practice such as that of *L=A=N=G=U=A=G=E*? Or does the appeal to the human beg the question? Is it, to use Bernstein's own words, more "a whole heap of letters" ("From A to Z")?

We are now in a position to return to issues of how authorship was put in question in *L=A=N=G=U=A=G=E* and to investigate the handling of gender and racial politics within the magazine's ambit. To begin with, *L=A=N=G=U=A=G=E* had almost nothing to say directly about confessional poetry, but its contributions did occasionally acknowledge the new identity-based poetry that was becoming an important part of the cultural politics of feminism and African American arts. Barbara Barg's untitled text in the form of a multiple-choice questionnaire presents the double binds of identity in its question 12 on "women writers": "a) are only concerned with content b) don't have happy marriages c) should always have men edit their works d) are naturally gullible e) are always referred to as 'women writers.'" Lorenzo Thomas justifies attention to the poet Lance Jeffers because he is "a powerful Black poet" whose "first collection was not published until the militant atmosphere of the 1970s made his voice much more than necessary"; his "language is masculine, bent in ways that tease syntax and recall the florid eloquence of early Afro-American oratory." Jeffers's authorship depends on this African American male voice: "Jeffers' voice modulates between outraged roar and lush, sentimental praise song for those and what he loves." There is a consonance here between *L=A=N=G=U=A=G=E* and what Daniel Kane attributes (with perhaps a trace of irony) to *C* magazine (1963–1966) which also published material by Thomas, a poem with the resonant title "Political Science": "Thanks to Thomas, *C* could claim to contain a political consciousness that would otherwise be seen as lacking" (*All Poets Welcome* 119). Erica Hunt's comment in her 1988 talk "Notes for an Oppositional Poetics" is relevant here: "there is nothing inherent in language centered projects that gives them immunity from a partiality that reproduces the controlling ideas of dominant culture" and so "there are serious shortcomings in any opposition that asserts its technical victories and removes itself from other oppositional projects" (204). However she is not, I would argue, opposed to the kind of project undertaken by *L=A=N=G=U=A=G=E*, because she goes on to contend that what is needed is "to think . . . how writing can begin to have social existence in a world where authority has become highly mobile, based less on identity and on barely discerned or discussed relationships" (204). This I would argue is the possibility that many of the contributors glimpsed in the shared social space of the magazine, even if in practice it remained hard to follow through on this cognitive extemporization around the authority of authorship.

How then did the magazine handle conflict and difference, and what were the consequences for poetics and the idea of poetry as a collective enterprise? Take gender politics. Despite the fact that, as Ann Vickery points out, "many women remember Andrews and Bernstein as actively encouraging their writing," sexism in the magazine is a persistent, troubling though low key presence (30). Peter Seaton in "Texte" quite casually refers to "the term for balance, the pattern, the magazine, aspects of pussy, period, boundaries of confusion, complexities;" John Taggart, in his review of Thomas Clark's *A Still Life*, refers to Lorine Niedecker's work as "the lady's poems;" Robert Grenier alludes to "thought density wife-ing quintessence passion" and "womanly devotion's license, romance, logic's guises" in Lyn Hejinian's *Writing Is an Aid to Memory*; Alan Davies describes the "curvaceous experience" evident in Diane Ward's *Theory of Emotion*; James Sherry reviews Lynne Dreyer positively, saying that "the issues are embedded in the woman." Is it sexism when Ed Friedman calls Susie Timmons "an original nutso genius" even though he goes on to say that she is "brilliant and everything she does is worth seeing," since casting doubt on the rationalism of women is a long-established ploy?

The women contributors do notice, and they try to instigate discussion that the male contributors noticeably decline to engage with directly. Maureen Owen points out that "a woman must continually face the struggle of being taken seriously at all." Gail Sher observes in a review of a book by Beau Beausoleil that his poetry overuses references to the gender of the speaker: "Four times in the same short poem for example, he'll say 'she said' and you think 'she said so what' but 'she said' is very much what. The logic of 'she said' is the nature of language itself." The dilemma is forcefully addressed by Susan Howe in a review of Owen's *Hearts in Space*. Howe eloquently argues that gender's implications for authorship cannot be fully predicted in advance of writing; gender is produced in the process:

> Virginia Woolf once said: "it is fatal for a woman to lay the least stress on any grievance; to plead even with justice for any cause; in any way to speak consciously as a woman; and fatal is no figure of speech; for anything written with that conscious bias is doomed. It ceases to be fertilized." [. . .] How do we navigate our way? How do we crawl under the barbed wire and sit on our own sacred land? What unity will be pulled from multiplicity? What dreams? What new language? Who ever (female *or* male) knew for SURE what was left, right, center, true, false? It is in questioning that really interesting work occurs. Women who are poets of the calibre of Owen, recognize the precious gift of their UNcertainty.

And these questions imply another: what unity of purpose even amongst the contributions to *L=A=N=G=U=A=G=E* can there be in the face of such uncertainty and the divisions and oppressions of gender? In the same issue, in a section entitled "Letters to the Editor," the Women Writers Union from the Bay Area assert that "not only have women been silenced as a sex, we have been oppressed—and silenced—on the basis of our race, our class, and our sexuality" and therefore as women writers they not only connect art and feminist politics, they engage in a "multi-issue approach" to politics. And as if to confirm what the women writers are saying about men and silence, Peter Schjeldahl is found saying that he thinks of himself not as part of "a little tribe of atavists or band of subversives" but as a poet who is "really completely alone and slipping through the interstices of the world." Not an empty poet but an empty identity?

I have said that the men contributors do not directly engage with these arguments from women writers, but of course the two (male) editors have selected these various feminist statements, and in doing so have given them public voice and a place in the network of authorships represented by the magazine, and to this degree the collaborative authorship of the magazine has a successfully fractal gender. But as the persistence of unaddressed sexist asides discussed earlier demonstrates, this fractal possibility is constantly at risk of being pushed aside in favor of a single masculine identity. At times, neither strong editorial selection nor the ideal of a shared commitment to a socially responsive poetics proves sufficient to resist such masculine takeover of authorship. This problem is not discussed explicitly anywhere in the magazine. We can however gain some insight into the difficulty the editors faced when confronted with resistance to fractal authorship by examining one of the rare open disputes contained in the pages of *L=A=N=G=U=A=G=E,* a sometimes bad-tempered exchange between Silliman and Jackson Mac Low. Although what is at issue here is not gender, but political identity, it is still a question of what identity and responsibility can be ascribed to an author within the framework of the magazine.

In issue 7, in an extended feature in which twenty-four writers responded to an invitation to "list five non-poetry books that they had read in the last few years that have had a significant influence on their thinking or writing," Silliman inadvertently upset Mac Low and the subsequent rift tested the limits of the model of the magazine as a network of friends, by mocking *WIN,* the magazine of the pacifist War Resisters League, on whose editorial board Mac Low had formerly been a member. Mac Low blamed not Silliman but ideology: "To hell with the know-it-alls who entrap generous spirits such as Ron Silliman into their exploitative ideological mazes" ("Letter to the Editor"). In his response, Silliman claims that his own poetry "recognizes an audience that possesses a bourgeois origin, is educated (to the point of being conscious of literary history), predominantly white & even male" and that "becoming political does not mean abandoning this audience, but making it instead look at itself" ("Particulars"). Even male? Silliman aspires to a discursive community in which white, male participants are made to look at themselves, and he hints at a doubt that *L=A=N=G=U=A=G=E* can do this. The two poets clash because their practices of authorship are so opposed. Silliman may believe that "words are never our own [. . .] they are our own usages of a determinate coding passed down to us like all other products of civilization, organized into a single, capitalist, world economy" ("If by writing"), but he does not conclude that the best aesthetic to adopt is something like what Mac Low describes as the use of "chance operations & other quasiobjective methods to generate artworks" ("Museletter"). For Silliman this would be surrender. Poets are still responsible for the codes they pass on through their actions as authors. What is needed is the reverse of what Mac Low offers, an intensive self-examination at both the individual and group level that challenges the "social positionality" of the author and examines the "constituent elements" of this social structure in "a quasi-scientific fashion" ("If by writing"). This public exchange between Silliman and Mac Low shows how the magazine's format struggles to frame the tensions arising from different intellectual and political commitments. Ideas about authorship entail political commitments that might not be reconcilable within the sociality projected by the magazine.

I use the awkward term "sociality" in order to avoid the more obvious model of "community" because Bernstein explicitly rejected this model of a literary movement like that of Language writing, and his explanations will help us see why the magazine was constrained when faced with attributions of identity that entailed membership in a community. *L=A=N=G=U=A=G=E* could readily be imagined to be a projective version of a new poetic community, as so many poetry magazines strive to be, placing emphasis on the celebration of membership through reciprocity of attention and support. But this is not how the editors see it. In his essay "Community and the Individual Talent," Bernstein expresses a wariness about the actualities of such apparently good intentions: "Many poets that I know experience poetry communities, say scenes, as places of their initial exclusion from publication, readings, recognition" because "to have a community is to make an imaginary inscription against what is outside the community." Bernstein then goes on to argue that "some poetry will want to work against received ideas of place, group, ethnicity, gender, sexuality, person, member, individuality, tradition, aesthetic tendency," some poetry will want to be "outside" (177). Although this argument sounds plausible to someone resisting interpellation by an ideologically constructed identity, it doesn't allow for the sort of argument that Thomas makes about Jeffers.

If community is not a viable model of how poets might interact, what is? Bernstein proposes that instead of trying to create a community, a better goal might be the constitution of a social space: "If I resist the idea of a literary community, while working to support the 'actually existing' communities of poets among which I find myself, it is because I want to imagine reading and writing, performing and listening, as sites of conversation as much as collectivity. I want to imagine a constellation of readers who write, to and for one another, with the links always open at the end, spiralling outward—centrifugally—not closing in" ("Community and the Individual Talent" 179). To create in other words the sort of space offered by *L=A=N=G=U=A=G=E*. The price however may paradoxically be another sort of exclusion, the exclusion of the identity discourses of communities.

The emerging conceptual paradigms of the subject and language that would dominate literary theory in the 1980s were not only hard to challenge, their differential benefits for differently positioned authors were also hard to articulate within the cognitive resources of the time. To see just what was at stake around theory, it will be useful to step away from the pages of *L=A=N=G=U=A=G=E* for a moment and leap forward a few years to the 1984 "Women & Language" issue of *Poetics Journal* edited by Hejinian and Barrett Watten. Kathleen Fraser laments a "lack of representation by an organized poetics" for women poets ("Overheard" 99).[7] Johanna Drucker takes up Fraser's concern in a wide ranging theoretical essay in which she argues that "the central issue seems to be the degree to which the authority located in language is a patriarchal order which determines the position of writing according to an already fixed hierarchy, reinforcing the situation of 'muteness' and 'exclusion' which traditionally has been women's place in that order" (Drucker 57). Drucker's essay reveals as forcefully as any document of the time just how coercive the new poststructuralist theories of language had become.

They appeared to block all efforts at autonomy, especially of political authorship, and so her strategy in the essay is not to hit the theory head on (perhaps by querying its exaggerated generalities and epochal claims) but to argue that new feminist Language writing is a valuable transformative *development* of the poststructuralist conception: "the 'feminine' must be the positive exploration of a practice which may continue to lie beyond the domain of the definable and theoretically containable and which emphasizes and demonstrates the relativity of the implied authority of language" (Drucker 65). This is a clever strategy, but one that requires an explicit feminist politics, an avowal of female identity, and that was just what was made difficult by the politics of literary friendship transcending difference on which *L=A=N=G=U=A=G=E* based itself.

L=A=N=G=U=A=G=E magazine attempted to create a zone for the "UNcertainty" that Howe valued, a space for controversy, elucidation, swapping of ideas and information. Its curious editorial practice, arising from the constraints of space in the stapled issues of the magazine (before the *Open Letter* issue), meant that the magazine itself became a collaborative work, a shared authorship, that often managed to find areas of intelligible, common purpose in the midst of aesthetic differences. Poets need not be empty, they need not cede authority to the new theories of language, nor treat their identity as fate. Avant-garde poetic exploration of forms of poetry without an author as expressive origin could seem to endorse a restrictive and dogmatic poststructuralist theory of the unalterable nature of language. For readers for whom the new social movements were crucial modes of political liberation, this avant-garde poetic exploration also risked suppressing too much of the necessary recognition of identity that had come to play such a large part in American politics. So the magazine became an agony / advice column for discussing authorship under many names, and the editorial arrogation of a directorial style of authorship through excerpting and anthologizing helped the readership face these issues. All of this was premised on the possibility that friendship would act as an equalizer and be enough to replace the rigidities of community identity or institutional drives, but as the dissension around Marxist politics demonstrated, the magazine's format struggled when friendship encountered the resistances of political difference. The next decade saw a precipitating out into distinct networks and social spaces for publication by writers of closer mutual interests and identities. Yet *L=A=N=G=U=A=G=E* magazine, as is evidenced by the way its name became attached to a wide range of poetic activities, remained a provocation as much as a resource, and an indication of what might be possible.

NOTES

1. Susan B. Laufer (Susan Bee) is credited with the layout and should, I think, be given credit for the way in which the material and visual structure works so distinctively. The first three volumes of *L=A=N=G=U=A=G=E* which I am discussing in this article were issued as unpaginated, folded and stapled pamphlets, and therefore my references to citations give only the issue number, date, and name of the article. A distinct volume four, not discussed in this article, was co-published with the Canadian journal *Open Letter* in 1981 and had a perfect bound black cover, pagination, and full-length articles. A helpful "Table of Contents" was issued around 1981. The entire magazine is available as an online facsimile, including a new hypertext index, at the University of Utah website http://english.utah.edu/eclipse/projects/LANGUAGE/.

2. For this reason I have not tried to place it in a wider literary history. Critical studies that reflect on the importance of *L=A=N=G=U=A=G=E* include Perelman, Perloff, Simpson, Vickery, and Watten.

3. The correspondence he is referring to can be traced back at least five years, but of course some of these poets had known each other much longer. Both editors have recently written accounts of the magazine that reflect on the magazine's origins (see Andrews, "*L=A=N=G=U=A=G=E*," and Bernstein "The Expanded Field of *L=A=N=G=U=A=G=E*").

4. Ann Vickery offers an informative description of the magazine in *Leaving Lines of Gender* 28–32.

5. Barthes continues that "the Author is thought to nourish the book, which is to say that he exists before it, thinks, suffers, lives for it," meaning that this is what literary critics tend to think (145).

6. Bernstein is quoting from an advance copy of Stanley Cavell's *The Claim of Reason* (125). The extract appears under the title "From the Claim of Reason" in *L=A=N=G=U=A=G=E* 8 with an explanatory note from the editors.

7. Kathleen Fraser had founded *HOW(ever)* a year earlier with the aim of making up for this absence. *Poetics Journal* itself was also attempting to develop a more articulate and theoretically aware poetics by publishing substantial articles by poets and critics on poetics and politics. An account of the work of the complex interrelations of feminism and literary theory, as well as the history of struggles for representation by women poets at this time, is beyond the scope of this article.

FIVE | BARRETT WATTEN

After Literary Community

The Grand Piano and the Politics of Friendship

I RETURN TO THE project of *The Grand Piano,* our multiauthored "experiment in collective autobiography" that recounts the emergence of the San Francisco Language school of poets from 1975 to 1980, from a later moment of its history.[1] While *The Grand Piano* was primarily devoted to producing a written document, ten volumes over the course of as many years, its writing has always been reflexive, moving between the past and present, and its work continues in the reading and writing that follows. I want to focus on the nature of this (collective or individual) practice of "reading out," of the continual production of new interpretative horizons in the present and future.[2] The work of *The Grand Piano,* it seems now, continues to be to rethink and reevaluate the radical politics of the emergence of Language writing in relation to subsequent history, personal, aesthetic, or political. The specific window for my rethinking and reevaluation has been the period between the publication project's completion and its series of performances through Fall 2011, which sampled and re-presented the work via nonlinear textual sequences.[3] It also happened that in this period there occurred a substantial change in the group's self-understanding, something like a crisis of community and even belief in the project, which may not be resolved. The crisis took place at a moment of instability of *aesthetic community,* of collective assumptions of *multiauthorship,* and finally of *friendship.* In writing on *The Grand Piano* now, I am called to reflect on its political negotiations, both during and after publication, of these terms in my reading of the work. I want to frame the changes in the nature of literary community that took place between two temporal moments before and after the work—the past in which we first met and wrote, and the present that succeeds the end of publication. In so doing, I bracket the material and spatial forms of *The Grand Piano* (developed in the longer version of this essay) and consider how our work reenacts the *beginnings, middles,* and *ends* of collaboration and friendship, also speculating on how a more horizontal than vertical model of literary transmission stems from its gender politics. I thus consider every detail of this discussion in terms of an overarching question: how *the politics of literary community* developed from our collectivity and friendship, through the temporal unfolding of our work, seen from an ever-advancing present.

Beginnings

The form of *The Grand Piano* is anchored by multiple time frames: what it means to write in the present, to reflect on what was written in the past, and to have written *in the present* at some time in the past. The theme of textual memory recurs throughout *The Grand Piano,* not simply as the intersection with specific memory (in the present) and a specific past (as it is reconstituted through memory up to a horizon of historical narration).[4] At these moments of disjunction between present and past, it is clear that temporality, phenomenality, memory, and finally narrative have different values in *The Grand Piano* than in the writing it remembers, reenacts, or narrates. In the early work of the Language school, it would be hard to find a like concern with the representation of time apart from the time of the work itself, which is imagined as either atemporal (existing *ab eterno* on the page as material text), punctual (a moment of time), or accretive (a nonnarrative sequence of moments characteristic of the use of parataxis).[5] Language writing generally constructed its time as textual, throughout its spatial form, seeing itself as temporal through processes of writing and reading. This atemporality of the work on the page matches the synchronicity of its mode of production and was part of the argument for Language writing as a new literary movement, regardless of any similarities to its antecedents. Just as the separation of synchrony from diachrony was a hallmark of structuralism, so the synchrony of the language-centered avant-garde made a break with the past and tradition and thus—in a kind of cunning of poetics—made a claim for its place in the succession of tradition. A radical genealogy argued then, as now, against conventional narrative forms of literary inheritance—such as the hermeneutics of the New American tradition that emerges through readings of Emerson and Whitman, Stevens and Pound—due to the specific kind of literariness occasioned by the temporal break of radical form. Here we move from the construction of atemporality in the work to the question of literary tradition, in comparing our radical past with our unfolding, retrospective present. Did the Language school enter literary tradition as just another step in a narrative from modernism to the New Americans to an ever-emerging New, or did it make a break with that series? Is the atemporality of Language writing still central to its unfolding narrative, or not?

I have argued that any narrative of inheritance comes undone with the Language school (rejecting, specifically, the Pound tradition as its master narrative).[6] As a supplement to volume 7 of *The Grand Piano,* one of four published over the series, the authors compiled a literary chronology of publications important to us in the period in which we began to write, and which may be read alongside the work we produced in the period.[7] *The Grand Piano*'s formal experiment in juxtaposing multiple strands of influence, supported by its documentation of publication history, led to a significant conclusion: it is not possible to position the Language school within a single narrative of inheritance, New American or otherwise. The asynchronous origins of the Language school—what has been called, within Marxist theory, its "combined and uneven development"—support an account of temporality in the work that is *neither* a single break with the past *nor* a mere continuation of tradition.[8] Multiple time frames produced the textual atemporality of early Language writing, and these are reinterpreted in the multiplicity of times of *The Grand Piano*. The work's scenes of reenactment are *never* simply sharp divisions between past and present, while its serial form of narration will *always* include aspects of discontinuity rather than present a continuous time. *The Grand Piano* is at once a compilation of microhistories, each differing from the next within the many time frames of its serial form, *and* an explicit argument for literary history arising from its discontinuous moments and intersecting genealogies. While the nonlinear form of *The Grand Piano* itself undermines any univocal narrative of development or futurity, and hence any account of literary tradition that might be read from these moments, there are many instances where specific historical accounts are put forward or contested. We may read the work's commitment to historicity at such moments of "beginning," in Edward Said's sense, where the "origins" of the group are proposed or contested or where new perspectives are developed in the present.[9] *Not* beginning at the beginning of the work, we may cite numerous moments dispersed throughout the text where the writing of a literary predecessor (often from the Surrealist, Objectivist, Black Mountain, or New York schools) is invoked as a touchstone for an author's poetic development. At such isolated moments, a fragment of poetry, a caught remark, or an anecdote become memorial sites at an intersection of language, desire, memory, or futurity that will be essential to the author's understanding of the literary.

In an early passage, Carla Harryman recounts the arrival of Robert Creeley's *For Love* at a book drop during the Vietnam War, virtually *deux ex machina*, which a friend found to be life-changing; she contrasts this moment of transformation with the repetitive playing of Creeley's "The Door" in the basement of the state university where she worked as a poetry archivist in the early 1980s (Armantrout et al., *The Grand Piano* 1:29–32, hereinafter *GP*). In the next volume, Bob Perelman interrogates the everyday present of Frank O'Hara's "The Day Lady Died" ("It is 12:20 in New York"), seeing it as an imperative to continue to write poetry and literary history in the degraded present of a later historical moment (qtd. in *GP* 2:76–87).[10] Both literary anecdotes are implicitly genealogical, but in substantially different ways. In both, the writers Carla and Bob will become are figured in terms of a *future anterior* of the literary moment, insofar as their writing in the present anticipates it. This is not simply retrospection but an inquiry into the prospective horizons of the literary as they were experienced and lived. Carla's response to Creeley was to question the gender of the literary in terms of her participation in it; Bob's was to call for a return to the present as always slipping away in any form of representation, to renew Creeley's "charge of the command" (*Collected Poems* 199) Two forms of literary transmission (or its refusal) are inscribed in these responses; between their microhistorical moments we may begin to construct a literary genealogy that is anything but progressive or chiasmic (an unfolding of literary tradition or an Augustinian conversion). These intersecting, contradictory genealogies are reinforced in the chronology of book publications, which comprise a multiple set of influences.[11] Each of these influences would be prospective and unfolding, within the larger ensemble of production characteristic of the periods we are writing about and within.

Such microhistorical moments, each conferring a different genealogy, provide a way of reading the various openings of *The Grand Piano* without claiming a causal connection between beginnings, middles, and ends. In comparison to the heroic origins of the New Americans, who valorized above all else their emergence into literary history as "making it" in every sense, the beginnings of *The Grand Piano* are underwhelmingly provisional. In volume 1, for instance, Bob opens by challenging the group not to be caught up in the dissociation of "desire-writing" but to focus on what is truly of value, which he names as "love":

> Playing, veering, upsidedown and backwards—yes. But also how to say what stays put?
>
> Love isn't limited to the language-furthering relation of parent and child, of course of course. But at the moment, it is my guess that love, in writing, does depend on some deep-set stance turned toward permanence.
>
> Not that any of our identities, subject positions, station locations, is permanent. But for now, to consider the question of permanence—relative permanence—and its relation to love.
>
> Our group has done lots of desire-writing, I think. All of our invention comes from near there, yes? No? (*GP* 1:11)

Bob's contrast of "desire" and "permanence" amounts to an opening-in-reverse, where early Language writing is seen as evanescent, a mere "veering" and play, in relation to experiences of value that come later such as parenting a child. Yet his opening also repositions Language writing firmly within the discourse of origins (and influence) of the New American poets, for whom "into the company of love it all returns" (*Collected Poems*, 258). In one sense, Bob makes a clean break with the poet he was in the past; in another, he claims a place in a more enduring set of values that, finally, aligns with literary history. While the author does join "the company of love" and thus literary community, he experiences this as an individual moment—the experiences that give rise to it (parenting his son Max) are unique and not distributable. Taking up the challenge of Bob's opening, in the next section I resituate the literary hermeneutics of "love" in our literary community with the staging of Louis and Celia Zukofsky's *"A"–24*, a defining collective event for the San Francisco Language school. My skepticism toward a horizon of value identifiable with literary tradition in the Zukofskys' work—which interprets the multiplicity and material signifying, even cacophony, of his poetry as a four-fold unity rendered by means of Handel's formal inventions in the sonata form—brings forward a series of more mundane and often political interpretive frames. The contingency and irresolution of these moments, past or present, is the point: I picket Wayne State University as a member of the faculty union; meet Bob at the Iowa Writers' Workshop; attend the Human Be-In in Golden Gate Park (or imagine I do); and am married in the same Alameda County Courthouse that was the locus of militant politics in the 1970s. Occurring in no chronological order, these events serve to unlink origins from event, public from private, and finally love seen as collective from love as personal and singular. The result is a return to the materiality of signification that is historical and political, rather than a narratively suspended form of "desire-writing." The resulting tension between these contrasting accounts of origin and end (and their entailment for literary value) describes the course for *The Grand Piano* as a collective, rather than individual, autobiography in the suspension of any particular account of origin and end.

Granting their plurality, one may follow a discourse of "beginnings" across the horizontal axis of the work's matrix, seeing each as an opening move in a multiauthorial game.[12] The vertical axis of the work also provides a series of openings in which each author has the chance to set the theme and tone of a volume, allowing each a beginning right up to the end. Bob's opening opposition of desire and love has occasioned, in a discontinuous manner that refuses to privilege any "beginning," a series of concerns that continue to recur in subsequent volumes: literary community, friendship, and writing. A parallel reading of the vertical series of openings of each volume—which the reader may pursue—further complicates the poetics of "beginnings" into a productive matrix along the sliding scale between present and past.

Middles

Bob's distinction between "love" as experience and "desire" as writing was in certain ways a provocative lead but in others a false start—although with the advantage of ungrounding or defamiliarizing our discourse, as well as putting life commitments that came after our early embrace of desiring language into a relationship with them. A more consistent register of beginnings is the many instances where an author turns to a specific work—a literary or personal breakthrough of one sort or another—and charts the subsequent "life" as an entailment of its prescience as "writing." We see this in Kit's discussion of the "brat guts" experiment in distributing authorship, to which nearly every author returns as some kind of touchstone. By volume 3, a common thread emerges where an author returns to a specific textual moment, reading it not in terms of its predecessors but toward their own work (a focus reinforced through our discussions online). Steve Benson reflects on his early struggles with identity and sexuality by quoting from journals, whose primary interest for him is stylistic or methodological:

> I wanted him to kiss me on the lips and fold me in his embrace so I paused forever, told him I was very nervous, asked him if he wrote that poem about me, told him I was about too dizzy, finally that I was very affected by having the conversation about sex with him once before, and unsure of my feelings but compulsively concerned lest I had hurt him, i.e., done the wrong thing. [. . .] (After pointing out that I still seemed to be having some problems about breaking up with Carla. His poem had been about his her. I never wrote poems re Carla until we broke up.) (*GP* 3:13)

The plot thickens here, between love, desire, writing, and friendship, and it will be the work of *The Grand Piano* to bring these elements in relation. Lyn Hejinian, while seemingly more literary in her account of beginning to write *Writing Is an Aid to Memory* (1978), identifies a germinal moment of dialogue between two male members of the group-to-come:

> I began *Writing Is an Aid to Memory* not long after moving back to Berkeley from Mendocino County. Our house was (and is) just three

> doors down from the northwest corner of College Avenue and Russell Street, and in the fall of 1977 there was a small café on that corner. At some point within a few weeks of our move to Berkeley, Barrett and Ron were having coffee in that café and spotted me walking by. They invited me to join them and immediately one of them—I don't remember which—remarked that they had just been wondering if I had read Milton. (*GP* 3:58–59)

The homosocial moment of interpellation here is important beyond the admission of belatedness (usually associated with narratives of beginning). The two men's anxiety over Milton's influence on a woman poet, an association with Lyn's (imagined) class background and (real) Harvard education, works to unlink patrilineage and homosociality in early stages of group formation. Lyn likely remembers this moment of challenge and opening because that is what it was: in asking into her literary credentials, the two friends attempt a modification of their "original" compact that will be deepened as collectivity develops and expands.[13]

This intertwining of writing and friendship develops, by the middle of *The Grand Piano,* into writing on the nature of friendship itself, a theme that is explicit in volume 5. Ron Silliman's account of the Brat Guts group, for instance, stands as an alternative fantasy of origins where authorship, friendship, and writing combine until they are indistinguishable.[14] As a result, it is impossible to tell who wrote the notorious line, "Instead of ant wort I saw brat guts"; the author has truly died and been distributed in the text (*GP* 5:22–25). What succeeds the author in a literary sense is multiauthorship, at a crossroads where friendship, community, and writing meet. It is important that this result is achieved through the negotiation of language, form, and performance, the latter of which creates a quasi-public space that gives a new value to the initially private collaboration of the group.[15] In Ron's account, the line "Instead of ant wort I saw brat guts" could have been written by any of the authors, and hence none of them—authorship is suspended, as a performative and political act. But at the same time, the line as *collective* generates new interpretive values for *individual* authors: "Does this sentence look more like Bob, Steve, or Kit? My guess is *all of the above.* Or, perhaps more accurately, none. It has qualities I can think about in relationship to each" (*GP* 5:25). Ron is "on the way" toward a community that is based in the radical individuation accomplished by poetic form in its possibilities for interpretation. For Jacques Derrida, drawing from Jean-Luc Nancy's notion of the "inoperative community," the radical contingency of friendship (demonstrated by Nietzsche's repeated use of the adverb *perhaps*) entails the likelihood of its continuing toward a larger horizon of community.[16] In the "brat guts" line, such a possibility exists at a contradictory and self-canceling intersection of syntax and semantics such that no intention could be said to ground it—thus yielding a wider horizon than that guaranteed by authorial intention, where the entirety of language itself becomes a model for interpretive community. Ron goes on to imagine how the line, as a kind of sliding signifier, might appear and be singularly interpretable in the work of any number of poets. That the line, written by one, *could be* a part of their work, that it would interpret it and become interpretable by it, is a generalized effect of friendship as produced in writing the line itself. At the intersection of writing and friendship, collectivity is imagined as a ground for meaning.

Writing is thus located in the midst of friendship and collectivity, in a state of not-yet-achieved community, after Nancy. This negotiation of the "middle" occurs at once as language and form, by means of the interaction of the ten authors, seen not only in terms of their likenesses and identifications but in their differences and conflicts. It is not the merely textual "middle" of autonomous form, it should be emphasized, though such a construction was a hallmark of early Language writing; rather, the social relations and differing histories shared (or not) between authors are inescapably the ground for the making of collectivity.[17] *The Grand Piano*, in its formal architecture, thus rethinks the formalism of early Language writing as relational and social; it demonstrates how negotiations of friendship subtend the literary values developed by the members of a group, tendency, or school (however its "social formation" may be imagined). In other avant-gardes (or simply of communities of taste) such as Surrealism, Objectivism, or the New York School, relations between friends have tended to be under-described; either they are generalized as a politics of tendency, with its exclusions on principle (Surrealism), or reduced to merely personal rivalry (such as undoubtedly took place between first or second generation New York School poets).[18] Rivalry, in *The Grand Piano,* becomes elevated to a formal principle through the construction of the work, so that each individual account necessarily abuts its difference from its neighbors' and must negotiate its place in the whole. In volume 5, this negotiation circles around the concept of "friendship" to the extent that the mechanics of literary group formation are demonstrated as an entailment of form, even as the specific contexts for the expansion of singular authorship into collectivity are often discontinuous or conflicting (rather than homogenous or like-minded).

If Ron sees the "brat guts" line as a "general equivalent" that would render any number of authors into a collectivity or even interpretive community, Carla explores social and literary regions to show how they are discontinuous and nonidentical:

> If community has to do with responsibility or being useful, [h]ers is an impossible community, one without borders, that accommodates idiosyncrasy, unpredictability, and social chaos. It makes itself up as it goes along, imagining that it can interfere with or accommodate anything that either pleases or displeases it. [. . .]
>
> Resistant to commerce, the story, the novel, the community that is not, faces its opponent [fn. 5: "Keyword: 'useless.'"] (*GP* 5:118)

Throwing down the twin gauntlets of theory (after Nancy) and gender (explored more fully in later parts of her section), Carla presents a discontinuous account of community as value *within* the writing of *The Grand Piano.* With the cunning of genre hybridity typical of her work, Carla performs a double negation of poetry and prose that refuses to invoke community in positive terms but that achieves it in the negative relation between genre and gender. In so doing she comments on and transgresses the homosocial community that informs both the "brat guts" experiment and arguably the larger literary tradition, in her camping on the Pound-Zukofsky-Creeley lineage as an object of fascination for many of the male Pianists:

> Zukofsky. Or Zukofsky and Pound. Or Zukofsky and Pound and Olson. But Zukofsky . . . Creeley gets stuck in somewhere, then Pound.

> Williams, back to Zukofsky. I say Balzac! And not just to be a brat. Or even more outrageously, what about George Sand? (not as good) so what? (as Eliot) but . . . a game I play in my head. Blake, Rabelais, Spicer, and Sappho if you want some poets. (Rabelais?) He-he-he. Gertrude Stein. Frank O'Hara and Anne Waldman wandering in the woods! (*GP* 5:120)

Carla's move on the tradition, however reinforced in microscopic ways in *The Grand Piano*, creates an alternative space that redefines its imagined community as not yet solidified in any particular judgment of taste—as members might *disagree* about the literary value of George Sand or Anne Waldman, and that is the nature of their community.[19] It is thus no accident that her section creates, on principle and through literary transgression of the genre of the essay, an alternative polity of writers more concerned with gender and narrative than would be typical of *The Grand Piano*'s "taste." And she names them, in a string of keywords that performs a "language-centered" critique of friendship and community *within* the developing form of the work, which it must take into account: "Number, communication, come upon, motion, mall theory, useless, El teatro campesino, George, not, *Socialist Review*, documentary, unworking, queer, Daniel, Ed, continental, Bob [Glück], Camille [Roy], Mary [Burger], Gail [Scott]" (*GP* 5:127). In queering *The Grand Piano*, Carla opens it to a larger form of collectivity than the one condensed and redistributed in the general equivalent of the Brat Guts group.

Writing in the middle of things, *nel mezzo del cammin di nostra vita*, establishes the nonnarrative "middle" of *The Grand Piano*; in volume 5 this correlates with "friendship." If one were asked to select a representative volume of the project for an extraterrestrial, there is no better example of its concerns or methods than those in volume 5. Here it is important, as well, that significant moments of *dissensus* as much as *consensus* emerge among its positions, taking their value in relation to more positive claims.[20] We have seen this contrast between Ron's valorization of the Brat Guts group and Carla's dissension from it by means of an alternate list of names and different set of genre procedures. My own contribution to the volume begins with an announcement of the centrality of "destructive envy" to an account of friendship or community, seen as a hallmark of literary negativity. Desire as negativity is a formal component of both friendship and literary form; in describing a series of friendships that failed, I reposition their individual (and individuating) forms of destruction as crucial to the work's formal architecture, as well as to friendship itself. Friendship is thus purely contingent: "The art of friendship is the care with which one seeks to ground a mutual consensus in the open terms of contingent dialogue. It does not have to be, and that is why it increasingly is" (*GP* 5:53). Underscoring his increasing feeling of dissent from collective norms in *The Grand Piano* (which for some might contradict the nonnormative writing practices that founded it), Bob titles his section "Odi et amo" ("I hate and love," from Catullus), tracking his dissent from a question of the epistemology of translation (of Catullus, by the Zukofskys) that became a primary fault line between the aesthetics of the New Americans, grounded in theories of originary language, and the Language school (who dissociated synchrony from diachrony, after structuralism, and severed poetry from etymology).[21] Bob worries that the turn to language cancels the presence and immediacy he finds to be a central concern of writing (and of the contingency of community, as present rather than an artifact of the past), throwing out the baby (presence) with the bath water (tradition), leads him to preserve the fault lines of negativity between us as a fact of literary value and friendship:

> How about disagreement now, in this project? In writing, it seems, much can be accomplished via disagreement (or a range beyond disagreement: difference, parody, polemic, disgust, hatred). In fact, isn't it true that pure admiration is an especially problematic attitude for a writer? [. . .] Disagreement doesn't always become the springboard to something new: it can become a sticking point. (*GP* 5:97)

Bob is exactly right to want for disagreement and difference something more than any copacetic voicing of objections that would encourage the illusion of democracy in the collectivity. Disagreement demands an exteriority to the project, not just a structurally reinforcing part of it—and indeed the disagreements registered by any of us (Carla's account of gender, mine of destructive envy) might be the straws to break the camel's back of imagined community. In one theoretical tradition —from Bataille and Derrida to Nancy and Rancière—such contingency is all to the good, and the anti-essentialist critique of literary community can go forward. Bob's anxiety will not rest, however, with pitching in the mere perspective of his dissensus; even as he claims to be a good citizen, to play by the rules of normative argument, underneath his critique is a sense that it could in fact be otherwise: "I saw on a recent flyer the phrase 'the Language school' and I disagree with it. Barry and I had a small unproductive exchange about it: for him, it's a normative critical term; for me, more impressionistically, I dislike the tone (I hate it, I suppose)" (*GP* 5:97). Bob might exit the group if the group insists on continuing to see itself as the "Language school"—as would in fact occur. Pushed far past the limits of tolerance that are stabilized by homosocial community, which happily folds all dissensus and negativity into the "great tradition" as a tolerable rivalry (the avatar of such a move being no less than Robert Duncan, as in the debate over translation), Bob seeks an emergency exit where dissensus is fatal and community fails. It is this risk, posited in the middle of things, that anticipates the "ends" of *The Grand Piano*, in more than one sense.

Ends

What is the *end* of *The Grand Piano*?[22] The question goes much farther than "how will we end *The Grand Piano*?" though that is included in it. We may consider questions of the *end* of history, literature, postmodernism, theory, or collectivity likewise to be part of it. To begin with, the end of *The Grand Piano* was a literal matter of argument and form—how to end a work that represented our multiauthorial rethinking of beginnings, undertaken "in the middle of things" that are the conditions we then found ourselves in? Who would ever want to imagine an *end* to their work in that sense, however our matrix of ten authors and volumes necessitated it? The end of the project *would* come, and each of us was charged to write it—both in the sense of making sure nothing necessary had been left out, and accounting for all that is still not represented. Finally, the end of *The Grand Piano* called for a self-conscious attunement with all that had gone before, in order that each individual end could serve as a keystone for the structure of the whole. In narrative terms, closure offers the retrospection necessary for an organizing perspective on the development that precedes it—which is why endings are the most crucial components of "beginning, middle, and end" as mimetic. The arch of the work's completion seems to demand a keystone in place to locate elements of the past as they are required by the structural whole. How would a collectivity that proposed "the rejection of closure" in every sense of writing, life, and politics enact the closure necessary for satisfactory completion of the work?[23] Or would concepts of the "end" be distributed everywhere throughout the work, so that no one ending could fully complete its narrative? Tensions between narrative and nonnarrative, explored and debated throughout the work, came to a decisive point in determining the proper value for closure of the work's reenactment. In that sense, the degree of lack of closure of *The Grand Piano* necessitates its continuation; what happens *after* the completion of the work, in its ten volumes, will be equally decisive.

The formal matrix of *The Grand Piano* offers many ways to rethink the question of the end within nonnarrative form. Each section, of course, negotiates its point of departure, development, and where to break off in relation to the next contribution, with a wide range of formal values. Throughout the project, Rae Armantrout enacts something like the "short session," after psychoanalysis perhaps, where *less* narration becomes *more* evocatively poetic; this achieves high autobiographical impact in the section where she discloses her diagnosis of cancer (*GP* 4:86–88) but it also is crucial for her literary account of the lyric (*GP* 8:35–41). On the other hand, a number of us spurred on our compatriots by finding formal means to extend our sections to increasingly greater lengths (Ron, Lyn, Carla, and I all weigh in heavily at times), a dynamic visible in the increasing length of volumes and sometimes found to be a problematic raising of the stakes of the project in online discussions. Either end of our sliding scale of page counts (a challenge to the democracy of equivalence and its figuring through one hundred unit-valued sections) had implications for closure.[24] The end can be found anywhere, as in Rae's accounts of cancer or the lyric; or it may be endlessly deferred, by means of formal procedures that tack on ever more numerous time frames and themes. Yet another approach to the question of ending could be found in individual authors' sequences, and the specific choices they make in ending the volume in which they appear in final position (the reader is free to construct a narrative of endings from these sections if she likes). The formal matrix of the ending, however, is disrupted with volume 8, where Alan Bernheimer's narrative of filmmaker Warren Sonbert's work and premature death becomes the 101st section, by the eleventh author, inadvertently coopting the closure of Carla's final section in the volume. The memorial section to Sonbert also anticipates the dedications of the last three volumes to him, David Bromige, and Leslie Scalapino—the latter two having died during the writing of volumes 9 and X. Thus at the end of the collective project, particularly in volumes 9 and X, deeper implications of the relationship between formal ending and autobiographical content start to engage, and the authors' strategies in response are manifold. Again, the reader is free to construct her account of the work's ending (and in so doing achieve the narrative benefits of provisional closure) through a consideration of any subset of the final volumes' sections. Even so, many of the final sections pursue strategies in stark contrast to their neighbors'; our narrative closure, as a result, will be as much a matter of dissensus as of consensus.

Throughout volume 9, one senses an anticipation of the "end" in our determination to expand our investigations toward that which has been neglected or not yet formulated: from "What's Missing from *My Life*," Lyn's revisionist history of her own autobiography; to Kit's "Notes Toward a Phenomenology of Time," which sequences a series of paragraphs that each describe a presentist moment; to Carla's essay on the feminine as destruction and / or abjection in "Siren Song"; to my own "Double Negative," which explodes the fault line between poetry and criticism (and / or academia). At the same time, in the process of stretching out many of us go deep, locating specific conjunctions of argument around the mortality of friends or events that convey some kind of destruction. Ron and Bob's essays on David Bromige, for instance, organize their accounts of the literary around David as missing friend, while Ted and Tom present uncanny or unrealizable friendships in their anecdotes of Ted's grandmother's retreat into madness or Tom's encounter with a third-world terrorist. Similarly, Rae identifies the "unheimlich" with San Diego itself, where she moved in 1978 as the first of the San Francisco Language poets to leave the Bay Area, through the specter of a homeless dwarf banging on the door of her house (quite evidently not a friend), while Steve develops an account of his process poetics by reproducing a moment of antagonistic community, the site-specific performance piece *Views of Communist China*, which was interrupted (by me) as a moment of negativity our notion of community then had to take into account. In each section, a negative moment congeals within an elaboration that seeks its termination as endless, anticipating a decisive confrontation with the end of our digressive series in volume X.

The range of attitudes toward ending in our final volume approach a value for community as a kind of unreachable "social sublime," a form of self-overcoming in company with others. This process of social becoming in relation to self-overcoming is given a timely and literal value in Lyn's account of university-wide protests at UC Berkeley (2009–2010), as she places strictly literary values under erasure, or Bob's narrative of hospitalization and recovery for an "ablation of the heart," followed by his organization of a poetics conference at Columbia University (June 2010), where he "seems to have lost my avant-garde card // in the laundry" (*GP* X:37). Many of us decide that "in my end is my beginning" (Eliot, *Four Quartets, Collected Poems* 183), taking the opportunity of ending to present material that in most autobiographies comes at the beginning; Bob, Steve, Ron, Rae, and I all return to early, often vulnerable, moments. The strength of the volume, however, may be how the demand for closure is folded into a form of narrative or essay (or even list) that cannot be understood as ending per se. Ted's opening essay, for instance, produces a rigorously structured account of the work as site:

> A "chronotope" is the formal array and spatial elements on which a narrative is based. Hence, this project may be read as a chronotope—not as a monument to a community, but as the dynamic *of* a community in its endless weaving of past experiences, present practices, and a future—even now unfolding. (*GP* X:22)

Carla interrogates "the essay as form" (after Theodor Adorno's essay), combining memorial accounts of two friends—Kathy Acker and Lorenzo Thomas, whose writing was thought to have little to do with each other's

—in a nonnarrative that comprehends both as co-present.[25] Further interrogating the ghostly presence of friends who are missing or nonexistent, Tom creates a phantom community member named "Bea Hookry" as a partial deferral of ending:

> I may have created [Bea Hookry] as a way to give myself *my Grand Piano*, a *Grand Piano* not "collective" but only mine. Or else she stands for one or more poet friends that might have, perhaps even should have, participated in our project but somehow do not figure among the ten who write and edit it. Perhaps this problem seems the more acute now that we have reached our final episode. (*GP* X:183)

Tom's trickster figure, as both condensation and displacement, identifies the tension between community as closure and the self as distributed through a fantasmatic othering of the friend. In almost every section of volume X, the formation of community is left open or interrogated in terms of the status of those who have not been named, are not part of our autobiography. If for Steve and Ron the end of the project is the proper site for a retelling of the formation of our collectivity—Steve narrates a series of earlier moments of group identity; Ron recalls the first time he met many of us—for Tom and Bob, the possibility of an alternative community, not restricted to the ten authors of *The Grand Piano*, is enticing or troubling. Tom dreams a nonexistent member of the group as a displacement for those not included ("Will Bea vanish? Or does she stand in for someone—say, Jean Day, Erica Hunt, Abigail Child, given that Bea is a woman" [*GP* X:183]); Bob anguishes over the seeming disjunction between his past hopes for community and its present decline: "I was hoping, I suppose, that the conference would summon what I remember as the open-ended immediacy of the Talks. That didn't happen, to say the least" (*GP* X:39). The conclusion of our project, in its first phase at least, may therefore be seen as split if not necessarily divided: between Lyn's militant affirmation of collectivity as a literal ground for the social action within the public university ("A movement now exists. Its participants [it would be a misnomer to call them members] are a diverse and [to some degree by intention] array of groups and individuals" [*GP* X:98]), and my own pessimistic account of community as contingent, even the site of destruction:

> I have been reflecting on a condition close to *social death* I have experienced in Detroit over the last several years—whatever hopes I may have had for community seem to have vanished into thin air. [. . .] *Social death* occurs in arts communities when one is perceived to represent a principle inimical to the aesthetic order that binds the community—one fails to reinforce its personal histories, taste formations, or conventions of artistic technique. One is then offered the role of negative principle of construction, and group solidarity is reaffirmed in the act of exclusion. (*GP* X:212–13)

To sum up the "ends" of *The Grand Piano*: the authors refuse to separate beginning, middle, and end, leaving suspended any conclusion. Our refusal of closure occurs precisely along the fault line separating friendship, as generally affirmed, from community, as questioned. At the same time, the "ends" of friendship, community, writing, theory are left open, as yet to come. Only further reading, performance, critique, or elaboration of its project will elucidate them.

Coda

It is impossible to say *before* or *after* in *The Grand Piano,* except in a literal sense: with the completed publication of its ten volumes in October 2010, a division occurred in our project that we have since struggled to redefine. At the same time, the print publication was never imagined to be the sum total of our effort: one of the ways it has continued, even before its culmination in print, is through establishment of an online site to assemble and archive ancillary texts, reviews, documents of performances, photos, and links. The site will ensure further opportunities develop content and create links beyond the ten original authors, while continuing the dynamics of collective process. Even more important has been the series of performances by varying subsets of the group, at conferences and other venues, since 2008. The prototype of *The Grand Piano* reading models itself on the matrix that was given at the outset as the work's formal constraint: ten authors in ten positions over ten volumes. As has been noted, within the form of the matrix as constraint is embedded a theory of democracy, as split between quantitative (as the *demos* as a form of counting) and qualitative (as skill in public speaking in the *polis*) registers. The conditions of democratic polity are further reproduced in the performance structure: unit-valued series of samples of each participant's sections, given equal time and building to larger structures of collectivity. In June 2008, three performers (Kit, Steve, and I) reenacted the Brat Guts moment, which was a key to the work's literary genealogy; in October 2008, seven performers produced a more complex structure, built from individual recitations to two-, three-, and multi-voiced sections, in Detroit. This structure continued in three distinct performances in 2011: a group reading at the January meeting of MLA in Los Angeles (seven readers); a performance at Poets House, New York, in April (eight readers); and a last series of events in Berkeley and San Francisco in November (seven readers). The performances developed in structural complexity over this series, the most difficult being the final two, scripted by Ted and Carla.[26]

While all the performances up until the one in New York were received enthusiastically by large, crossover audiences, the response to the latter event was noticeably chilly. The bicoastal emergence of the Language school, on both West and East Coasts, inscribed in the split sections of Ron's epoch-defining anthology, *In the American Tree*, had hardened into a fault line between divergent assumptions of community.[27] In the question and answer session after the reading, none of our New York Language school colleagues ventured to ask a question or comment, and there was a noticeable acting out before the event when a professional photographer arrived on the scene.[28] Bicoastal tensions continued at social events following the event, which lacked the celebratory unity after the performance in Los Angeles. Any community imagined in the performance was split by competing claims of its regional counterparts, and the rivalry we had worked out over ten volumes surfaced with stunning clarity. An agonizing and soul-searching exchange among members of the group, the details of which will remain on the listserv, precipitated Bob's departure from further activities with the group.[29] We headed for the last of our year's performances and are in the midst of negotiating translation of a selected *Grand Piano* in French, now lacking an original participant.

None of this turn of events was unanticipated. The disquieting speculations about the nature of community in volume X, along with the sense of being haunted by those who had been "left out" by our structure, evidently set the stage for the *contretemps*, even as community, and specifically our project, was confirmed by many. Bob, particularly, had complained about the politics of community from about volume 4 on; his section, titled "UTOPIANOPLACE," reports a conversation with Bruce Andrews, who insists that Language writing as such can only be defined by formal features, along with a general sense from younger writers at the party Bob was attending that Language writing had become a brand name or market niche (*GP* 4:125–26). Whispered or audible feedback from New York Language poets, it is true, had become known to many of us, as evidenced here and there throughout the publication. At the same time, the serial form of *The Grand Piano* allowed for considerable reflexivity in its claims to collectivity; as feedback was offered, from one quarter or another, it was incorporated into the narrative in decisive ways.[30] The ongoing project of making chronologies of readings and bibliographies of books and magazines often involved fact checking and cooperation with many writers outside the immediate group, as well as with libraries. But finally, the politics of community in *The Grand Piano* boils down to a debate between form and content: whether the general compact we had agreed on at the outset (ten authors, ten volumes, one per position, collectively edited, published at regular intervals, on deadline) still permitted a great enough range of speech to count as democratic. Subtending this, there was also an implicit question whether the unit-valued matrix in fact discouraged hierarchies and made possible the formal equivalence of friendship as the prior condition of community; further, since such an equivalence would involve the politics of gender (seven men, three women are not equal numbers), the question of the gender politics of the project could be raised (as it often was by Carla). None of these formal decision structures, however, explains the volatility of the tensions that led to the New York moment of dissensus. Whether the group dynamic to account for rivalry and hierarchy failed; whether pressures from New York poets eroded confidence in the objectivity of our collective process for some; whether the specter of "groupness" itself exerted undue pressure on the creative independence of an individual poet; or whether it was merely the fear and loathing of terms such as "avant-garde" or "Language writing"—are all debatable.[31] The status of the "end" of *The Grand Piano* was highly uncertain in New York, given the palpable split between differing accounts of collective history.

A better "end" of *The Grand Piano* after publication did occur, however, with two performances in the Bay Area in November 2011. Coinciding with the upsurge of political activity around the Occupy movement, at Berkeley, Oakland, and San Francisco, the events reinterpreted the collective practice of *The Grand Piano* through forms of collective participation enacted in these events. The fact that many younger writers interested in *The Grand Piano* were active in the Occupy movement guaranteed that it would be received in present terms, rather than as a monument to the past. Eight members of the group performed the complex score developed by Carla and Ted, followed by a question and answer session at Berkeley nearly as long as the performance itself. In San Francisco, on the other hand, audience involvement preceded the performance, providing both audience and performers with a strong reciprocal bond. In the end, there was not a question of the coherence of the group, or of differences among us, as the boundaries of the project extended outward, in real time and space, to a thinking of aesthetic and political agency at a historical juncture where collectivity is being redefined. Given the encouragement of these new forms of collectivity, I will go on record as believing that our project will continue, in similar ways, in forms that are as yet unimagined by any of us. At the same time, I have to wonder if Bob and I are still friends.[32]

NOTES

This essay is derived from a series of lectures in Europe as *The Grand Piano* neared completion: at Université Paris VII; Université Lyon II; École des hautes études en sciences sociales, Lyon (October 2009); and Universität Erlangen-Nürnberg (June 2010). Thanks to Abigail Lang, Antoine Cazé, Isabelle Alfandéry, Noura Wedell, Heike Paul, and Harald Zapf.

1. *The Grand Piano: An Experiment in Collective Autobiography, San Francisco 1975–1980* is a ten-volume, multiauthored "experiment in collective biography" begun as an online collaboration in 1999 and serially published from 2006 to 2010. The authors, all active participants in the reading series at the Grand Piano on Haight Street, and more generally in the emergence of Language writing on the West Coast, include Rae Armantrout, Steve Benson, Carla Harryman, Lyn

Hejinian, Tom Mandel, Ted Pearson, Bob Perelman, Kit Robinson, Ron Silliman, and the present author.

2. The present essay is one of a series of reflections based on the experience of collaborating on *The Grand Piano*. See Watten, "First Response" and "How *The Grand Piano* Is Being Written."

3. I will discuss these events in more detail in the Coda. Earlier readings occurred at the Poetry of the 70s conference, University of Maine, Orono, June 2008, and at the College for Creative Studies, Detroit, October 2008. Our website, where new material will continue to be developed and displayed after the end of the project's publication, is located at http://www.thegrandpiano.org. The project listserv—which generated tens of thousands of emails during the process of composition—has continued as a site of discussion, focused both on the project itself and on everyday life.

4. For a reading of three moments of *The Grand Piano* that negotiate the gap between present and past in and as writing, see Watten, "Presentism and Periodization"; the cited moments are Harryman, 1:30–31; Perelman, 1:76–77, 86–87; and Watten, 4:67.

5. On forms of nonnarrative, see Watten, *Constructivist Moment*, 198–206; *Poetics Journal* 5, *Non/Narrative*; and the recent *Non/Narrative* issues of the *Journal of Narrative Theory*, ed. Carla Harryman.

6. Watten, "Language Writing and the Mediation of Modernity."

7. The four bibliographical supplements archive the readings at the Grand Piano (part 1); related readings at other venues in the same period (part 4); a chronology of book publications during the period of the emergence of Language writing (part 7); and a chronology of little magazine publications in the same period (part X).

8. On the 1970s and Language writing, see Watten, "After Radical Particularity"; see the works of David Harvey and Ernest Mandel on "combined and uneven development"; Ernst Bloch on asynchronicity; Raymond Williams on "dominant, residual, and emergent" forms.

9. Said, *Beginnings*.

10. I discuss these passages at length in Watten, "Presentism and Periodization."

11. These would include, but not be limited to, French and Soviet theory; revisionist modernism after Stein and Zukofsky; mid-career accomplishments of the New Americans; emerging liberationist aesthetics—black, feminist, Hispanic, gay; theoretical debates in Marxism in the 1970s; and parallel activities in other arts, genres, and media, and so on.

12. In the longer version of this essay, I chart a series of moments—in no sense presented in a linear sequence—in which the authors present a moment of "beginning" important to them.

13. On the distinction between "community" and "collectivity," see Nancy, *The Inoperative Community*.

14. The "Brat Guts group" was an early experiment in multiauthorship con-

ducted by Kit, Steve, and Bob. The three would meet off and on and engage in improvisatory reading and writing sessions in which one person read rapidly and discontinuously from a stack of books while the other two would type as fast as they could, writing down what they heard or imagined or both. The resulting material made its way into each author's poetry.

15. In this sense, "collaboration," suggested by Catherine Taylor as a more accurate term for the writing of *The Grand Piano* (in her introduction to the New York reading, 2011), is an inadequate term for the public and political values achieved through its collective processes.

16. Derrida, *The Politics of Friendship*; Nancy, *The Inoperative Community*.

17. See Harryman's chapbook *The Middle* for a prescient critique of aesthetic autonomy in the early Language school, rethinking radical form at the intersection of multiple genres.

18. In Kant's notion of the *sensus communis*, nothing is said about the relations between its members who "would agree" with the judgment of taste, except that the "genius" has a special role in convincing the aesthetic community of a new "rule" for what counts as aesthetic. While members of the aesthetic community *are* defined in terms of a commonality of "taste," nothing is said about other interests or disagreements they may have—or how their mutual regard for the aesthetic is negotiated or achieved. Opening up the differential and negative relations of aesthetic community is a particular contribution of Rancière's work, specifically *The Politics of Aesthetics* and *Aesthetics and Its Discontents*; and also Hinderlither et al., *Communities of Sense*.

19. Waldman was not included in the canon-making anthology of the New York School, Padgett and Shapiro's *An Anthology of New York Poets*.

20. On dissensus and community, see Rancière, *Dissensus* 27–44. I am indebted to Antoine Cazé's presentation at our January 2011 group reading at the MLA for his development of a Rancièrean reading of our project.

21. This conflict over the poetics of presence and translation was enacted at an evening, sponsored by the San Francisco Poetry Center, devoted to the poetry of Louis Zukofsky shortly after his death in 1978, between me and Robert Duncan. Numerous references to the event appear throughout *The Grand Piano*.

22. It is important that *end* as telos and as narrative may be dissociated in a nonnarrative work such as *The Grand Piano*; I am deliberately exploiting the disjunction between them here.

23. The *locus classicus* here is Lyn's essay by that title, "The Rejection of Closure," in Hejinian, *The Language of Inquiry*.

24. See Rancière's discussion of the *demos* as defining citizenship quantitatively, in terms of census numbers, rather than qualitatively, in terms of participation in debates; *Dissensus* 45–61.

25. Adorno, "Essay as Form," in *Notes to Literature*, 1:3–23.

26. Recordings of the performances are available at the Grand Piano site. The 2008 performances were scripted by Kit, and the 2011 performances by Kit and Ted.

27. While there were questions about Silliman's splitting of his anthology between "West" and "East" sections, and seeming to prioritize the former, the distinction has generally not been determinate in the reception of the Language school, though it has been a persistent subtext.

28. On arriving at the venue Charles Bernstein, Bruce Andrews, and Pierre Joris quickly got into a group photograph with some members of the group, and Bernstein later posted photos of the event, with himself prominently featured and excluding some participants, on *Jacket 2*.

29. This narrative attempts to take into account only the public aspects of the events in New York and Bob's withdrawal, which was confirmed in his nonparticipation in the West Coast readings, and is meant to substantiate the link between friendship and community.

30. A good example of this was Juliana Spahr's early online response characterizing the Language school in racial and class terms, which resulted in considerable attention to race, particularly in subsequent volumes; see also my online reply, "First Response."

31. An explanation for Bob's disquiet may partly be found in his rejection of the politics of the avant-garde; see Perelman, "My Avant-Garde Card."

32. This narrative was submitted for comment to the online listserv of *The Grand Piano*, and my collaborators' extensive comments have been incorporated into the present draft.

SIX | MARIA DAMON

Between Friendship Network and Literary Movement

Flarf as a Poetics of Sociability

FLARF, WHICH WAS hailed as one of the (first) two "avant-garde superpowers of the twenty-first century,"[1] is both a method of writing poetry and a de facto friendship network. The method is characterized by so-called "google-sculpting" (generating material through google searches for key words and phrases and stringing together the results with some authorial massaging) and other internet features, and by its humorous and knowing deployment of "sublime terribleness."[2] While the term "Flarf" and the characteristic embrace of assaultive, funny, and parodically politically incorrect content are attributed to "founder" Gary Sullivan (many others in the poetry world before Flarf's inception have experimented and continue to do so with using internet materials), the energy with which a group of loosely connected friends coalesced around this method and sensibility has made it a collective enterprise. Today Flarf comprises a listserv of about fifteen members, though over the past decade-plus many poets and fellow travelers have passed through stages of active participation. In the friendship network that now comprises the listserv and characterized it in the past, no particular friendship stands out as especially germinal, although several members are or have been domestic / romantic couples, and the collective mutates in response to friends getting friends "on the list." (The Flarflist is now closed, though there have been festivals, readings, and individual book and anthology projects, as well as an open and highly active "Postflarf" listserv.) I will thus not be addressing one singular friendship in what follows, but rather exploring both some literary friendships as cross-millennial influences, and the success and productivity of this affective circle as a model of anti-dyadic friendship in the contemporary techno-poetiscape.

Flarf's generational reinvention of and its relation to the recent or distant literary past have been noted with regard to the Surrealists and Dadaists, Oulipo, and certainly the New York School (indeed one could loosely describe the Flarf aesthetic—its casual veneer, its insistence on the detritus of daily life as subject material—and its members as third generation New York School). There are differences between Flarf and these groups as well: earlier avant-gardes, for example, sometimes evolved into fairly rigid and exclusionary structures, with a kingpin calling the shots—André Breton among the Surrealists, Filippo Marinetti among the Futurists, or Guy Debord among the Situationists. No such mechanism has arisen in Flarf. Nor is there a Flarf manifesto; such a thing would be considered too serious, too coercive. Any Flarf poem, the more vulgar the better, could be a manifesto, but it would not speak for the group (poems are not collectively composed, but shared on the collective list). There are counterintuitive forebears as well, primarily Dante Alighieri's and Brunetto Latini's *dolce stil nuovo* circle—my focus here. Such older antecedents suggest that, while Flarf's origins were organically rooted in a friendship network, it can be placed (and to some degree, depending on which "Flarfie" you ask, places itself) in a self-conscious literary tradition of iconoclasm that nonetheless retains a malleability responsive to its shifting contexts.

Flarf's deliberately awful parody of contemporary poetic tics and all-out revels in the most banal internet detritus raised to the status of poetry are a form of demotic revolution, a poetic claim for the vernacular, the "life-giving" vulgar, which at least one friendship-based poet—Frank O'Hara—has explicitly linked with love. In this essay, the rubric of friendship and mentorship firmly linked to the vernacular (Dante's and Latini's poetics emphatically advocated use of the demotic) arches over the paired phenomena of collaborative friendship and un/timeliness; that is, the phenomenon of being out of step with one's times, a step ahead, behind, or both simultaneously. It does so through calling up a curious (but not completely misplaced) intertext; if Flarf provides a snapshot poetics (hello Allen Ginsberg) of the present moment, then Book XV of Dante's *Inferno,* which chronicles the (fictional) meeting of Dante the pilgrim with his maybe-sodomite mentor, the encyclopedist, banker, lawyer, poet, orator, exile, and statesman Latini, looks backward to a paradigmatic recognition of the linguistic and homosocial queerness (I intend "queerness" both in terms of sexuality and in broader terms of torqued, deliberate "wrongness") of literary and civic mentorship in the wake of a ruined civic experiment and a millennial turn.

Dante's complex encounter underscores the inequality of the mentorship relation, suggesting the uncomfortable and often tacit unevenness in friendships in general, the push and pull of eros, competition, and companionship, and how a younger generation gets to rewrite and hence judge its guides. More importantly, though, the polemically literary use of the linguistic register known variously as the demotic, the vernacular, or the vulgate, plays into this mélange / mêlée as an ongoing project stretching at least from Dante's time and influence via "sweetness and greatness" through to current experimentation with internet as vernacular, and has been central in the Flarf project, as has its corollary, encyclopedism, particularly as a response to catastrophe (Duncan, "Sweetness" 142–46).[3] (The two are linked through expansiveness and collectorship: a perceived need both to account for everything and to give every form of language a "hearing"—they must be represented!) Use of the vernacular in intimate friendships has been exquisitely written about by Jean Genet, who refers to the secret language and whisperings of homoerotic prison relationships, which are as intense as they are provisional. This relationship between a highly demotic poetics, queerness, and companionship has been likewise celebrated by poets and Dante enthusiasts Robert Duncan and Robin Blaser, participants in the queer "San Francisco Renaissance," yet another descending tributary of the medieval romance tradition of Dante and Latini that makes up a nearer ancestral voice informing Flarf.

Again, as one might imagine, there are distinct differences between these two radical styles and the friendship circles in which they were nurtured. The near-millennial distance separating Flarf from the *dolce stil nuovo* mandates attention to three elements of Flarf: gender, technology, and the relationship between them. The active participation of women in Flarf (and sometimes their self-parodic stripper pseudonyms), as well issues of queer / gay / Oedipal lineages in literary communities, the camped-up (satirically exaggerated) machismo of Flarf (during the 2008 presidential campaign, Mitch Highfill wrote a series in which every first line read: "Hello voters!! / My name is ________ [John McCain / Hillary Clinton / Barack Obama / Mike Huckabee / Mitt Romney, etc.] and I have a huge cock") versus the unself-conscious machismo of classic avant-gardes, issues of sexuality and power in the mentor-protégé relationship, and suspicions of sexism and racism by outsiders are elements in Flarf's evolution. At the recent millennial turn, Flarf poets, especially Gary Sullivan, look back to the last one for a communal model of queering poetics to establish a vernacular poetic idiom; Flarf's reliance on the internet and its social forms (listservs, chat groups, social networking sites, search engines) rather than the ideal of the city-state (Florence) and its governance, provide the structure and motivation for this new poetic language. The networked sociality of the present day positions Flarf at the intersection of poetic and affective activity.

Timeliness: Belatedness as Vanguard

Let's consider John Ashbery's catchy epithet for O'Hara, whose commitment to friendship and coterie as indispensible to poetry hovers over these pages, mediating the premodern Dante and the postmodern Flarfies: "too hip for the squares and too square for the hips" (81). Although we have thought for some time now (at least since 1968) that to be "ahead of one's time" is to be in fact deeply representative of one's time, let's revisit this banal formulation, not to make special claims for misunderstood genius but rather to ask questions about time (generational time, creative time, etc.). What could it mean, for example, as the description of O'Hara suggests, to be so far ahead of one's time that one is hopelessly behind? Or, conversely, so atavistic that one appears messianic? Flarf is deliberately untimely; it deliberately Others itself, freezing time through its stupidness (its inability to progress or "build upon" itself), a caricature of poetry whose vulgarity rather than sublimity trumps time. Flarf festivals have included theme music for each reader, including "MacArthur Park" (the most Flarfiest song possible), "Summer Breeze," "Afternoon Delight," and other 1970s drivel, songs that reference time but inanely so, making the references mere mood-setting clichés, and for Flarf, the mood is always hilarity.

This notion of temporal in-betweenness, first off, evokes the concept of transhistorical mentoring such as that between Dante and Sullivan, whose comic strip, *The New Life,* which has run in *Rain Taxi Review of Books* since Sullivan moved to New York in the late 1990s, riffs on Dante's declaration of a new poetics.[4] But the trope of in-betweenness also suggests a specific intertext through the poignancy of the following lines from Canto XV of Dante's *Inferno,* which describes the circle of the Sodomites, or those who have been condemned for "crimes against nature." After a conversation famous in Dante scholarship for the complexities of the affectionate and mutually respectful encounter between Dante-pilgrim and Latini, in tension with the obvious fact that Dante-poet places his former mentor quite far down in the concentric circles of Hell, the sinner from an older generation must part from his former protégé, spurred on by the urgency of catching up to the cohort he has fallen behind and by the fear of being caught up with by another group of sinners in their endless circling in a burning desert of fiery rain. In taking leave of his former student Dante-pilgrim, Latini races to rejoin his group of infernal comrades as another group approaches from the rear ("people are coming with whom I must not be," he says cryptically):

> Poi si rivolse, e parve di coloro
> che corrono a Verona il drappo verde
> per la campagna; e parve di costoro
> quelli che vince, non colui che perde. (*Inferno* XV: 121–24)

> [he turned about and seemed like one of those that run for the green cloth in the field at Verona, and he seemed not the loser among them, but the winner.] (Alighieri 196–97)

To clarify: as Latini is caught between two sodomitic, homosocial communities, it is impossible for a moment to tell whether he is in the vanguard or the rearguard, although—and because—the concept of anteriority or posteriority is mostly askew in this context of eternal circumambulation. At the same time, anteriority, posteriority, and eternal closed-system repetition obliquely invoke Dante-poet's pious critique of homosexuality: Who's in front (on the bottom)? Who's coming from the back (on top)? Either way there's no issue from these sterile hierarchies. The Canto seems to come down on the highly compromised side of the vanguard-as-wishful-thinking, evincing Dante's deep ambivalence toward his teacher; although Latini occupies an abject position of nakedness, fending off and dodging falling flames while trudging the burning sand on a barren, fiery desert, scurrying to catch up to his appointed band of cosodomites, the pilgrim concedes that his former teacher and literary model seems, in a momentary visual trick, to be a young athlete triumphing (the green flag of victory) in a footrace held in a beautiful field—the annual footrace at Verona.

The pain of seeing one's mentor, a kingpin in Florence's political and intellectual life, brought down to such a state is mitigated by the explicit affection with which the two men address each other and in the final image in which Dante casts Latini as a glorious athlete taking the prize. But is this redemptive, or is the delusionally palliative image itself an instance of the perversion—linguistic, literary, rhetorical, sexual, civic—that momentarily seduces the pilgrim? After all, it is Dante-poet who puts Latini in Hell, so in a sense the pilgrim is responding with shock and sorrow to the cruelty of his own alter ego's hindsight. Latini and Dante were both proponents of the vulgate—writing in Italian (or, in Latini's case, also French) rather than Latin, so Latini was directly influential on the "sweet new style," which used secular topics like romantic love and a secular / vernacular tongue to achieve the sacred in poetry—like Flarf, which uses a new style to articulate new relationships between affect and language in a supermediated world. Is Flarf atavistic in its use of crude, lowbrow materials, or is it on the forward edge of an aesthetic breakthrough that blends the vulgar with high poetic aspiration? As Dante-poet poses a complex problem for literary heirs and their mentors throughout Western literary history, Sullivan invokes Dante's stability as a foundational canonical figure to launch a poetics that has destabilized that tradition.

Latini is so commonly thought to stand behind Dante as the latter's most influential mentor that a fresco in Florence's Bargello attributed to Giotto di Bondone puts them side by side; moreover, the modern translator of *Il Tesoretto,* calling Latini the Cicero of Florence, also names him Dante's "cicerone" ("guide"; qtd. in Holloway xi). What then of the overly intimate queering of mentorship or friendship? To belabor the point, why is the beloved guide in Hell? Although some argue that the *Tesoretto*'s dedication to Guido Guerra, who appears alongside Latini in Hell, suggests that Dante suspected a homoerotic link between the two, much of the commentary on Canto XV suggests that Latini's true "crime against nature" might well have been linguistic perversion, rhetorical deviance or torsion (i.e., queering), rather than sodomy or homosexuality; same-sex practices among men were well known at the time, but since Dante and Virgil encounter sodomites in Purgatory as well, there must have been something more or other for Latini to have merited such harsh treatment in the poet's work. That is, Latini's very investment in eloquence and its relationship to knowledge and civil governance, as well as his influence on Dante both as a poet and as a social actor and philosopher —i.e., "his example of using erudition and intelligence in the service of the city"—may constitute dangerous and punishable gifts or come to appear as liabilities even as his protégé absorbed and reinvented Latini's revolutionary legacy with his own imprimatur (Raffa 62).

Dante's bedrock status as Sullivan's legitimating mentor should not obscure the chaotic civic crucible in which the former's "sweet new style" was honed, a crucible that included a tight "boy gang" of poet friends involved in the same aesthetic project (Guido Cavalcanti, Cino da Pistoia, Lapo Gianni, and others), or the controversial and embattled career of his mentor. Latini, 1210–1294, was a Guelph, like Dante, during the vicious civic wars, as well as notary, statesman, philosopher, and perhaps most importantly, orator. After the 1250 Guelph revolution established a democratic government in Florence, he was sent as ambassador to France to secure aid against the opposing Ghibellines. While he was there, the revolutionary government in which he was a key player was overthrown and his civic dream temporarily shattered; in Parisian exile he composed both of the works for which he is known: *Il Tesoretto* (Little Treasure), a long, allegorical poem in Italian on which Dante's *Commedia* is clearly modeled, and *Li Livres dou Trésor*, written in French prose and subsequently translated into Italian by a contemporary as *Il Tesoro*, an encyclopedic compendium that "treats of all things that pertain to mortals," namely government, ethics, oratory. Importantly for discussions of Flarf and the demotic, *Il Tesoro* was the first encyclopedia written in the vernacular: French, then Italian. While Latini's investment in encyclopedism clearly leans toward statesmanship and ambition marked by a desire for civic and social order, and Flarf's expansive embrace of all information has an anarchic, bricoleur sensibility, there is a shared desire to account for all human social activity as it transpires through language.

In both cases, moreover, emphasis on the demotic rather than the high language of either Latin or capital-P poetry and on heavily appropriated material (Latini borrows from Cicero, Aristotle, and St. Isidore of Seville; Flarf from random e-sources) in a ragtag assemblage emphasizes the collaboration of unknown "friends" (invisible companions) as well as close relations with actual interlocutors. Friendship is a kind of theft, especially if, like this premodern public intellectual and these postmodern scavenger-poets, one doesn't believe in originary authorship.[5] The push-pull of Dante / Latini and of Latini toward the front / back of the line allegorizes the ambivalence of poetic apprenticeship, cross-generational friendship, intertextual appropriation, and queer vanguardism; but more than that, it confuses and suspends history and imagination, cloaking civic ruination in a terrible beauty verging on the hallucinatory.

Blink and you miss it. The hell-tormented Latini appears momentarily as a triumphant golden athlete capturing the green flag of hope. The Flarf poets, a group of irreverent iconoclasts dedicated to anything-goes hilarity and comradeship in the old bohemian style and in the new cyber-café of listservs, look for a moment like wraiths walking the white-dusted streets of New York in the post–9/11 hours of hellfire raining downward. How do they do it? How do they embrace the impossible world they lived in with pleasure and spontaneity? How do they conjure this world of inane silliness and pleasure? They do it through poetry. The last shall come first and the abject be raised to the stature of role model and FatherMother Poets of generations to come.

The linguistic queerness with which Latini has been charged is rife in Flarf (which, like "queer," has become an interesting verb whose potential outstrips the nominal), though currently its members comprise an exclusively heterosexual roster. Some of this queerness is simply a parodic exaggeration of the mainstream machismo fueling current US politics as usual, such as exaggerated adolescent or even infantile profanity or toilet humor, women writing intensely bawdy work that borders on the comically violent ("kiss my . . ." and "scissors" were the keywords of one google poem by Katie Degentesh aka "Flarfette Jones," a nom de Flarf selected for its stripper-ish sound). The very campiness of Flarf's excesses vitiates gestures of conventional aggressive masculinity and competition; as Ron Silliman has observed on his flagship blog for contemporary poetry and poetics, Flarf is noteworthy for the absence of a single strong male personality setting the terms of the discourse. The Flarf men were pleased with this, imagining themselves off the sexism hook, but the Flarf women said, yes, that's true, there isn't a single strong male personality, there are several! Indeed, strong personalities cross the gender line among the Flarfies, though in most academic and media discussions of Flarf, it is the men (Drew Gardner's "Chicks Dig War," Sullivan as founder of Flarf, and K. Silem Mohammad for his conceptualist leanings and Shakespearean rewrites) who draw most of the attention. Sharon Mesmer (especially her book *Annoying Diabetic Bitch*), Nada Gordon (though her published volumes are not especially "Flarfy" nor are they intended to be), Mel Nichols, Degentesh (whose *The Anger Scale* received positive attention both from pro- and anti-Flarfies), and more recently Elisabeth Workman are powerful samplers of expressive mass-mediated culture, and their work often addresses sociality itself. In an earlier essay ("Electronic Poetics Assay") I addressed Flarf and gender, declaring the overriding tone to be the smart-alecky, adolescent male associated with *Mad Magazine* and wild shtick. Although the tone of Flarf has remained consistent, I would revise its analogs now in a more gender-equal direction: Sarah Silverman, Sandra Bernhard, and, in Gordon's case, opulent performances of hyper-femininity that have their closest analogs in Mae West–style burlesque, belly dancing, or Bollywood with an erudite verbal soundtrack.

Friendship itself always, in spite of friends' claims to be in perfect synch, soulmate-style, involves being both in step and out of step with each other in a playful/ominous agon that subtends relations that expand and contract over time. The way in which Flarf poetics evolve on the listserv, through extensions of themes (Elmo, swan vomit, unicorn boners) or particular phrases (for example, "that's what it would be like to fuck Valerie Bertinelli," "except language poetry," or "except Flarf" as final lines of any classic or new poem or poetics statement, which circulated May to June 2010) and the complimentary banter that follows any new poem, is warm, comradely, and light; it is also a stuttering, a fuzzy sheath of discourse that builds up relationships but also creates minor fissures of differentiation.

As Flarf evolved into a world-acknowledged poetry phenomenon, it no longer solely drew on the intensity of proximity, and friendship became a more flexible mantle than is possible in more tight-knit circles. This is a different kind of friendship, to be sure, from the hothouse dyad of a William Wordsworth / Samuel Taylor Coleridge, an Ezra Pound / T. S. Eliot, Li Po / Tu Fu, Arielle Greenberg / Rachel Zucker, O'Hara / you name him / her relationship, or my own intense collaborative friendship with mIEKAL aND. And it differs from the (sometimes tragic) collaborative relations between erotic or domestic partners: Patti Smith / Robert Mapplethorpe, Arthur Rimbaud / Paul Verlaine. This is a looser kind of friendship, nondyadic, enhanced by the erotics of distance, fluidity, and lack of projective expectations and personalized competition that can plague more intimate friendships. In a sense, like Dante-pilgrim's and Ser Brunetto's friendship, in which the respectful distance of generation and mentorship mitigates the potential intensity of the bond (though Dante-poet wreaks his Oedipal revenge full force), Flarf's friendship bonds are attenuated by the contemporary conditions of friendship mediated by social media technologies and spatial distance. If we accept Simone Weil's observation about the difficult non-instrumentalism of "perfect friendship"—that it would be similar to Eve's wanting the apple with all her soul and body but not reaching and eating—it could be said that Flarf is that, but without the twisted ambivalence that gives Weil's prescription its masochistic pathos and uncanny rightness (135).

Can this be called friendship, in a sense that is deeper than, say, friendship à la Facebook? Yes, because there is teaching and learning, give and take, support and encouragement in times of crisis. So while it is not modeled on intense dyadic "frenemy" pairings, Flarf is an outgrowth of already extant networks, dyads, and triads. As Mesmer, who joined the Flarflist in the summer of 2001, says, "it was born of friendship [. . .] I thought we were just goofing around. I had no idea this was going to become a verb, a noun, in contemporary poetry. None of us did. It was so uncommercial but it's become a household word." One of the reasons it has lasted, she maintains, is that, while it started with friendship, these friendships, as they manifest on the listserv, are handled with a light touch and "a kind of weird maturity" where expectations for intense emotional bonding are low (Mesmer). Flarf is loose, "like the internet itself." It's "non-contiguous," as it has members in Oregon, California, Maine, Providence, Minneapolis, though primarily and originally in New York. While Dante wrote about his former comrades retrospectively after a cataclysmic exile, Flarfies are already in diaspora, encountering each other already at a distance, so the possibilities for bitterness and riven histories are highly abated.

Daniel Kane's appealing phrase "poetics of sociability" captures Flarf's position somewhere between the rigidity of a self-conscious avant-garde movement and the haphazardness of a mere poetic tendency (*All Poets Welcome* 162). There is a zeal around Flarf, but it's the manic zeal of having fun, of reveling in "our inappropriate body fluids swarming animals and antisocial tendencies," of spinning poems off of other poems in flurries of internet activities that also call into question and justify the non–work-related ways in which urbanites, information workers, teachers, and white-collar professionals use their diurnal clocktime (Davis). "His Whiteness Writes a Poem" by one poet begets "Beyond the Complexity of My Whiteness" by another (who is not white); "Houston, We Have a Problem" begets "My Problems with Flarf" begets "My Problem with Gary Sullivan's Problems with Flarf" begets "'My Problems with Flarf' Business Model" begets "What is Your Porblem" begets "No Porblemo." While these could be called linked poems, they do not follow the forms of renga or exquisite corpse; indeed they could not be said to be forms in the, um, formal sense. They are more like contagions of poesis.

Flarf's contagious nature outside of its circle of participants has led to its institutionalization in the poetry media and course syllabi, with concomitant critiques of elitism, apolitical impulses, and a bad-faith relationship to the mass culture it thrives on. It has been misunderstood as merely a method with no consideration of content, and it has been accused of both participating actively in the racism of some of its contents and of condescendingly disavowing its content through absurdist juxtapositions. Among its productions are—please note the high camp of many of the titles—K. Silem Mohammad's *Deer Head Nation*; Drew Gardner's *Petroleum Hat*, which contains quote "our generation's 'Howl'" unquote "Chicks Dig War"; Michael Magee's *My Angie Dickinson* and his Mainstreampoetry blog ("Mainstream Poetry for a Mainstream World"); Mesmer's aforementioned *Annoying Diabetic Bitch*; and so forth.

A friendship-based collaboration (individual poems are not cowritten, but the project functions as a collective) can collapse male- and female-coded attributes, can be a weakening or interweaving of distinctions, of category, of intactness; a bleeding across, a writing-through, a trans-experience. The benefits of friendly collaboration are obvious. What are some of the problems? After all, if we think of Latini and his commitment to democratic Florence, to a public ethics of eloquence, to training a younger generation of statesmen and intellectuals—why is he in Hell? What could be wrong with sodomy? The Western theological tradition links it with solipsism (metaphorically, the nonreproductive aspect of same-sex love and its same-sexness), sterility, narcissism, and stasis; the Flarf analogy would be its circle-the-wagons, embattled, "we're misunderstood" response to criticism. The downside of this kind of community is that it can be too contained; it can develop its own language and its own system of reference (think of iconic subway maps on t-shirts: New York, Paris, London; yes they're on t-shirts that travel worldwide, but these subway systems are also self-enclosed, they only go where they go, they have internal complexities that boggle the mind). Flarf has developed a private vocabulary that doesn't necessarily translate; decontextualized from Flarf's studied hysterical idiocy, some of it, because there is no overt critique provided for the internet detritus that shows up on the page, looks like sexism, racism, homophobia. It's not unusual for one member of Flarf to feel a line has been crossed, to the complete surprise of other Flarfies who see the transgressive moment as perfectly within the continuum of Flarfable material. This private vocabulary, based as it is on throwaway language, could also be described as fluid and mobile, like the friendships in Flarf. One can't take anything too personally, even friendship.

Crisis

Dante's poignant scenario of semi-articulated queerness, the mixed-up vanguard / rearguard circularity of queer time, the strange physical and emotional awkwardness of the encounter, diasporic encyclopedism, and the ambivalence of poetic / intellectual friendship take on a strangely contemporary twist when we consider the cataclysmic background against which the conversation takes place. Firefall rather than rainfall, itself a perverse phenomenon in that fire normally rises rather than falls (Kay 21), provokes images of the World Trade Center catastrophe in which incinerated matter comprising the debris of human commercial discourse (including human remains) rained on New York City, covering everyone and everything with a thick, malodorous white dust. And Flarf, the gauchely brilliant poetic development that had started a few months previously, raised perversity, awkwardness, intimacy in the face of hellfire to comically obscene heights and depths.

What does friendship mean in disastrous times, and what specifically can mentorship mean in circumstances under which the future's uncertain and the end is always near? Dante wrote the *Commedia* after having experienced exile and a millennial turn, and he places his former community of poets and public intellectuals in various circles of Hell or Purgatory; the Flarfies, many of them New York–based witnesses and participants in the aftermath of 9/11, write in the context of millennial change and civic catastrophe as well. As noted, Flarf had its roots in crisis. Although it started in early spring of 2001, it came into its own and was irrevocably stamped by its crucible experience, 9/11, when the World Trade Center towers (I'm writing this on the ninth anniversary of that cataclysmic event, sitting in a café in the Midwest) were brought down by airplanes hijacked by members of Al-Qaeda, providing a hellish context for Flarf's comparatively blithe and unhellish sensibilities. Like Dante, the core Flarfies of New York witnessed the end of their world, their city, during 9/11, the imagery of which is eerily similar to *Inferno* Cantos XIV–XVI: burning flame and ash raining from the sky, rivers of blood and tears, a vertical scale of horror and conflagration combined with the denizens of Hell's endless horizontal and circular trek.

Though the true catastrophe came almost two years later, Flarf members, like Dante, experienced a millennial turn, a momentous occasion that threatened to end the world through the very tool that had made it manageable: the internet and computer glitches. All such moments are fraught, however arbitrary we recognize these turning points to be; and while this was not true at the moment of inception, Flarflist members have come to see their bathetic literary discreations as a bellwether of the twenty-first century, a kind of provocation to rethink the role of the aesthetic in everyday life; as Mesmer says, "For almost a year [after 9/11, people were still asking] 'Where were you on September 11?' Maybe Flarf was an outgrowth of the need to get together, to reinforce each other's existence by getting together and talking." Is Flarf the sweet new style—which for Dante's circle, came from the Arabic via the Crusades—for the twenty-first century? Sullivan's haunting account of 9/11, an email to the Poetics listserv posted on 14 September 2001, brings together elements of friendship during crisis, encyclopedism, and Dante-esque apocalypse. It is encyclopedic in its need to salvage everything, capturing the importance of poetry friends and also diverging sharply from his contemporaneous Flarf poems in its serious sincerity. Starting with a description of a dinner with other Flarfies, Sullivan writes that the friends discussed "whether or not this was something we could or should write about. Never mind how, just whether or not it would be contributing to the general deluge, contributing to what has already become a media spectacle, whether or not we might have anything to add," adding that there was a compulsion to hear and tell first-person anecdotes and accounts. "Nada said she felt it was like some awful privilege to be so close to the events," as if witnessing as a poet gave one a particular mandate ("Last Couple").

Sullivan had been at his midtown job when the towers fell. After heading to the St. Mark's Poetry Project to join other poets, he describes his foot-journey back to Brooklyn across the Williamsburg Bridge covered with human and information-society equipment ash:

> [I walked] across the bridge with hundreds of others, very slowly, turning back every now and then to see the skyline of downtown Manhattan, a huge plume of smoke rising from where the WTC had

> been. Above us, the occasional J train was creeping along, every passenger's face pressed to the window. When we got to the other side, descending down into Brooklyn, there were about 40–50 Hasidic Jews waiting there with cups of water, which they silently handed each of us as we walked into Brooklyn. Very few words were exchanged except "thank you's." (Sullivan, "The Last Couple of Days," hereinafter "Last Couple")

The tiny gestures of goodwill that offer respite, like Dante-pilgrim's approaching Latini in Hell, take on auratic significance: Dante's encounter because it gives the damned a chance to tell his story in an otherwise isolated context, the water-giving because it takes place silently in a usually over-amped city. Sullivan makes a point of mentioning the strange smell and ubiquitous burnt matter spreading out all over the city, and then imagines the victims' experiences, comparing their feelings to when he'd been caught in a subway fire a year previously: "it's an intense adrenaline rush that you can't even describe as fear, although I guess that's what it is. I'm guessing or projecting that thousands of people were experiencing something like that at one moment. I can't stop thinking of that" ("Last Couple").

Contrast this tentative prose account with "Fast-posting Flarfy," Sullivan's contemporaneous and equally encyclopedic send-up of Anne Waldman's anaphoristic "Fast-Speaking Woman," posted to the Flarflist on 1 October 2001, in which he gets comedic mileage out of his own post-traumatic stress:

> I am a scared and pissed off Flarfy!
> [. . .]
> I am a retaliating in ever-widening circles Flarfy!
> I am a gas-mask and antibiotics buying Flarfy!
> I am a suddenly blurting out hateful things in public without
> realizing it Flarfy!
> [. . .]
> I AM A WRITING ABOUT IT NOW WITH SOME CLARITY
> AND DISTANCE FLARFY!
> [. . .]
> I am a hopefully losing myself in work will be healing flarfy.

I am a suddenly fearful of being fired flarfy.
I am a realizing that without a job I won't have medical insurance
  and won't be able to afford anti-biotics flarfy.
I am a fuck it I'm going outside for another cigarette flarfy.

Although Waldman's declaration of self-confident universalism contrasts with Sullivan's epic confession of the banality of failure, abject confusion and fear, the latter performance in turn displays a mastery far from his prose's anguish. It's clear that Flarf serves as an aesthetic, distancing device as much as any Wordsworthian lyric, though hilarity rather than tranquility marks its recollective reframing. Moreover, that reframing occurs in the trauma's immediate aftermath, thus functioning as an active processing of trauma rather than an attempt, as Jack Spicer might say, to cast it in amber.

Encyclopedias, Exhaustiveness, Queerness, Diaspora

Consider how Latini's status as encyclopedist and as an exile plays into these musings on the Flarfies, internet-infatuated progeny of the New York School. Though Latini has become, through his more renowned protégé, a canonical figure, his status as (ambiguously) queer and (temporary) exile indicates that this encyclopedic impulse is here not envisioned as imperialist but as Other-inflected survivalism.

What compels interest more than the encyclopedia's claim to order knowledge is its implicit acknowledgment that true thoroughness is impossible, which frees up the project of salvage, accumulation, and accounting-for to be one of sheer eccentric, disinterested passion and commitment to letting, in Walter Benjamin's words, "nothing that has ever happened [. . .] be regarded as lost for history" (254). Benjamin's *Arcades* project epitomizes a method that embodies the urban labyrinth: endless, fragmentary, circular, made up of quotations and off-the-cuff, unintegrated but mutually resonant aperçus and analysemes; its principle of composition moved from the dialectic to the "constellation," an apt analog for the New York School's mapping of friends, places, and objects as an alternative mode of relational and creative self-placing. (Benjamin's is, I would argue, a queer project.) Encyclopedism, especially, but not only, as a response to crisis, draws together the figures of Latini,

Dante, Benjamin, O'Hara, Ginsberg, and the Flarfies, in a chronologically linear, but formally and thematically nonlinear and highly malleable line of mentorship / friendship that is manifested in their written lines and the lines of their city walks and underground travels, mapped haphazardly and subject to light-touch, oblique navigation.

Like Latini's *Tesoro*, like the *Arcades Project*, like O'Hara's mapping of queer Manhattan, Google is encyclopedic, a tool of both navigation and disorientation for Flarf. Latini navigates the civic politics of Florence from both intimate proximity and exilic distance, with rhetorical eloquence (this queer project might be usefully distinguished from Dante's and Virgil's orderly and hierarchic trek through Hell, Purgatory, and Paradise as through a magisterially decreed catalogue of human conditions, though Dante's proximity and indebtedness to the queer should never be entirely back-burnered), a map not only of the city but of the self. Like Wikipedia, that strange and arbitrary bri / collaged, ongoingly amended and emended "people's encyclopedia," and the growth of phenomena like queer oral history archives in cities and towns around the country and even the world—Flarf's internet psychogeographies partake of these sensibilities.

These desires to, if not account for everything, at least declare oneself open to every (social) phenomenon and to harness that awareness in a broadly pedagogical or public project, suggest some articulable relations between friendship, mentorship-through-history, and encyclopedism. Flarf's collecting internet debris is a form of historicism, like the first generation New York School, declaring that phenomenological attention to "the moment," especially those shared with friends, is worthy of poetry. The gathering (verb) of dross is analogous to the gathering (noun) of friends whose circle of support can do more than a dyadic friendship in times of stress; the tensions and anguish are distributed across a wider network, and Flarf survived while dyadic relationships (especially domestic couplings) throughout New York suffered.

The word Google itself has a felicitously fuzzy etymology. The neologism "Googol" was coined by American mathematician Edward Kasner based on a word uttered by his nephew (reminding us that, as Black Mountain potter M. C. Richards observed, poets are not the only poets), indicating an unimaginably huge number—a one followed by one hundred zeros; arguably, the multiple "os" and the one "l" in the word mirror its mathematical value; the word also resembles "boggle," as in "mind-bogglingly large." It suggests the contradictory encyclopedic impulse to name and to remain inarticulately awestruck. But "google" also implies "googly-eyed," a derivation of "goggle-eyed": infatuated, awestruck, . . . moonstruck. Overwhelmed to the point of being not quite right in the head, so dumb you're smart and vice versa. Like Flarf. But while "goggle-eyed" literally means pop-eyed like a sailor or a frog (or like the comic strip character Barney Google), "googly" somehow also suggests indeterminate focus, a slipping of intention, perhaps a covert rivetedness, a cruising alertness that is no less infatuated and attentive for its obliquity. "Squinting at each other under a new moon" is how Dante describes the sodomites eyeing his pilgrim-self and Virgil before he has recognized Latini as he who "many a time in the world [. . .] taught me how man makes himself immortal": "Each looked at us as men look at each other under a new moon at dusk, and they puckered their brows on us like an old tailor on the eye of his needle" (*Inferno* XV:18–21). In the liminal light of dusk, in the liminal time of the new moon, in the liminal space of underground travel (the collabyrinth of the New York underground), in the liminal space between millennia, underground men and women check each other out with sideways passion, always careful to keep it light in the claustrophobic darkness. This googly cruising, even in Hell, intended to tip us off to the nature of the crime against nature, becomes, in light of current thinking about queer survival, a remarkable display of, in Benjamin's words, "courage, humor, cunning, and fortitude" (255).

The link between exhaustiveness and the demotic, that intimate argot, expresses itself in the "courage, humor, cunning, and fortitude" of whispered connection. They share the democratic impulse toward a minimally hierarchic experience of multiple presences and voices, while still "saying something" coherent. Dante's great polemic, "De Vulgari Eloquentia" ("On the Eloquence of the Vernacular") marks a literary revolution that will occur many times over: the invocation of the power of vernacular in a reworked poetics of the new.

Latini encouraged the *dolce stil nuovo* of Dante's circle. Latini's encyclopedia queers language, democratizing it by defying a social norm.

Internet languages are also vulgates, demotics; netspeak is both a cyborg language and a *vox populi,* both natural and unnatural. The vernacular is natural in that it is mimetic, but it is unnatural in that it flouts a hierarchy deemed natural as a way to preserve a top-down social ordering. Often in poetry or aesthetics that which is more natural, more reflective of the everyday, is deemed revolutionary or unnatural precisely because it transgresses the rule of aesthetic difference, that is, that poetic language should be different from quotidian language. At the same time, the initial move to the vernacular is itself a declaration of difference—from the established poetic order. The poetic "voice" of the individual lyric, which has reigned in (and reined in) Western poetry for the last several centuries, is loosened and attenuated not only by collaging techniques but by the medium of the internet self; however, it is not fully done away with: one can tell Mesmer Flarf apart from Ben Friedlander Flarf, Sullivan Flarf, or Nichols Flarf. And Benjamin, after all, is exquisitely attuned to how social openness functions in the intricacies of difference, objecting mightily to the mass demonstrations of nationalism that wore the cloak of democracy because they allowed the people representation (in the form of the chance to "express themselves" at these mass rallies) without political, economic, or cultural enfranchisement. Flarf, then, is no grand panacea (it would be laughable—most notably to the Flarfies themselves—to make claims for Flarf as a genuine political intervention), but a prism through which some forms of freedom and affective pleasure may be glimpsed. Perhaps any friendship network that also acts as a site of hyperproductive and innovative creative nexus holds the seeds of utopian possibility.

The many issues suggested by Canto XV and by invocation of Dante in general in a consideration of Flarf—among them intellectual mentorship and ambivalent disillusionment, literary / rhetorical legacies and generational triumphalism, queerness and civic citizenship (*pace* Walt Whitman), and the polemical use of the vulgate in literary endeavors as paradoxically natural and perverse—indicate a literary self-consciousness in movements that see themselves as radical departures. And rather than see these intertextual encounters as necessarily or solely Oedipal in the Bloomian sense, one can understand them as experiments with alternative associative forms that go beyond the standard though fraught / filial, sibling / hothouse, or domestic / romantic bond and reach into the realms of collaborative friendship, queerly coded platonic cyber-relationships, textually and electronically mediated public courtships, and public literary ventures such as send-ups of standard poetry readings, play performances, and endless debates about what "we" (Flarf, etc.) "are" as a socioliterary entity.

Vernaculars, like Flarf names or internet handles, enable users to navigate the net like navigating a city . . . anonymity leaning against the john door of the five spot, hurrying to or from an assignation,

> *Under thy shadow by the piers I waited;*
> *Only in darkness is thy shadow clear.*
> *The City's fiery parcels all undone,*
> *Already the snow submerges an iron year . . . (Crane 46)*

Hart Crane waits for an assignation, anonymous or known, friend or transient lover. The bridge and the city are already friend and lover to him; he holds the space, temporal and chronological, in an out-of-time demi-monde where intimacy is by definition elusive as moonlight. The iron gate clangs shut: on Hell, on 9/11, on the millennial turn. Imperceptibly delicate strands of non-desiring, nonexploitive friendship, sometimes clothed in the grotesque, the quotidian, and the banal, map out a poetics within these disasters.

NOTES

1. See Bök. Conceptualism is his other "super power."

2. See, for example, Hilton Obenzinger's statement that "Melville's poems were of extraordinary terribleness approaching the sublime" (*Poetics List*). "Google-sculpting"—different Flarfists have different techniques and guiding precepts; Drew Gardner offers a relatively concise explication of his own: "When I use sought text I am often fusing modes. I start with multiple sources. I break them up, recombine them and use them as a kind of environment for the writing of the poems. It's not exactly collage—I think of it as improvising on harmonies (themes, vocabularies, perspectives) that emanate from the sources. There are lots of different dynamics possible—dialogue, dialectic, contradiction, pile up, etc., with this way of going about writing. It's a kind of cybernetic steering through a sea of information and communication and subjectivities, and a way of reaching and stretching the range of themes and materials I'm dealing with. That steering

creates flow in the poem, the flow of rhythm but also the flow of information. It allows me to expand my range and to fuse modes—satiric, lyrical and meditative, for instance. Using materials from the web also keeps me connected to the poetic values of the vernacular, and helps me to discover poetry in places where poets might not always look" ("Message to Flarf Listserv").

3. Robin Blaser, like Duncan a member of the San Francisco Renaissance, gave a keynote lecture at a Dante Society meeting (1997) entitled "Great Companion: Dante Alighieri" and laughingly remarked that "Dante Was My Best Fuck," the title of a 1974 lecture he gave on Dante.

4. *The New Life,* like *La Vita Nuova,* is the poet's manifesto of a new poetics based on a life change. Sullivan started the cartoon when he moved to New York City from Minnesota, where he'd previously moved from California drawn by Minnesota's reputation for supporting the arts through plentiful grant money and foundations and relatively inexpensive overhead.

5. Sullivan: "Language itself is collaborative! Period. And beyond that, our understanding of ourselves as 'poets,' the whole culture of poetry, that's a collaboration, too. The idea some people have and perpetuate of the solitary poet coming up with his or her work alone is, as far as I'm concerned, a complete misrepresentation of reality" (Interview).

PART THREE

Inclinations

SEVEN | ROSS HAIR

Jargon Society

The Remote Relations of Lorine Niedecker and Jonathan Williams

A certain remove seems to be the way I operate best.
—Jonathan Williams (*Prospect into Breath* 54)

We are the long range people.
—Lorine Niedecker (qtd. in Corman 61)

IN *BEAUTIFUL ENEMIES* Andrew Epstein reassesses the Romantic notion of lyric subjectivity, arguing that it "should not be seen as an utterance issuing from an isolated subjectivity but as a social text, caught in a web of interpersonal and intertextual relations" (*Beautiful Enemies* 15). Epstein proposes this in relation to the first generation of New York poets whose socializing in various New York City coffeehouses, loft spaces, and bars, reified their sense of group identity and fellowship. Such venues are, Epstein suggests, "densely interwoven cultural, intertextual, interpersonal spaces" that ensure tangible, if often fractious, notions of poetic community (*Beautiful Enemies* 5). But where does a geographically remote poet such as Lorine Niedecker, who spent most of her life living and working in rural Wisconsin, fit in relation to such networks? Frequently compared to Emily Dickinson, the enduring image of Niedecker as a solitary poet makes her particularly susceptible to the myth of "isolated subjectivity" that Epstein is keen to dispel.

I want to suggest that far from perpetuating "the Romantic myth of the poet as solitary genius," Niedecker in fact exemplifies how poetic community can occur outside of major metropolitan centers of activity (Epstein, *Beautiful Enemies* 10). To demonstrate how Niedecker does so, this essay considers her poetry in the context of the transatlantic milieu that published her—particularly the Jargon Society—and the influence

Niedecker had on the poetry of Jargon's founder, Jonathan Williams. As I discuss, Jargon was instrumental for what Peter Middleton describes as the "elective affinity between American and British poets, readers, and publishers" that helped "shape the reception" of an eclectic transatlantic poetry "society" within which Niedecker assumed considerable stature from the 1960s onward ("The British Niedecker" 248).

Despite her relative autonomy from any group, even the Objectivists to whom she remained peripheral, Niedecker's poetry, I propose, constitutes a complex "social text" that is defined by, and responsive to, a poetic "society" that claims no geographical center nor advances any specific group identity. By considering the tacit dialogues that Williams's poetry establishes with Niedecker's, I want to argue that poetry itself provides a kindred space for otherwise isolated and, in the sense of being "remote from the centre" and "out of the way," *eccentric* poets who adopt discrete positions within their immediate and literary communities.

THE NAME "JARGON" was suggested by the painter Paul Ellsworth at the Institute of Design in Chicago in 1951, where Williams briefly studied. Far from being concerned with hermetic "jargon," however, the scope of Williams's press is open and inclusive, and has published a range of books, from Louis Zukofsky to Ernest Matthew Mickler's *White Trash Cooking*. The social inclinations of Jargon became more pronounced in the 1960s when Jargon became "The Jargon Society." It did so in order to become eligible for receiving government arts grants from funding bodies such as the National Endowment for the Arts, the North Carolina Arts Council, and the John and Cara Higgins Foundation. Funding and private sponsorship have ensured a steady publication of Jargon titles, right up to Philip M. Jones's *Roadside Memorial Polaroids* (2012), which was funded by private sponsors. Williams tells Robert Dana: "It seemed people would not give money unless they had particular tax benefits. Also, to get money out of the National Endowment or any of the foundations, you had to do this. So that made us become more social, then, than perhaps we had been before" (204). Thus, as well as being a way to secure funding, the addition of "Society" to

Jargon's name also reflects the press's social inclinations. According to Williams, there has "always been kind of a group or community aspect" to Jargon: "it's not a one-man band, it's a backwoods symphony" with "a lot of people helping me, you know, advisors, people writing letters" (qtd. in Dana 204). A Jargon letterhead from the mid-1980s emphasizes this, describing the press as a *"Non profit, public corporation devoted to charitable, educational, & literary purposes"* complete with an *"EXECUTIVE DIRECTOR," "DIRECTORS," "PRESIDENT,"* and a number of *"COHORTS,"* including Basil Bunting, Guy Davenport, and John Furnival.[1] This Anglo-American cohort is indicative of how Jargon was pivotal in encouraging a transatlantic "society" of poets and artists to flourish from the 1960s onward. When Williams, with his partner Thomas Meyer, began "living on the margins of the Modern World" in 1969—"opting out in [the] old world" of Dentdale, Cumbria, for part of each year, and spending the rest in Highlands, North Carolina—these transatlantic networks became even more tangible (Williams, *The Magpie's Bagpipe* 132, hereinafter *Magpie's*).

Williams expressed interest in publishing Niedecker as early as 1957, but it took another twelve years before Jargon published its first Niedecker book, *Tenderness & Gristle: The Collected Poems (1936–1966). From This Condensery: The Complete Writings of Lorine Niedecker,* followed in 1985. Williams considered Niedecker a friend and an influence. In 1961 he visited Niedecker at her Fort Atkinson home. "I was so happy to talk an hour or so this past fall with Jonathan Williams who stopped at my place on his trip thru the mid west," Niedecker writes Cid Corman: "He gave me *Amen/Huzza/Selah* which seems to me an important book of poetry" (Niedecker, *"Between Your House and Mine"* 31–32, hereinafter *Between*). A friendship ensued and, despite her occasional frustrations with Williams's publishing schedule, Niedecker regarded him enough to give him, for Christmas in 1964, a gift book of "Handmade Poems." This token indicates Niedecker's affection for Williams, as only Zukofsky and Corman, her closest friends in poetry, received similar gifts. Williams visited Niedecker again in February 1967 when she accompanied him to his reading at the University of Wisconsin, Milwaukee. She writes Corman:

> I couldn't help as I looked around at that quiet little gathering of somewhat select persons [wonder] what it would be like to live in a community of poets ! a little too cold to speculate while there and now each one of us is an isolate dot on the page again. (*Between* 114)

Considering the popular image of her as a solitary poet, Niedecker's analogy of isolate dots is striking. Elizabeth Willis has questioned the common tendency to see Niedecker as "an anomalous rural savant" (*Radical Vernacular* xiii, hereinafter *Radical*). As Willis notes, as much attention has been put on Niedecker's "working-class Wisconsin identity as to her poetics; we are told that Niedecker was isolated, washed hospital floors, lived most of her life in a small cabin, and sewed her clothes by hand" (xiii). Niedecker offers a different perspective, however, as it is not just her but *all* the poets gathered in Milwaukee that are otherwise "isolate dot[s]." Indeed, isolation is a condition of many of the poets in Jargon's society: Corman in Japan and Boston, Zukofsky in New York, or Ian Hamilton Finlay in Edinburgh—even the peripatetic Williams—all these poets with whom Niedecker corresponded remained relatively isolated from one another. For this reason, Lisa Pater Faranda notes, "the little presses" such as Jargon became "vital centers of activity" within this transatlantic milieu (*Between* 35, fn.4).

The importance of society is apparent in Williams's review of *My Friend Tree,* in which he emphasizes Niedecker's remoteness: "No phone, almost no neighbors—I'm sure none with whom she can talk about poems, about the latest book from Louis Zukofsky off in Brooklyn Heights" (*Magpie's* 22–23). On first impression, Williams appears to reiterate the popular "misperception that Niedecker worked in isolation and that her work was unmediated by cultural forces beyond the local" (Willis, *Radical* xiv). Likewise, on the jacket of *Tenderness & Gristle,* Williams describes Niedecker as being "faithful and recurrent, as beautiful and homely, as my favorite peony bush." Willis considers this an "unintentional slight" on Niedecker and an example of her publishers' "paternalistic" tendencies (*Radical* xiii). However, Williams's botanical allusion can also be read as an acknowledgment of his and Niedecker's mutual regard for relatively solitary poets such as Buson and Bashō whose haiku frequently invoke peonies and other flowers.[2]

Such allusions are significant for the society both poets kept. It is therefore notable that the word "cohort," used on Jargon's letterhead, possesses a botanical meaning that refers to the taxonomical ranking of plants, which, as the botanist Donald Culross Peattie proposes, also have a "social life" (47–48). Indeed, flowers assume considerable social significance in Williams's poetry. In "Enthusiast" he claims that, "we flower in talk" quoting Edward Dahlberg's assertion that literature is "the way we ripen ourselves / by conversation." (*Jubilant Thicket* 250, hereinafter *Jubilant*). And, in "The Deracination"—meaning, to tear up by the roots or be displaced from one's environment—Williams puns on the "root" (*racine*) meaning of the word:

definition: root,

"a growing point,
an organ of absorption, an aerating organ,
a good reservoir, or
means of support" (*Jubilant* 241)

Poetry roots *and* it branches. As a "growing point" it propagates the exchange of ideas, but it is also a "means of support," absorbing at the root but flowering, pollinating, abroad: "the mind / glows and the wind drifts," dispersing seminal ideas in multiple directions (*Jubilant* 241).

Thus in comparing Niedecker to a peony, far from presenting her as a parochial curio committed exclusively to the provincial, Williams uses botanical imagery to emphasize the reach of her work. Like the peonies flowering in Fort Atkinson, Niedecker's poetry is rooted in its environment, "feeling it as a living center and source" while flowering out beyond it (Niedecker, qtd. in Penberthy, *Lorine Niedecker and the Correspondence with Zukofsky* 76, hereinafter *Correspondence*).

Niedecker's poem "Consider" develops similar botanical analogies, demonstrating how flowers, like poetry, traverse their immediate locale and disseminate across geographic and cultural distances:

Consider

the alliance—
ships and plants

The take-for-granted bloom
of our roadsides
Queen Anne's Lace
Black Eyed Susans
rode the sea

"Specimens graciously passed
between warring fleets"

And when an old boat rots ashore
itself once living plant
it sprouts.

(*Collected Works* 283–84, hereinafter *Collected*)

"Consider" is concerned with the transplantation of plants and humans; how both can, to quote "The Deracination," "pull up / from roots" and establish themselves in new climates (Williams, *Jubilant* 241). Trees, in providing timber for ships, transport not only additional plant cargos but also themselves; for, "when an old boat rots ashore," its timber encourages a whole new cycle of propagation to begin. But "ships and plants" also function as verbs, so that human culture "ships and plants" itself in new soils, because ships transplant people as well as plants. And transplanted people, Ric Caddel notes, bring with them "take-for-granted" names to new shores:

> In the case of Queen Anne's Lace, a little used name for one (English) umbellifer became transferred to another, in New England, "in memory" perhaps ironically, of an English Queen left behind (the English name is associated with St. Anna): the name in other words, came with the people who named it. So too the native [Black Eyed Susan], a compositae with yellow petals and a black center, takes a name from an imported English folk song [. . .] about taking ship. (285)[3]

It is worth noting that "alliance," like "cohorts," has a specific botanical meaning. It is a term, coined by the botanist John Lindley, synonymous with "cohorts" and refers to plant groups allied to each other in their general structure. For Niedecker, however, "alliances" are cultural as well as biological and imply the symbiosis of ships, plants, people, and culture.

Niedecker addresses further ideas about transplantation by quoting Loren Eiseley's remarks about the French scientist Georges-Louis Leclerc, Comte de Buffon (1707–1788), who "had his specimens passed graciously through warring fleets" and "corresponded with Franklin" (45). According to Eiseley, Buffon's major contribution to evolutionary theory was his awareness of "the significance of animal and plant distributions":

> He said of the New World species which differed from those of the Old Continent: "They [. . .] have remote relations, which seem to indicate something common in their formation, and lead us to causes of degeneration more ancient, perhaps, than all others." (44)

Buffon's term, "remote relations," and the intellectual context in which it occurs, resonates pertinently with Jargon's sociopoetic networks. As a society connecting otherwise remote writers, Jargon recalls the American Philosophical Society that Buffon's correspondent, Benjamin Franklin, with John Bartram, established in 1743 to disseminate a "common stock of knowledge":

> But as from the extent of the country such persons are widely separated, and seldom can see and converse or be acquainted with each other, so that many useful particulars remain uncommunicated, die with the discoverers, and are lost to mankind; it is, to remedy this Inconvenience for the future, proposed,
>
> That One Society be formed of Virtuosi or ingenious Men residing in the several Colonies, to be called *The American Philosophical Society;* who are to maintain a constant Correspondence. (Franklin 14–15)

This society indicates another "web of interpersonal and intertextual relations" relevant to Niedecker's and Williams's interest in natural history. Jonathan Skinner, citing Peter Whalen, notes that Niedecker shows a "'poetic correspondence' with the heroes of the American Philosophical Society" (45). These "heroes" also figure in Williams's poetry via the legendary shrub, *Franklinia alatamaha,* which Bartram and his son William, upon discovering along Georgia's Altamaha River in 1765, established as "the head of a new tribe" and "honoured with the illustrious name of Dr. Benjamin Franklin" (Bartram 369). Williams's book *An Ear in Bartram's Tree* (1972) refers to this shrub and reproduces William Bartram's drawing of it on its cover. The shrub and its discoverers are also invoked a number of times in *Blues & Roots: A Garland for the Southern Appalachians* (1971). In "The Leaf of Galax and the Habit of Pyrola," the shrub poignantly symbolizes "the America of [André] Michaux and Bartram," that, Williams writes, "has been going down a rathole for a long time" (*Blues & Roots*, hereinafter *Blues*).

Extinct in its native habitat, the shrub now only exists as cultivars that descend from Bartram's specimen. The shrub's "metaphorical uniqueness" and its deracination from its native Georgia soil offer a pertinent metaphor for the eccentric, remote positions of Jargon's society (Irmscher 50). The reach of this society is also exemplified by the publication history of "Consider" which was initially published, sans title, in *Origin* in 1970 and later reprinted as "Consider" in the posthumous collection, *Harpsichord & Salt Fish* (1991), by Ric and Ann Caddel's Durham-based Pig Press. Under the auspices of an allied society of poets, publishers, and readers, "Consider," as part of an "expatriated" book, was "graciously passed" across the Atlantic like the flowers and names it describes (Middleton, "The British Niedecker" 248).

BOTANY, AS CADDEL SHOWS, is implicated in the folkways of vernacular culture. Both Niedecker and Williams possess a "folk base" that reflects their interaction with their communities and their interests in natural history. In a letter to Williams, Niedecker writes that her "folk base" is her "only claim to any difference between most poets and meself" ("Letters" 54). She suggests that Williams is "folk too but [with] an intellect beyond it also" ("Letters" 54). These folk bases derive from the poets' immediate communities. For Niedecker, this is the small Wisconsin town of Fort Atkinson and Black Hawk Island, a flood-prone peninsula protruding onto Lake Koshkonong. In Williams's case, there are two locales that his folk base draws on: Highlands, an area located within the Macon and Jackson counties of his home state of North Carolina, which forms part of the Appalachia region; and Dentdale, a rural valley farming community in Cumbria.

"Folk art," Zukofsky suggests, "occurs with inevitable order as part of the growing history of a people" (70). The knowledge exchanged amongst a community becomes ordered into collective forms: folk songs, ballads, nursery rhymes—even the "sociology" of plants, with "their own ecology and folkways"—"order" peoples' histories (Peattie 157). These forms "emphasiz[e] a thing over and over again—with the body, with the hands, with the feet, with the voice—so as to make certain the sincerity of an emotion [. . .] has been conveyed" (Zukofsky 99). Zukofsky's emphasis on sincerity dovetails with Williams's interest in the "homemade things made by people on the Outside": "Isolated people who made poems, hill farmers who made beautiful dry stone walls, artisans who made proper Lancashire cheese or onion relish or chutney" (Williams, *A Palpable Elysium* 14). Williams finds in these artisanal practices testimony of "the days of one-to-one relationships, of things made by the hands and talents of persons with a feeling of kinship for you" (*Magpie's* 183). Such folkways emphasize a collective memory and communal knowledge that "is not the property of the few 'arty' but of everybody" (Zukofsky 103).

Both Niedecker's and Williams's folk bases emphasize regional dialects and idioms and the environs specific to them. "Niedecker," Willis notes, "found poetry in the gossip that flowed through the offices of Hoard's Dairyman in the 1940s as much as in her research on Wisconsin history and geography for the Federal Writers' Project" ("Possessing Possession" 98, hereinafter "Possessing"). Williams also values the vernacular. "I like to catch people speaking 'poems' who have never heard of the word *poet*," he writes in *Blues & Roots*: "It has been my business along with many of my superiors (W. C. Williams, Louis Zukofsky, Lorine Niedecker, A. R. Ammons), to try to raise 'the common' to grace, to pay very close attention to the earthy, for one thing."

Like Niedecker's "*folk speech*" that, Jenny Penberthy suggests, is based on "the common currency of routine interactions," Williams's folk base emphasizes social interaction, conversation, and community (*Woman and Poet* 60). Meyer calls this Williams's "kepology," a term from Epicurus: "That which is said, or spoken of, discussed, or 'taught' in the garden, or the orchard [. . .] well away from the hustle and bustle" (Meyer). Such "kepology" recalls Niedecker's own "earthy" concerns:

> I don't know how the old time poets did it—the poetic vein was the soft spoken, hushed, sweet-worded kind of thing, almost artificial, but maybe in their own time it was earthy enough for poetry [. . .] now I find when one hasn't been writing for a while, you start off in something like that soft vein, but as soon as you get used to writing again, you pick up everything for poetry, get into everyday speech etc. (qtd. in Penberthy, *Correspondence* 147)

"Earthy" speech also informs Niedecker's *New Goose* poem, "Grampa's got his old age pension":

> Grampa's got his old age pension,
> $15 a month,
> his own food and place.
>
> But here he comes,
> fiddle and spitbox . . .
>
> Tho't I'd stop with you a little,
> Harriut,
> you kin have all I got. (*Collected* 100)

The colloquial, demotic speech emphasizes what Middleton calls the "relational networks" that can otherwise go unnoticed when "folk speech" is simply exhibited in poems as "memorials of different cultures" ("Folk Base" 177). Grampa is doing well for himself, it seems. He has a pension, "his own food and place," and some modest pleasures—the spitbox suggests tobacco. However, his closing remark, "you kin have all I got," is ambiguous. Have his "kin" taken all he owns? Or, is Grampa's kin the only valuable thing in his life? Is Niedecker suggesting that familial company is more valuable than material wealth? It also remains unclear as to who the exploiter and the exploited are in the poem: is Grampa a miser or a victim? Perhaps Grampa knows how to "fiddle" his family, both emotionally and financially. Further questions are raised by the innocuous word "little." How long is "a little" period of time? The answer must vary considerably for retired Grampa and, one assumes, working "Harriut." Such ambiguities indicate that the folk speech Niedecker employs is not ossified but alive, sustaining a dialogue with the community from which it came, and implicating it in a range of issues concerning property, wealth, time, and family relations.

"Grampa's got his old age pension" develops a folk base that informs Niedecker's first published poem "Wasted Energy," which, Willis notes, "is a recasting of folk material, focusing on differences in class- and culture-based language usage" ("Possessing" 97). According to Willis, "Niedecker reports on her environment like an anthropologist," setting the poem's speaker "apart from the subjects whose speech-acts she records" (97). Williams adopts a similar position in *Blues & Roots* in order to record the qualities of Appalachia's natural and cultural histories. Williams likens the poet to a folklorist or anthropologist who, in the tradition of Cecil Sharp or William Bartram, goes out in the field to document his subject:

> Three men are hiking the Appalachian trail. The mycologist is the one who knows to look for oaks and apple trees on a north slope and, hence, for morels. The archaeologist won't have to stub his toe to spot the arrowhead or the potshard. The poet is the one who wants to stop with the local boy who is digging ramps on the side of Big Bald Mountain and hear what kind of talk he has in his head. (*Blues*)

Williams was fond of quoting from John Clare's "Sighing for Retirement": "I found the poems in the fields / And only wrote them down" (*Blues*)—which highlights the fieldwork of *Blues & Roots* (Clare 19). References to Appalachia's most famous natural historians—John and William Bartram, André and François André Michaux, Charles Sprague Sargent, Charles Wilkins Short, and Peattie—occur throughout *Blues & Roots*. Like Niedecker, however, Williams wants to preserve his found speech and praises Charles Ives—another adroit user of vernacular finds—"for *Bringing Everything Back Alive*" (*Blues*).

Williams's finds, Herbert Leibowitz suggests, "make up an unofficial oral history in verse of the Southern Appalachian folk" (Leibowitz). Recalling Niedecker's sentiments about "the folk from whom all poetry flows / and dreadfully much else" (*Collected* 142), Williams claims that his book is "the best of what mountains and I have found out about each other, so far. And a little of the worst as well" (*Blackbird Dust* 122). Thus, Leibowitz notes, "the redneck's bigotries are not sanitized;

they are part of the record." Parochial sexism therefore informs "The Nostrums of the Black Mountain Publican," which concludes with a warning against cunnilingus:

> but, boys, lemme
> tell you:
>
> DON'T EAT NO
> HAIRPIE
> ON FRIDAY! (Williams, *Blues*)

As the colloquial "boys" suggests, the recipients of this advice are exclusively male. That the title could be misconstrued as referring to Black Mountain College, where Williams studied, might be something he intended, as the college was notoriously macho in its fraternal bonds.[4] Indeed, Williams's poem indicates how macho culture—whether bar or avant-garde college—promotes exclusion. The word "Nostrums"—from the Latin *noster*, meaning "our"—stresses this in its implicit polarization of an "us" versus "them" mentality.

Perhaps it is for similar reasons that Williams shows aversion to poetic clubs and coteries. "I am as little interested in coterie as I can possibly be," he maintains: "Princeton was one club, and Black Mountain was another. I made distance from each as quickly as possible" (*Blackbird Dust* 119). Indeed, Williams's poetry shares what Ruth Jenison describes as Niedecker's "multiple tendencies," which defy the "classificatory systems that conflate clique with movement—or a shared historical moment with a shared aesthetic project" (134).

Williams's folk base also posits the poet as a pseudo-anthropologist, "an autochthonous mindless recording mechanism established ecologically within a mountain region" (*Magpie's* 164). "I like to get my ear right to the ground and listen to this Nation talk its trash," Williams writes: "In certain styles the South is impossible to beat: the billboard, graffito; e.g., like from nature" (*Magpie's* 166). One example of this trash is a found poem entitled "JOHN CHAPMAN PULLS OFF THE HIGHWAY TOWARD KENTUCKY AND CASTS A COLD EYE ON THE MOST ASTONISHING SIGN IN RECENT AMERICAN LET-

TERS:" which was "passed onto" Williams by Davenport in 1966 (Davenport and Williams 87):

> O'NAN'S
> AUTO
> SERVICE (*Jubilant* 191)

An Irish mechanic's shop sign takes on biblical proportions via an unintentional allusion to Onan, second son of Judah, who spilled his seed to avoid impregnating his sister-in-law, Tamar, during intercourse (Gen. 38:8–10). God killed Onan for his disobedience, but his name lives on in the word "onanism," another term for *coitus interruptus* and that other form of "auto / service"—masturbation.

The title's allusion to John Chapman amplifies the poem's implicit theme of dissemination. Known in American folklore as "Johnny Appleseed," Chapman was also a spiller of arboreal seeds and established apple tree nurseries throughout the Midwest. Niedecker also wrote a poem about the altruistic missionary: "When Johnny (Appleseed) Chapman" (*Collected* 118). Chapman shares a number of Niedecker's concerns: both show a respect for their nonhuman environs and both, to varying degrees, promote a nonmaterialistic ethos. Niedecker's poem also makes similar claims as Williams's. Chapman "was the early American apple," Niedecker writes, "who changed the earth by dropping seeds" (*Collected* 118). Like Williams, Niedecker sexualizes Chapman's activities, emphasizing that he had no bed, "Nor had he a wife. Nor creed / that embraced grafting" (*Collected* 118). In addition to its horticultural meaning, "graft" also means to integrate in, or attach to—in an inappropriate manner—something else. Thus, although Chapman, as a missionary for the Swedenborgian Church of the New Jerusalem, abstains from sexual relations, the word "grafting" connotes "embrace" and coupling. Indeed, Chapman "reproduced by seed," Niedecker writes, and implies erections when she claims: "His trees grew while he slept" (*Collected* 118).

Such self-reflexive innuendos, in Williams's and Niedecker's poems, promote certain priapic qualities and an eros of dissemination, which scatters the vital force—the mustard seeds—of one's visions and passions.

Williams himself earned the title of Johnny Appleseed for his own peripatetic "do-it-yourself" ethos. "Roaming the countryside and sowing cultural seeds gained Williams the admiration of Fuller," Tom Patterson writes, "who called him 'Indispensable!' adding, 'Jonathan Williams is our Johnny Appleseed'" (9). It is a fitting analogy for the intellectual seed exchanges occurring throughout Jargon's vast "society."

"JOHN CHAPMAN" and "The Nostrums of the Black Mountain Publican" are both pertinent examples of how Williams's folk base, like Niedecker's, stems from "the folk from whom all poetry flows / and dreadfully much else" (Niedecker, *Collected* 142). Indeed, both poets celebrate "the richness of folk language while acknowledging the brutality of the culture it supports" (Willis, "Possessing" 99). The irony of advertising practices such as masturbation on a shop sign in the heart of America's conservative Bible Belt is not lost on Williams, who has expressed a desire "never to meet" the equivalent "some 4,000,000 Baptists" of North Carolina (*Magpie's* 164). It is not surprising therefore that Williams and Niedecker should adopt ambivalent, marginal positions within their communities. Both poets show an uneasy awareness that liberal ideas may not be welcome in small parochial communities. For example, the "potted progressive principles" endorsed by Niedecker in her poem "When Brown Folk Lived a Distance" come at a humane and financial cost (*Collected* 136). "How dark / if to fight to keep my livelihood / is to bleach brotherhood," Niedecker wryly notes, emphasizing how ideals of racial equality have severe financial implications in a small-minded community (*Collected* 136). As Margot Peters notes, "as a property owner," Niedecker "dreaded selling to blacks because they put off other buyers, lowering value" (127). Williams is equally aware that liberal ideals can be alienating: "It amuses me to read members of the Urban Wolf Pack rejoicing on the liberality of the American character. If people in Macon County, N.C., read any number of my poems, my house would be mysteriously burnt down" (*Magpie's* 147).

The means available to Williams, such as two houses in two locations, meant he was better able to remove himself—and keep a "cool distance" —from his neighbors than Niedecker (Niedecker, *Collected* 160). But, as her letter to the poet Ron Ellis indicates, Niedecker also found removal the best way she could:

> Would like to ask: not too much publicity, please. Not local publicity. I've tried to stay away from it all these years. I came close to being written up in the Union a couple of times but *begged* it not to be done. I live among the folk who couldn't understand and it's where I want to live. I'd like not to appear a freak. If I appear a freak to you I wouldn't mind so much—might even be a compliment! ("Local Letters" 94)

A sense of marginality informs a number of Niedecker's poems, including "In the great snowfall before the bomb": "What would they say if they knew / I sit for ten months on six lines / of poetry?" (*Collected* 143). Like Williams's "The Nostrums of the Black Mountain Publican," the third-person pronoun, "they," in Niedecker's poem stresses how the speaker, "as writer and as woman," is displaced from the folk among whom she lives and works (Willis, "Possessing" 98). We become privy to the "other" perspective of such parochial polarities, witnessing sexism in the workplace ("I was Blondie"), the corruption, and "favor[s]" occurring within those dynamics (Niedecker, *Collected* 142). Gender roles go unquestioned—"The women hold jobs— / clean house, cook, raise children, bowl / and go to church"—and acquiescence to "church" values and the "radio barbs" of a media that hooks and catches its consumers on tenuous ideals (Niedecker, *Collected* 143). But, Rachel Blau DuPlessis suggests, Niedecker's "relationship to the people is never without judgment of an outsider: she is inside the social class. Yet outside by virtue of her artistic production" ("Lorine Niedecker, the Anonymous" 120, hereinafter "Lorine Niedecker"). The Heraclitian notion of being estranged from that with which one is most familiar becomes a necessary condition for the poet writing about, and within, their community. In this respect, a "folk base" becomes a significant resource for Niedecker and Williams, allowing, as Middleton notes, for "the doubleness of participant observation amongst a people that are also 'one's own'" ("Folk Base" 175).

The relations Niedecker and Williams have with their geographical communities also reflect their poetic society. Glenna Breslin is referring to Niedecker's Wisconsin life when she claims that Niedecker "cultivated a persona detached from her community and claimed her anonymity desirable and self-imposed," but it also reflects Niedecker's dealings with her poetry community (189). The two are not exclusive, as DuPlessis's consideration of Niedecker's "anonymity" highlights; this, she argues, "is both an advantage and a fate": "Niedecker worked to turn the non-elite, non-hegemonic literary career (anonymity, erasure, loss) to an accepted fate: she will disappear into the folk from which she came" (DuPlessis, "Lorine Niedecker" 118). The advantage of such anonymity, however, is that it can become "a gesture of career building" (118).

Niedecker's "career building" can be seen in her reflections on her social restrictions (DuPlessis, "Lorine Niedecker" 121). "Fate usually intervenes to keep me from being socially active—nicely social I mean," she tells Bob Nero:

> But fate has worked hand in hand too with my writing life—I don't mourn the lone-ness of it for poetry. In fact, I couldn't do it any other way and I have the presumption to feel that others writing should retire unto themselves deeper than they do. (qtd. in Nero 137–38)

Without underestimating the hardships of Niedecker's day-to-day living or her difficult marriage to Al Millen, it is evident that there is some choice in Niedecker's "lone-ness."[5] But "lone-ness" makes Niedecker's proximity to her Wisconsin community and her poetic community more tenuous. Without a readily available fellowship of writers to converse and share ideas with, one increasingly retires deeper into one's self for confirmation and resource. There are, however, as Peter Quartermain proposes, a number of advantages for the poet whose identity is not reliant on identifying with a specific poetry group: "Working alone, you can't (or don't wish) to hang onto the coat-tails of others, you *have* to make do with what you find around you, you *have* to accept the situation in which you find yourself" (279). Niedecker not only accepted her situation, she used it to her advantage. Poetry may have caused Niedecker to feel a "freak" and marginal within her community, but it also enabled her to participate in an *eccentric,* a remote, society, while maintaining a "cool distance" from the inevitable gossip and disputes.

If Niedecker has to be compared to another writer, then T. E. Lawrence is more appropriate than Dickinson. "He was," Niedecker tells Zukofsky, "in the center of his own silence no matter how much action went on around him" (qtd. in Penberthy, *Correspondence* 337). Niedecker's remote relations with both her Wisconsin community and her society of poets put her in a similar position; rooting deeper into herself and her surroundings—like her local peonies—in order that her poetry prosper more emphatically. And, as her poem "T. E. Lawrence" suggests, such autonomous "silence" is more a social act directed outward than an inward retreat:

How impossible it is
to be alone
the one thing humanity
   has never really
moved towards (*Collected* 198)

Niedecker did feel alone. "I wish you and Louie and Celia and I could sit around a table," she writes to Corman: "Otherwise, poetry has to do it" (*Between* 48). Poetry did "do it," on many occasions, making it relatively impossible for her "to be alone" in Wisconsin. In a letter to Williams shortly after Bunting visited her in 1967, Niedecker writes that it was "a high point in my later life" ("Letters" 52). Bunting suggested Niedecker visit him in Madison before he left for Canada, but she was unable: "I told B. he, LZ and I would see each other around August in *Poetry*—LZ's *"A"*–18 in Aug. and B and I sometime thereabouts—there we'll be in our dog days" ("Letters" 52). That Niedecker found consolation in this missed opportunity by way of a mutual appearance in Chicago's *Poetry* magazine indicates how poetry reinforced the bonds of her friendships.

Finlay summarizes the remote relations of Jargon's society in *Detached Sentences on Friendship*: "Friendship is *inclination,* / acquaintance *geography.*" Friendship, Finlay implies, is borne out of mutual affinity rather than proximate convenience. Henry David Thoreau makes a similar point in *Walden,* perceiving community not as the place "where men most congregate" but as "the perennial source of our life, whence in all our experience we have found that to issue, as the willow stands near the water and sends out its roots in that direction" (121–22). Thoreau's pun on the root of "community"—from the Old

French *comunete*, meaning "reinforced by its source"—would not have been lost on Niedecker and Williams. Neither would have Thoreau's botanical analogy of the willow tree rooted near its nourishing source, its *root*. One source for their transatlantic society, as we have seen, was kinship. The other was poetry itself and the people from whom, and for whom, it flows.

NOTES

1. Whit Griffin, a former intern with the Jargon Society, kindly provided this letterhead designed by A. Doyle Moore.

2. "To see Niedecker as tree or flower is lovely and not inaccurate," Jane Augustine proposes in her review of Niedecker's *Collected Poems*: "It reflects the influence of haiku on her short forms and the Asian use of the natural object as 'always the adequate symbol,' as Pound noted" even if, as she argues, Williams's "feminine stereotype, 'woman' equals 'nature,' does not do her justice."

3. Williams also addresses the "alliance" of botany and folk song in *Blues & Roots: A Garland for the Southern Appalachians* (1971). The book's title derives from Charles Mingus's 1959 album of the same name, which appropriates traditional blues and gospel music. "Roots" also puns on the references to Appalachia's bluet flower and rue shrub as well as invoking the region's transplanted "roots" music—"bluegrass"—which, Robert Cantwell notes, is an "Americanized strain of English, Irish, and Scots-Irish traditional music, shaped by Afro-American rhythms and tonalities" (6).

4. For Williams's relation to Black Mountain College see Hair.

5. For further discussion of Niedecker's marriage see Peters (164–65).

EIGHT | ANDREW EPSTEIN

The Volley Maintained Nears Orgasm

Rae Armantrout, Ron Silliman, and the Cross-Gender Collaboration

IN 1982, Rae Armantrout and Ron Silliman, two central figures in the avant-garde movement known as Language poetry, decided to collaborate on a poem. First one poet wrote a fourteen-sentence paragraph of prose poetry, then mailed it to the other, who then added a fourteen-sentence paragraph and returned it by mail, until they had accumulated fourteen such paragraphs. The resulting poem, entitled "Engines," appeared in the literary journal *Conjunctions* in 1983; it was later published as a section of Silliman's long poem *The Alphabet* in 1992, and in a collection of Armantrout's own selected poems, *Veil*, in 2001. Like many collaborations, "Engines" is a self-conscious text that reflects on its own status as a jointly created work; it overtly reckons with both the excitement and the ambivalence engendered by the creative exchange between friends, particularly when those friends happen to be of the opposite sex.

It is not surprising that such a collaboration would have been undertaken by writers associated with Language poetry: community, collaboration, and the social have been central concerns of the Language movement since its inception in the 1970s. Inspired by the communitarian ethos and the poetics of sociability espoused by the "New American" poetry of the postwar period—led by the New York School, Black Mountain, Beat, and San Francisco Renaissance poets—but skeptical of its residual individualism, Language writers developed a rigorous, sometimes utopian model of poetic community. They staged intensive debates about the nature of their own collective, and about their community more broadly. At the same time, they began to experiment extensively with collaborative writing practices. The list of collaborations by Language writers is long, including book-length, multiauthored works like

Legend (1980) (by Bruce Andrews, Charles Bernstein, Ray DiPalma, Steve McCaffery, and Silliman), *Leningrad* (1991) (by Michael Davidson, Lyn Hejinian, Silliman, and Barrett Watten), *The Wide Road* (2011) (by Carla Harryman and Hejinian), and the recent *Grand Piano* series (2006–2010) (billed as "An Experiment in Collective Autobiography," cowritten by ten members of the Language community). But "Engines" stands out as one of the relatively few poems jointly authored by a man and a woman to have emerged from this particular scene.

In this essay, I argue that "Engines" is a fascinating example of a cross-gender avant-garde poetic collaboration, and as such, is an unusually rich site for an examination of how friendship, gender, and writing collide in contemporary American poetry. In recent years, scholars have begun to explore the importance of community and friendship to the development and practices of postwar avant-garde poetry, from the New American Poetry to Language writing and beyond.[1] Such discussions have analyzed, and often celebrated, collaboration as a crucial, exemplary instance of literary friendship and avant-garde community in action.[2] There is also a growing body of scholarship that focuses more generally on the nature of collaboration, often without special attention to the avant-garde or to poetics.[3] In such work, critics have explored the erotic dimensions of collaborative practice, most notably in Wayne Koestenbaum's *Double Talk*, a groundbreaking book that argues that male literary collaboration is driven by sublimated sexual desire.[4] At the same time, recent feminist criticism has delved into the history of women working as coauthors with one another, while also reevaluating the role of gender in literary relationships between men and women more broadly.[5]

However, little attention has been given to the phenomenon of cross-gender collaboration, in part because it has been a rather rare practice.[6] As Holly A. Laird has observed, "the great majority of the books written about literary coauthorship devote themselves to writing partners of the same sex (including alleged or avowed sexual partners)" ("A Hand Spills" 351). When scholars do consider literary relationships between men and women, they have often sought to expose the long tradition of casting women as auxiliaries, secretaries, and assistants to powerful male writers. Such studies have done the important work of uncovering the often invisible presence of crucial, creative women lurking in the shadow of male "geniuses," but have not often considered what happens when men and women attempt to cocreate literary works as equals.

In Koestenbaum's study of male literary collaboration, he quickly dismisses cross-gender collaborations as little more than "an appropriative relation," a perpetuation of "an old tradition of wifely subordination" (14). For Koestenbaum, this paradigm—"the union of a male writer and his female amanuensis: Sylvia Plath typing her husband Ted Hughes's poems"—is less "fruitful" than "the history of female (and lesbian) collaboration" (14). Similarly, in her study of "women's literary partnerships," Bette Lynn London notes that "women's more complex authorial engagements, however, have tended to be dwarfed by the dominant model of spousal collaboration that defines most cross-gender writing arrangements—a model that relegates women to the role of helpmeet and amanuensis. Trained to read these roles as ancillary, we lack the vocabulary to describe them otherwise" (20).

Although there is hardly a robust tradition of cross-gender collaborations upon which to focus, the practice has become increasingly visible in contemporary literature, just as the old hierarchical, sexist paradigm of male creator and female helpmeet has given way to more egalitarian models of such relations.[7] Thus, it would seem that the time is ripe for readers to consider more closely the distinctive nature of the cross-gender aesthetic collaboration as a unique forum in which gender, writing, subjectivity, and friendship all intersect. More specifically, recent cross-gender collaborations display—and sometimes explore thematically—the subtle power dynamics and sexual dimensions of male-female relationships in a world transformed by feminism and rapidly shifting gender roles.

In what follows, I argue that "Engines" is an exemplary case in this regard. Given the facts of its authorship, this collaboration provides us with an unusual, valuable window into the internal dynamics of the Language writing community. Both Silliman and Armantrout had spent much of the previous decade immersed in the intense creative ferment and dialogue of the evolving Language collective, a group that was dedicated to meta-conversation and self-reflection on the problematic nature of community and gender within avant-garde movements.

The poem they composed in 1982 embodies the broader debates about group identity, individual subjectivity, friendship, gender, power, and authorship that were pulsing at the heart of their own collective. As we will see, "Engines" deliberately encodes, often playfully, the erotics of exchange and dialogue, the presence of unequal power in cross-gender relationships, and the tension between individuality and union inherent in any collaboration or indeed, in friendship itself.

FROM THE FIRST, the Language movement insisted on the importance of collectivity, rejected the idea of "the poet as a solo egoist," and enthusiastically embraced collaboration as a key aesthetic practice (Hejinian, *The Language of Inquiry* 171). While some of the poets, like Bernstein, worried about "groupism" and warned of the dangers of a "Conspiracy of 'Us'" (as the title of one of his important early essays has it), Language writers generally celebrated the generative potential of a close-knit yet fluid, shifting coterie of like-minded avant-garde poets (*Content's Dream* 343).

However, the preoccupation with community and collaboration in early Language poetry did not manage to paper over the persistent problem of gender and the perceived marginalization of women within the formation and evolution of Language writing and its community. Critics have recently begun to analyze the complex positioning of women within the evolution of Language writing, most thoroughly in Ann Vickery's exhaustive history, *Leaving Lines of Gender: A Feminist Genealogy of Language Writing* (2000). As Vickery argues, "the critical reception of Language writing has therefore tended to represent women as secondary participants or its passive benefactors" (12). Her study demonstrates how Language writing's "consolidation as a group practice (within its respective communities as well as institutionally) was both enabling and problematic for the women writers involved" (6).

During the 1970s and 1980s, many experimental writers both within Language poetry and beyond began to draw attention to the fraught gender politics that continued to roil even the most progressive poetry communities and to mark the reception of new writing. Dissatisfaction with the masculinist ethos of the avant-garde exploded in the work of second generation New York School poets like Bernadette Mayer and

Alice Notley, and led Kathleen Fraser to found *(HOW)ever,* a groundbreaking and influential journal entirely devoted to a wide spectrum of experimental poetry by women, in 1983.[8]

As Vickery's study shows, both male and female poets began to wrestle with thorny questions about feminism, essentialized gender categories, and the politics of poetic form versus identity politics (37–49). Among the male Language writers, Silliman seemed especially drawn to such questions, both in his critical writing and in his poetry. For instance, in a much-discussed, extended debate that was published in 1991, Silliman and Leslie Scalapino carried on a heated, public conversation about identity, women's writing, and the avant-garde. The exchange was triggered by a controversial 1988 essay in which Silliman argued that women and other marginalized individuals are less likely to write formally innovative work because, unlike white heterosexual males, they "have a manifest political need to have their stories told" (Scalapino and Silliman 51).[9] At the same time, as I have argued elsewhere, Silliman uses his poetry both to challenge sexist ideologies and practices and to acknowledge his own complicity with them.[10]

Like Silliman, in the 1970s and 1980s Armantrout became an influential contributor to such discussions about gender, community, and poetics. In widely discussed essays like "Why Don't Women Do Language-Oriented Writing?" (1978) and "Feminist Poetics and the Meaning of Clarity" (1992), Armantrout plunged into the fray, as she too grappled with charged questions about experimental poetic form, the politics of representation, and women's writing (*Collected Prose* 13–15, 38–48, hereinafter *Collected*).

Highly sensitive to the gendering of the avant-garde and its poetics, Armantrout spent the early years of Language poetry's development rather strenuously resisting assimilation into a community identity, that "Conspiracy of 'Us'" which Bernstein feared. Like many women writers, Armantrout remained wary of a group aesthetic, in part because she felt pushed to the margins of a male-dominated scene. In the 2007 preface to her *Collected Prose,* she recalls that in her early essays she was reacting to "the (mostly) male theorists of the new language movement" and "was struggling against (what I saw as) over-restrictive definitions of what a new poetry should look like" (*Collected* 9).

For example, in "Poetic Silence," a deliberately provocative essay that she delivered as a lecture in the important Language community "Talks" series in the early 1980s, Armantrout challenged the dominance of "the new sentence," a form of prose poetry composed of disconnected statements arranged paratactically that, by the late 1970s, had become the preferred mode for many of her peers within the Language writing community, including Silliman, Hejinian, Bob Perelman, and Watten.[11] At the time, Armantrout had resolutely continued to write her extremely compressed, lineated poems filled with gaps and white space. In the talk, Armantrout takes aim at the prevailing house style:

> As we know, a new sort of long prose poem has developed and gained increasing influence over the last few years. I want to argue, not against this sort of prose poem, but for the value of the lyric format, and its greater potential for evoking silence. To describe it simply, this new prose poem is most often composed of non-narrative, declarative sentences. The declarative sentence declares. Thus such poems tend to create a tone of certainty, of resolution and completeness which leaves little room for the experience of silence. (*Collected* 22)

By juxtaposing her sense of the closure and decisiveness of the "new sentence" prose poem with a celebration of the mystery, ambiguity, and "silence" of her own lyric mode, Armantrout was consciously distancing herself from the Language community, aesthetically if not socially.

In more recent years, Armantrout has discussed this resistance in several interviews and has made clear that the politics of group identity and individual style was a factor in her aesthetic choices, which also had repercussions for her links to the collective.[12] As she told Tom Beckett in a 1999 interview, "I mainly avoided the move to the prose poem that happened in the late 70s and early 80s. At that point there was some controversy within the group, I think, about whether I really 'belonged.' And I know that, since then, some people outside that group who happen to like my work have told me that they don't see me as one of 'those people'" (*Collected* 130–31).[13]

At times, such anxieties surface quite palpably in Armantrout's work, like at the end of her poem "Leaving": "So I was hidden / among fashionable allies" (*Veil* 87). At such moments, Armantrout's poems dramatize her "sense of precarious belonging among the Language writers," her mixed feelings about her alliances and friendships within the Language community and their impact on her sense of self ("An Interview" [Keller] 221). Armantrout's reluctance to merge her own identity fully with the Language writing community and its house style was tied to her sense that the scene remained dominated by male voices, perhaps in spite of its best intentions. In her interview with Beckett, she offers an assessment of the gender dynamics of the West Coast Language poetry community in its formative stages. Although she insists that the "San Francisco LangPo scene was utopian by contrast" with the "sexist" environment she grew up in, she does say that the Language poetry community

> was perhaps unnecessarily masculinist in style. People argued with each other openly and sometimes fiercely. If someone didn't like the reading you gave, he might tell you so. You were expected to give as good as you got. There was, perhaps, a bit of a warrior mentality. I remember that at the Talks series, first held in Bob Perelman's loft, it was difficult for women to participate [. . .] It wasn't that we were dismissed —but it was sort of a free-for-all. You had to be quite aggressive to get the next word in. I don't hold anyone individually responsible for that. Individually, these guys encouraged me. (*Collected* 132)[14]

As Armantrout has noted, her "experience as a young woman among the mostly-male language writers" was a formative one that generated the enduring fascination with power dynamics and gender that underlies so much of her writing (*Collected* 131).

IT IS NOT INCIDENTAL that Armantrout and Silliman composed the 1982 poem "Engines" right in the thick of these contentious debates that were circulating within feminism and the experimental poetry community. At a moment when both poets were embroiled in discussions about the role of women in male-dominated avant-garde movements and the relationship between women's writing and experimental form, the idea of engaging in *cross-gender* collaboration may have seemed particularly alluring. As Armantrout and Silliman must have sensed, a two-person, cross-gender collaboration offers possibilities that run quite counter to a "masculinist" collaborative project like *Legend*, conspicuously written by five male poets, or a collaboration coproduced by two women, like *The Wide Road*, by Harryman and Hejinian (a piece jointly composed between 1991 to 2010).[15] The opportunity to stage an extended conversation between a male and a female member of an avant-garde community seems to have offered both poets a way of broaching some of these vexing questions about gender, power, authorship, and avant-garde community, but within the space of poetry itself and not outside of it, in the usual realm of lectures, debates, or critical discussions.

In a 1985 interview, Silliman contrasts the collaborative book *Legend* (1980), which he cowrote with four male Language poets, with the 1982 poem "Engines," his collaboration with Armantrout, which he seems to see as a more fully realized collaboration:

> To my own eye, ["Engines"] has a tension and a density that I was never able to achieve in my portions of *Legend* [. . .] In a two person collaboration, there is an intense chain of action and response, attention and reaction, which one finds in such other interactive events as tennis or love-making. I'm much more sensitive to the nuances of interaction than I was five years ago. (40)

As we will see, the Armantrout-Silliman collaboration is extremely self-conscious about the "intense chain of action and response" that gave rise to the text. In a 2003 post on his widely read blog, Silliman explained the quite deliberate and lengthy process of exchange, revision, and dialogue that led to the poem's creation: "I would type a paragraph and send it to Rae in the mail. She would add one and send it back. We suggested revisions to one another's paragraphs & played off of the themes as they arose—my helicopters were a direct translation of her angels, for example" (*Silliman's Blog*). By offering specific details about the give-and-take procedures that generated the poem, Silliman's 2003 comments also added considerable stability to the indeterminate, fluid collaborative text. Prior to these remarks, readers could only speculate about the nature of the poem's collaborative process, who wrote which sentence or section, whether the poets traded off words, sentences, or paragraphs, and so on. But these comments serve to reestablish the boundaries of individual authorship: we now know that the poets each wrote entire, separate paragraphs sequentially and then exchanged them by mail; we also know that, as Silliman has stated, "my helicopters were a direct translation of her angels." This perhaps offhand comment actually offers a significant clue about the authorship of each paragraph: because the recurring images of helicopters *only* appear in the odd-numbered paragraphs of the poem, and because we now know the authors traded off paragraphs, it seems safe to conclude that Silliman wrote the odd-numbered paragraphs, and Armantrout the even (where most, but not all, of the "angel" images appear). Although I do not wish to claim that this is a definitive explanation of the poem's authorship, in what follows I entertain this possibility, in part because it intriguingly illuminates aspects of the poem's colloquy. That said, it is not my intention to reduce unnecessarily the poem's play of textual identities, not least because "Engines" continually teases and hints at questions of authorship, individual signature, and who wrote what.

SO WHAT KIND of poem does this collaborative process of composition yield? "Engines" is a prose poem fashioned out of disjunctive, non sequitur sentences arranged paratactically and deliberately eschewing any linear progression or fixed, overall subject. The piece juxtaposes observations of the minute details of everyday life ("the noise of the fan cooling the slide projector is punctuated with clicks" [Silliman, *The Alphabet* 37], "pearls perch on crinkled lobes" [39], "in the ashtray, the cigarette burns to the filter" [41]); fragments of unattributed, quoted language ("I think something happens in the end" [37]); ironic metacommentary on the poem itself and its processes ("for this paragraph, attach separate form 1040-ES" [37], "narrative suppresses immediate attention" [39], "content seems increasingly prescribed" [41]); politically inflected cultural critique ("at the base of their neck, each wears the small scar of tenure" [40], "only the policeman's horses appear neutral to the sight of so much blood" [39], "Above Fashion Valley they're building Fashion Hills" [40], "In *Dallas,* capitalism and the family are the same thing, and no scene need last more than 90 seconds" [40]); and so on. In other words, it feels much like a textbook example of the mode that Silliman described as "the new sentence."

In that sense, "Engines" much more closely resembles Silliman's poetry than Armantrout's exceedingly spare, terse, lined poems, which tend to feature much less descriptive, observational writing than Silliman's. As Armantrout mentioned in a recent interview, "certainly on the surface my writing could not possibly look more different from Ron Silliman's" (Interview [Feldman]). Why, then, does her collaboration with Silliman "look" so much like her friend's work and so little like her own? Is the poem a melding of voices or a subsuming of Armantrout's into Silliman's own aesthetic? If it is the latter, one could argue that the poem merely re-inscribes the traditional hierarchical relationship between male and female coauthors. However, the poem, and Armantrout, seem highly conscious of this issue, as the text tackles questions of individual "style" and challenges masculinist aggression. Nonetheless, the unsettling recognition that the poem is closer to Silliman's aesthetic than Armantrout's lingers and complicates any easy conclusions about the poem's status as an example of postfeminist equality.

The poem is not "about" anything in the conventional sense. But, as Silliman has suggested, collaborations are always about what happens in the collaborative process, are always "opportunities to explore the boundaries of self & other" (*Silliman's Blog*). "Engines" obviously takes as its central theme the back-and-forth, dialogic process that generated the poem itself.[16] Right from the start, "Engines" deploys imagery of dialogue ("You stand in the glass booth, pretending conversation" [37]) and erotic intimacy ("An Interview with Ron Silliman" [Beckett]). It is interesting to note that a key image in the first paragraph combines the exact two activities, "tennis and love-making," that Silliman would soon mention as analogies for collaboration in his discussion of "Engines" in his interview with Beckett: "The volley maintained nears orgasm" (37). This phrase, and the poem as a whole, posits a key analogy: the cross-gender collaboration is an interactive act undertaken by two people, like love-making or tennis. With such imagery, the poets hint that the collaborative work is a space where the textual and the sexual overlap and blur. Rather than suggesting that collaborative works are fueled by subterranean, sublimated desire, as Koestenbaum argues, "Engines" foregrounds the fact that the sustained give-and-take interaction of a cross-gender poetic collaboration can be pleasurable and sexually charged.

Even the poem's basic structure hints that the text itself is a kind of "volley," an act of dialogue, as opposed to one of merging or melding. The poem features fourteen prose paragraphs, each consisting of fourteen sentences.[17] This creates a structured, balanced form within which to carry on a poetic dialogue, and the regularity of the structure means that the poem is symmetrical, founded on a measured, not chaotic, formal pattern. In that sense, "Engines" resembles the sort of orderly conversation one finds in improvisational jazz, where each member solos for a certain number of bars before turning the floor back over to another player, who will often riff off the notes played by one of the other musicians. The seesaw motion of the text's structure (mine / yours, mine / yours, mine / yours) reinforces the sense that it is on one level *about* the gendered dimensions of this very conversation, about the two poets' roles within the larger community they share.

This is enhanced by the poets' frequent recourse to contrasting sentences, some referring to a man ("He attempts a series of irrefutable statements [38]," "He came in from behind" [37], "His fear was of scale" [39]), and some referring to a woman ("Her one idea provokes disaster" [37], "so they laid her in a glass coffin" [37], "She likes to think time passes" [40]). Furthermore, through linguistic play and punning, the poem frequently makes explicit the call-and-response nature of its composition. For example, the second paragraph, presumably written by Armantrout, offers a fragment of what sounds like autobiographical reflection: "her face, like her mother's, is tense" (37). The following paragraph responds directly and playfully, with a punning riff on the sonic qualities of the statement that also seems to emphasize the contrasts between the "she" and the "he": "his face, like his mother's, was dense" (37).

Another example of the poem's playful, yet rather tense exchange occurs when the second paragraph states "unable to reply, melodrama skips ahead" (37); in the following paragraph, a voice seems to answer, skeptically, "Melodrama *skips*?" (38) as if to say: what does it mean to write that melodrama "skips" ahead? Not to be outdone, the very next sentence, which opens the new paragraph, the fourth, begins with the line "skeletons *bloom*?" (38). Not only does this syntactically and graphically mirror "melodrama *skips*?" but it is a direct response to an image in the first paragraph: "Skeletons bloom at the rear of the lab" (37). Thus the question about skeletons "blooming" seems to be an assertive reply to the question about the image of melodrama "skipping": an example of two writers, two friends, serving and returning, questioning and challenging, even poking fun at each other's figures of speech and imagery in the space of the poem itself.

However, this can also be read as an example of a woman writer using the space of the poem—as opposed to the loft or lecture hall, sites where Armantrout and other women in her community felt silenced—as a place to aggressively reply to a male interlocutor who has questioned and lightly mocked something she had written, by turning the tables on him. In this way, "Engines" becomes a site for a distinctly feminine response and act of resistance to the masculinist behavior that marks the social world of the larger avant-garde community.

"Engines" also meditates on the individual's relationship to the group, but with acute attention to gendered imagery, sexuality, and gender roles. It is hardly incidental that the poem opens with a striking image of a collective: "A herd of wild helicopters scuds in the night" (37). "Herd" is of course a negatively charged word for a group, with connotations of sheep-like conformity, and the helicopter takes on overtones of masculinity and violence throughout the poem. Later, the ninth paragraph revises the opening line of the poem, stating "I mean: *stampedes* in the night" (40), which further highlights the aggressive, overpowering element of this herd of choppers (40). The use of such imagery seems to allow both poets to acknowledge that the Language poetry community threatens to function as a kind of testosterone-fueled, cliquish boys' gang and to reflect upon the uncomfortably circumscribed options for women within and outside the herd.

Unwilling to simply liquidate their own poetic identities in a unified "voice" of a collaborative work, the poets seem to worry about the tension between individual "style" and the "herd," the collaborative or communal identity. Shortly after the image of the mob of helicopters, the first paragraph says "style is its own mark" (37), which invites us to consider what "style" might mean in a jointly composed text. Does the use of a particular style or voice denote an individual identity or not? References to "style" recur throughout the poem, as when the ninth paragraph notes that "style is the fiber in description which shrinks at the first wash" (39) and the twelfth responds: "By style marked" (40).

At one moment, the poets seem to hail the union of their two voices in a plural, jointly signed work ("the plural is restful and suggestive" and "pride is the plural" [40, 41]), while at another, they seem to hold fast to the inviolate self: "One grows more individual—uniquely marred and indescribably attired, unable to join the talk" (38). Because Armantrout seems to have written this sentence (as it is an even-numbered paragraph), it further suggests her ambivalence toward the group aesthetic of Language poetry—a reluctance "to join the talk," particularly since she saw the Language community as something of a masculinist "herd." In this way, the poem seems to reflect Armantrout's desire to remain "more individual," which we have already seen manifested in her quite deliberate decision to continue writing short, lineated poems in the face of the group's adoption of the prose poem as its collective signature, its chief form.

Many of the recurring figures and tropes in the poem underscore its fascination with the tense interaction between men and women, which indicates that both poets are overtly contemplating the intertwining of gender and power. For example, there is the imagery of helicopters that, as Silliman has acknowledged, runs throughout the poem, as can be seen in the following sentences taken from odd-numbered paragraphs: "Instinctively we crouched, disembarking the Sikorsky, darting swiftly in a bent-over manner beyond the wide sweep of the blade (which only became visible as it slowed to a stop)" (37); "They take on the countenance of helicopters, shuttling from the clouds" (38); and "Their wings are like blades" (39).

Even if we did not have Silliman's acknowledgment that "my helicopters were a direct translation of her angels," it is not hard to see how the helicopter becomes a gendered signifier in the complex "volley" of the poem. The governing image of the poem (encoded in the poem's title itself) provides the two poets an allegorical figure for the gendered social dynamics of their friendship and their community. With its whirring steel blades and other militaristic connotations, the helicopter imagery deliberately contrasts with Armantrout's more ethereal angels, which appear in the even-numbered paragraphs: "the spirits whom we call angels were never at any time or in any way darkness" (37), "It is more difficult to believe that the holy angels are now unaware of their eternal blessedness" (38), "You must be the angel, Gabriel" (38), "Metatron is called the scribe of heaven" (39), "Michael heals. Uriel descends in a chariot of fire" (41). Within the context of the poem's "he-said, she-said" dynamic, Silliman's stampeding helicopters seem to embody an aggressive masculinist impulse, and perhaps point to the "warrior mentality" Armantrout attributed to the Language writing community of the 1970s and early 1980s. One telling moment in this tug-of-war occurs when Silliman invokes "her" figure of the angel only to re-inscribe it. Perhaps indicating the tendency for male voices to absorb and drown out those of women, Silliman deliberately makes the image over into a trope of his own, a macho, car-chopper hybrid: "An angel named Mustang with blades of steel" (paragraph 13, 41).

At one moment, an even-numbered paragraph (presumably by Armantrout) says, "He attempts a series of irrefutable statements" (38), which seems to critique rather directly Silliman's poetics (what else is the "new sentence" other than a "series" of "statements"?). It is notable that the sentence conveys some doubt about whether this could be a successful endeavor in the first place ("he *attempts*"), mingled with the inveterate skeptic Armantrout's temperamental aversion to anything, especially any linguistic utterance, being "irrefutable." The association of "statements" with an unwelcome irrefutability closely echoes Armantrout's argument in "Poetic Silence"—her belief that the "declarative sentence" of the Language poetry prose poem creates "a tone of certainty, of resolution and completeness which leaves little room for the experience of silence" (*Collected* 22).

One can also sense an element of feminist critique at play here. In some recent comments, Armantrout has, somewhat hesitantly, connected "the 'masculinist' style of the Language scene" with the "assertive, statemental or propositional sentence that's characteristic of Language Writing in its west coast variety" (*Collected* 86–87). Thus, it is probably not an accident that, in "Engines," it is a "*he*" who "attempts a series of irrefutable statements," since it allows Armantrout to further challenge what she saw as the domineering tone and unpleasant certainty of the masculinist "new sentence." Once more, we see how debates about poetics, gender politics, and literary form have moved from the social sphere, from the café or living room, to the social site of the poem, where they are performed and hashed out.

Later, another even-numbered paragraph (presumably by the same author, and thus by Armantrout once again) revises this sentence in the following passage: "A point of pride. He attempts a series of irrefutable *movements*. By style marked. Genghis Khan Antiques, Godfather's Restaurant" (40). What the "he" now attempts are irrefutable "movements" rather than statements—which could mean either a series of gestures, or movements in the sense of a vanguard artistic movement. It is worth noting the constellation of images juxtaposed in this passage—the reference to "pride," the recurring nod to the masculine "attempt" to be "irrefutable," the hint about "his" attempt to create an avant-garde movement, the suggestion that "style" could serve as a marker of individuality or territory, the ironic references to violent, powerful male figures (Genghis Khan, the Godfather) turned kitsch and commodity. It stands as a powerful example of how "Engines" encodes Armantrout's subtle critique of masculinist ideologies and their unfortunate foundational role in the formation of Language poetry, and of avant-garde collectivity more broadly.

These moments of feminist critique coexist with a charged language of physical desire that lends the poem an agitated, unresolved tone, underscoring the tense back-and-forth structure of the piece. By placing rather raw erotic imagery, double entendres, and direct references to sexual practices at the heart of their poem, Armantrout and Silliman make overt the sublimated erotic dimension Koestenbaum sees as latent in male literary collaborations; they literalize the metaphor that collaboration is, by nature, an interactive mode of communication akin to conversation or sex, and reveal it to be a mode of acting out complex, often erotic feelings between its participants.

At the same time, the poem also exposes the tensions inherent in cross-gender friendship itself. On the one hand, it continually hints that an erotic subtext lurks within any interaction, any conversation, between heterosexual men and women. Simultaneously, it suggests that sometimes a chat is just a chat and not an act of seduction after all. Thus at one moment, we hear that "the volley maintained nears orgasm" (37), while at another, we are told that "some conversation is not a come-on" (40). These two possibilities both hover, unresolved, throughout the poem, which only adds to its erotic charge, perhaps in a way that is meant to parallel "real life" conversations between heterosexual men and women: is this, or is this *not,* a flirtatious or sexualized conversation? How does one know? What if I am reading the signals wrong and she is thinking "That is not what I meant at all. / That is not it, at all" (Eliot, *Collected Poems* 6)?

The idea that cross-gender conversation is a playful, flirtatious game of seduction and evasion runs throughout the piece. At times, the poets intentionally allow their imagery to flicker, double-entendre–style, between the sexual and the nonsexual. For example, in paragraph three, presumably a Silliman passage: "He came in from behind. There are several ways in which this can be taken, but we prefer air freight" (37). Similarly, in paragraph five: "Huge, well-hung balls of type" (38). At the end of this phrase, the locker-room anatomical reference with which it began is suddenly converted into a comment on typewriting or typesetting. As these examples suggest, the poets use ambiguity and punning to incorporate, deflect, and play with sexual innuendoes. This offers them another way to heighten the erotic dimensions of the exchange and to demonstrate how much ordinary language and mundane conversation are suffused with sensuality and erotic potential. There are even some teasing lines that hint that something more may be hidden beneath the surface, as in the three-sentence combination, apparently written by Armantrout: "Light flicks over those leaves in complete silence. That is a slippery tongue. Do we suggest relations that we aren't willing to declare?" (paragraph 2, 37).

Specific features of the poem's sexual imagery also further reinforce the masculine-feminine, "he-said, she-said" quality of the text's dialogue, as certain erotic references seem to be connected, deliberately, to a heterosexual man's point of view, and others to a heterosexual woman's. In the odd-numbered (Silliman-penned) paragraphs, one finds the word "penetrate," the phrases "he came in from behind," "he found hair flattened to the leg by the scrim of nylon intensely erotic" (38), "huge, well-hung balls of type" (38), "the head is both swollen and mottled" (39), "it has the look and feel of milky eggwhite" (39). Further, the actions in "his" paragraphs are described from a male perspective and seem to be deliberately penetrative and overtly masculinized: "more gentle than the art of pushing is the desire slowly to withdraw" (39), "this is inserted to test your response" (39), "I put in my thumb and you start to writhe" (40), "I put my tongue to the button" (41).

In contrast, the even-numbered paragraphs (presumably by Armantrout), implicitly critique Silliman's aggressive, even sexist way of expressing erotic desire. In her paragraphs, one finds physical experiences that seem explicitly gendered female, and often less focused on penetrating the other and objectifying the other's body: "pressure fills the channel nicely, not exactly wet" (39), and (perhaps less identifiably "feminine") "pleasure detaches from the stroke and spreads" (38), and "You twist your key in the ignition. A woman mumbles and shakes. Fucking as if to stimulate an ideal reader" (41).

The poem's pervasive sexual imagery culminates in this last trio of sentences in its final paragraph (presumably by Armantrout). Here the textual at last collapses into the sexual, as the act of literary collaboration merges with the physical act of "fucking," while simultaneously implicating the reader in the tryst. These lines would seem to up the ante on Koestenbaum's notion that a collaboration is "a metaphorical sexual intercourse" (3). Whereas Koestenbaum wishes to uncover the repressed homoerotic desire between men that is sublimated in the male literary collaboration, in the case of "Engines," one finds a more overt, teasing recognition that heterosexual desire and gendered power imbalances are inescapable in cross-gender collaboration and conversation. In other words, "Engines" is less "a sublimation of erotic entanglement" than a playful exploration of it, one that takes the metaphor of collaboration as love-making and makes it literal (4).

ONE COULD ARGUE that, by definition, the contemporary cross-gender collaboration challenges the traditional model of the woman as muse or helpmeet and the man as heroic creator. It explicitly makes men and women equal, coproducers of culture. In that sense, the cross-gender collaboration is an inherently political, egalitarian, and feminist act, and we might assume that is one reason both Armantrout and Silliman were attracted to the form. However, as we have seen, these two poets are too self-conscious, too politically sensitive to wholly embrace the idealistic notion that working together on a poem as equals means that gender equality and collective identity have been achieved. They never fully buy the idea that individual style, personal identity, or competitive individualism is so easily dissolved. They are too theoretically attuned to ignore the persistence of ideological constructions of gender, the implicit power relations and erotic dimensions of friendships across gender lines, the blurred boundaries between autonomous selfhood and collective identity—all of which surface throughout the poem in various ways.

The Armantrout-Silliman poetic tête-a-tête amply demonstrates why the collaborative work is one of the most important venues for poets not only to test their ideas and anxieties about friendship, community, and poetry, but also to reflect on how gender, authorship, and individual autonomy interrelate. In working together to write "Engines," Armantrout and Silliman seized the opportunity the cross-gender collaboration provides to compose a poem that probes, both playfully and uncomfortably, the gender dynamics that are inherent not only in friendship but also at the heart of the model of collaborative exchange so dear to the idea of the avant-garde itself.

NOTES

1. See, for example, my book *Beautiful Enemies: Friendship and Postwar American Poetry*, as well as studies by Davidson, Shaw, Kane, Rifkin, Vickery, and Gerald Izenberg, among others.

2. Many of the recent studies of avant-garde American poetry, community, and sociability focus on the important role of collaboration in the New American poetry of the postwar period, particularly within the work of Frank O'Hara and the New York School. For example, see Epstein, Shaw, Kane, Herd, Hazel Smith, and Reed (and other essays in Hampson and Montgomery). Collaborations have frequently been a focus of studies of Language poetry as well, as I will discuss.

3. For more on the body of scholarly work that focuses explicitly on the nature of literary collaboration (though not necessarily within poetry or the avant-garde) see Koestenbaum's influential book; Laird's essay and book; two issues of *PMLA* (March 2001 and October 2001), which featured special sections on collaboration and included pieces by Holly Laird and Linda and Michael Hutcheon; and books by Stillinger, Chadwick and de Courtivron, Ashton, Lunsford and Ede, and Stone and Thompson.

4. Koestenbaum's study examines collaborative works by pairs of male writers, including Sigmund Freud and Josef Breuer, William Wordsworth and Samuel Taylor Coleridge, T. S. Eliot and Ezra Pound, and Joseph Conrad and Ford Maddox Ford, and argues that "men who collaborate engage in a metaphorical sexual intercourse" in which "the text they balance between them, is alternately a child of their sexual union, and a shared woman" (3).

5. For examples of recent feminist criticism and gender studies that have focused particularly on women writing with other women, see Laird, London, and Kaplan and Rose. For a discussion that focuses particularly on feminist collaboration between women within the Language poetry community, see Vickery (249–64).

6. Several studies have given special attention to cross-gender collaborations—see, for example, Garrity and Latimer, and Karell. See also Stone and Thompson, Cohen, and Chadwick and de Courtivron, who focus on pairings of writers and artists, if not collaborations per se.

7. For example, see the recently published anthology *Saints of Hysteria: A Half-Century of Collaborative American Poetry* (edited by Duhamel, Seaton, and Trinidad), which includes a number of cross-gender coauthored works. See also *The Crown of Columbus,* cowritten by the married couple Michael Dorris and Louise Erdrich, and *Which Brings Me to You,* a collaborative epistolary novel written by two contemporary fiction writers, Julianna Baggott and Steve Almond.

8. For more on the historical and literary importance of *HOW(ever),* see Vickery (88–100) and Kinnahan (23–40).

9. This discussion can be found in *Poetics Journal* 9 (1991). It is worth noting that Silliman's comments about women's writing were made in a 1988 essay, six years after the writing of "Engines."

10. See Epstein, "There Is No Content Here," which discusses Silliman's attention to his own biases and assumptions as a white, heterosexual man in his long poem *Ketjak* (1974) (esp. 763–68).

11. For Silliman's definitive discussion of the "new sentence," see the title essay of *The New Sentence.* For an overview of the "new sentence," see Perelman (*The Marginalization of Poetry* 59–78).

12. See Armantrout's interview with Keller, where she discusses her uneasiness with the "faddishness" of the "new sentence" prose poem in the 1970s. ("An Interview" [Keller] 229.)

13. The question of whether Armantrout "belongs" within Language poetry as a movement and as a community has only grown more complicated in recent years, especially as her reputation has begun to soar. Although critics still associate her with Language poetry, they are quick to establish the differences, often to praise Armantrout at the expense of other Language writers. For example, see Dan Chiasson's recent review in the *New Yorker* of Armantrout's book *Versed,* which was awarded the Pulitzer Prize and the National Book Critics Circle Award

in 2010. Chiasson takes pains to sever Armantrout from her affiliation with Language poetry: "These days, it's difficult to remember how hard Language poets once tried to submerge or subvert their individual differences, as part of their program to demystify the 'individual' (feel free to supply 'subvert' and 'demystify' with scare quotes, too): the aim was to be understood as a collective. This happens, to some degree, in all self-conscious literary movements. Still, real differences among the individuals have since come to light, chiefly differences in talent, and Armantrout is by an order of magnitude the best poet in the group" (111).

14. In a 2005 interview with Eric Elshtain and Matthias Regan, Armantrout comments further on the "masculinist style" of the early Language poetry period, which was marked by "bold assertion and aggressive argumentation" and "seemed to cut women out of full participation, at least in some venues" (*Collected* 86).

15. Watten examines the inherent "homosocial," "masculinist" aesthetic of *Legend*, coauthored by five male Language poets ("The Secret History of the Equal Sign"). He quotes Harryman's belief that *Legend* "wanted to foreclose on the possibility of on-going collaborative experimentation by constructing [a work] so definitively masculinist. [*Legend*] was one of the least interesting manifestations of collaboration vis-à-vis its process to me: that's because of its monolithic (homosocial) affect, i.e., its intention seemed to create a monolithic edifice" (615). Watten goes on to argue that "Harryman and Hejinian's collaborative novel, *The Wide Road*, likewise offers an alternative to the homosocial/masculinist values for collaboration that Harryman complains of" (620). The cross-gender collaboration would seem to offer another, quite different alternative to the masculinist collaboration.

16. When asked a broad question about whether he consciously includes "thematic" content in his work, Silliman responded by singling out this poem: "*Engines*, the collaboration with Rae Armantrout, has a lot to do with the give and take involved in the collaborative process" (Interview [Sullivan]).

17. Carl Boon makes the intriguing suggestion that the poem's use of fourteen paragraphs made up of fourteen sentences each is meant to allude to the sonnet form and to cast the poem as a kind of sonnet sequence. Given the sonnet's long history of reflecting upon amorous relationships and sexual desire, the poets' evocation of the ghost of the sonnet could be another way in which "Engines" signals its preoccupation with the erotic.

NINE | ANN VICKERY

In / Complete

Locating Origins of the Poet in Jennifer Moxley's *In Memoriams* to Helena Bennett

IN *NEW SOCIAL TIES*, Deborah Chambers argues that friendship ties "are beginning to be viewed as an expression of intimacy that replaces the sense of social integration associated with the concept of 'community'" (2). Novel forms of socialization, global communication, urban movements, and sexual communities have all impacted upon discourses of belonging. As "community" is viewed alternatively as impossible or, at best, in flux, there has been "a postmodern shift of emphasis from kinship and community networks to personal bonds" to the extent that friendship is now the privileged term (Chambers 2).[1] This shift from community to friendship can be seen first in how poets themselves are imagining their relationships to one another. While the late 1970s and 1980s saw a more explicit theorization and enactment of the practice and values associated with community, particularly among Language writers, poets emerging in the 1990s were interested in exploring different, looser but still intense social bonds. The paradigmatic shift is also being registered critically, with recent books like Lytle Shaw's *Frank O'Hara: The Poetics of Coterie* (2006) and Andrew Epstein's *Beautiful Enemies: Friendship and Postwar American Poetry* (2006) tracing the sociality of poetry through the framework of friendship. Although community remains integral to an understanding of literary practice, the identification of a writing self to a community has become complicated and, indeed, rendered interpretatively awkward, by a recognition of relationships as incessantly mobile, dependent on circumstance, and variable in the degree of what Gerard Delanty calls their "thick" and "thin" levels (115).

As social theorists like Chambers discern, friendship and community share many characteristics, and there is often a slippage between the two terms. Aristotle argues that friendship is a foundational unit of community, enabling political consensus. Yet he also discerns that what people have in common in various types of community may be more limited than friendship. Whereas community has a public orientation, friendship is more personal, ambivalent, and complex in attachment. Karina Butera notes that friendship has often been treated as a "peripheral and seemingly accidental occurrence located outside core social structure" largely because, unlike marriage and kinship, friendship is viewed as "an individual choice based on emotional bonds rather than binding personal contracts." Friendship, as Butera points out, "receives no institutional status" (19). Whereas community can often be tracked through instrumental belonging, friendship is marked by a series of affective transactions. As Chambers suggests, it "conveys positive values about the voluntary nature and self-expressive aspect of relationships" (2).

This essay explores how Jennifer Moxley represents the formative making of self as poet in light of her friendship with the late Helena Bennett. Moxley's poetry falls within a particular tendency of twenty-first century new poetics that, according to Lisa Sewell, is marked by a "lyric mode that is historically aware, socially generative, and overtly interested in movement toward an expansive and connective consciousness" (4). In both her poetry and her extensive memoir, *The Middle Room* (2007), Moxley considers an intellectual and aesthetic fashioning in light of the jointly pursued life, as well as the shifts that may occur between *philia* (friendly love) and *eros* (erotic love). Against the association of eros with the highest form of friendship and the drive towards immortal union (the possibility of envisioning the "really real"), Plato contrasts a lesser, vulgar eros of sensual love. For Moxley, the role of desire in the interrelated concepts of love and friendship is continually brought to bear on any possible recording of a poetic past. And unlike Aristotle's highly gendered model of virtuous friendship, Moxley endorses an unreliable and radical constitution of intimacy between women.

While Classical analyses of complete or pure friendships construe them as elevated above all other social relations, Moxley contextualizes her friendship with Bennett within a mid-1980s social grouping teasingly coined "the San Diego Literati" by Stephen Rodefer. This group included emergent writers like Moxley, Steve Evans, Bill Luoma, Douglas Rothschild, Chuck Cody, Shelley White, Scott Bentley, and John Granger. As with Moxley, many of the group went on to write critically and creatively about the intimate social composition that informs poetic development, such as Luoma's *Works and Days* and Evans's work on coterie and gossip.[2] In light of the fact that contemporary language use is indelibly shaped by the totalizing forces of late capitalism and the effects of war, Evans identifies an American avant-garde after 1989 that manifests a heightened imperative to enunciate a "we" just as it seems increasingly inoperable ("The American Avant-Garde after 1989" 90, hereinafter "Avant-Garde"). As the writing of this generation was not only transforming conditions through its very production but also outpacing "the terms of its own recognition," any desire to "fix" a community would be frustrated (91). Still, a sense of affiliation, even in terms of the San Diego cohort, might be identified through small press activity such as the Subpress Collective series, which published Moxley's *The Middle Room*, Rothschild's *Theogony*, and Bentley's *The Occasional Tables*. Both Moxley and Bentley would also run their own magazines, *The Impercipient* and *Letterbox* respectively, and chapbooks by both Luoma and Rothschild appeared in the Situations series. These books, chapbooks, and publications are but a few of the many "fugitive venues" that supported a post-1989 avant-garde, fugitive perhaps because of their limited circulation and therefore difficult to know about if one was not part of the informal, mobile constellations from which they were generated (Evans, "Avant-Garde" 91).

Moxley is, in many respects, a fitting case for examining the heightened significance of friendship in poetic careers today. She has not only written extensively about friendship but has integrated it in her publishing and editing choices, and in other aspects of her poetic practice. In "Fragments of a Broken Poetics" (2010) she characterizes the "small exchanges of the friendship economy of poetry" as reciprocal and nonhierarchical (27). The contributors to her little magazine, *The Impercipient*, are, accordingly, viewed less like a "coterie" and more like a network, with the magazine providing space for "a conversation between friends, some longstanding and some new" (Moxley, "Pillow Talk"). Her 1996 collection, *Imagination Verses*, gestures toward openness and equality in its dedication, "To my Contemporaries." Produced in a limited edition of twenty-six, then a further fifty, the aphoristic series, "Fragments of a Broken Poetics" was sent as a gift to friends. Her other collections have been typically published through friends' presses, with *Imagination Verses* published by Lee Ann Brown's Tender Buttons Press, *The Sense Record* published by Rod Smith's Edge Books, and *The Middle Room* published by Luoma as part of the Subpress Collective series.[3] As this publishing history demonstrates, Moxley's focus on what could be called a self-conscious connective poetics is not singular but rather part of a broader trend among recent poets to declare an affective mapping in their publishing choices and details of their poems.

Epstein contends that "at the heart of experimental American poetry pulses a commitment to both radical individualism and dynamic movement that is sharply at odds with an equally profound devotion to avant-garde collaboration and community" (*Beautiful Enemies* 4). Moxley herself describes the "proposition of belonging to a community bonded by nothing more substantial than a passion for words" as "frustrating, sexy, and seemingly impossible" (*The Middle Room* 3, hereinafter *Middle*). For Moxley, social identification becomes a mechanism to better map what might be called an apprenticeship, a journey "towards the completion of what [Paul] Valéry called our 'whole training in the possible.'" She further argues that the poem is "an axis point through which the creator and the community of a shared language pass" (*Imagination Verses* ix, hereinafter *Imagination*). Yet at the same time it is "unjust" in its promise of history and might best be understood as an intervention, a "crucial and critical disjuncture" (*Imagination* x). As Jacques Derrida points out, grief is etymologically associated with grievance or injustice (ix). Aristotle's famous phrase, "O my friends, there is no friend," foregrounds the question of address: in citing the friend when that friend is no longer present, is the address or complaint only to oneself? In foregrounding loss ("there is no friend"), Aristotle's paradoxical proposition also foregrounds the possibility of friendship's return in the face of living on.

A fellow poet who died of cancer in 1990, Bennett is presented in numerous elegies by Moxley as formative to the sense of herself as writer. In an interview with Noah Eli Gordon, Moxley suggests that "the past holds the present hostage and shapes it" ("Mysteries"). Through a direct mode of address to Helena in "The Second Winter," Moxley draws Helena's figure into contemporaneity:

> Helena, my beautiful Helena,
> why do I persist in foolish visions,
> "fly to those ills you know not" she answers,
> with the sadness of unresponsive ghosts.
> I feel I might shrivel for lack of her
> but decide to leave off this illusion
> for the ancient place of my origin. (*The Sense Record*
> *and Other Poems* 29, hereinafter *Sense Record*)

As Giorgio Agamben points out, origin is "not only situated in a chronological past: it is contemporary with historical becoming and does not cease to operate within it." The processes of distancing and nearness which define contemporariness "have their foundation in this proximity to the origin that nowhere pulses with more force than in the present" (17). Helena's significance in Moxley's lived present is beyond the simple nostalgia, even illusion, of memorialization or archiving the self. This is reinforced by "the record of my leaves" being dismissed as "but dreams of mental making." Going back to an "ancient place of my origin," Moxley alludes to Helena's mythic namesake and speaks of a "delicate foamy birth, painted seascape." Helena functions here for the speaker as an artful and necessarily narcissistic projection of an ideal. The seascape also alludes to the beach backdrop of La Jolla, where they studied at the University of California, San Diego, signaling a drive to mythologize the past. Moxley notes, "though I am not old yet the old specter / of your waves still moves me hypnotically." The affective memory of, particularly her grief for, her friendship with Helena generates a loss of control in the subject. Moxley's declaration that "I feel I might shrivel for lack of her" goes even further in suggesting a diminishing of self without Helena (*Sense Record* 29).

In *The Politics of Friendship*, Derrida suggests that the traditional, idealized concept of friendship is about "believing in ourselves" through an *exemplum*, the "same as self but improved" (4). Helena is essential to the constitution of Moxley's self through embodying the beautiful and the desirable. In another poem, "During This Revolution," the speaker is "mirrorless" without Helena, reinforcing Helena's formative role in the primal scene of subjectivity (*Imagination* 41). "The Sense Record" also explores what Derrida calls the apparition's "haunting return" (*The Politics of Friendship* 3):

> when she came to me in the garden,
> a tall ghost in a white T-shirt
> lifting its arms behind its head
> to gather its shoulder-length hair
> in a loose spray of summer wheat,
> exactly the sort of thoughtless business
> she once so readily mastered. (*Sense Record* 68)

Here, memory is encapsulated through a familiar gesture of gathering hair together, which is likened ironically to a harvest "spray." The mastery of such action even as it is "thoughtless" contrasts with the speaker's own loss of command and the distraction of thoughts that are "too awkward, too erratic to rest / at ease in the beautiful iamb." Although Moxley suggests that the poem "must be a fit / condolence, a momentary / and ordered form," it remains instead a gathering place for the perpetually "moving / and needful Company of / thought" (*Sense Record* 5). The title of another poem, "Grain of the Cutaway Insight" echoes the "summer wheat" of "The Sense Record." The word "lonely" emanates discord or ugliness:

> Long lost friend, with whom I once
> spoke into the night of books and
> left, thinking to myself on my short
> walk home of all the things I wanted so
> to tell you
>   in a poem, I am lonely
>   in the in-*commiserate* word,
> its small sound remains
>   an incipient dis-harmony (*Sense Record* 5)

In coining the term "in-commiserate," Moxley brings together the lament and the incommensurable. The very sounding of the word foregrounds the "impercipience" of mourning and the gap between grief and elegiac representation. The term "cutaway" suggests loss (insight unachieved) but is also a personalized reference to the cutaway jeans that the beloved used to wear. Yearning for intimacy ("all the things I wanted so / to tell you") is heightened as lost opportunity, while the poetic form is inadequate, the speaker "wanting otherworldly metrics, / or the faith to overcome" (*Sense Record* 5). Derrida notes that engagement in friendship takes time, "for it carries beyond the present moment and keeps memory as much as it anticipates" (15). For Aristotle, complete friendship is underpinned by stability, constancy, and permanence, all values related to steeped maturation.

Written over ten years, *The Middle Room* is a testament to Moxley's "taking time" but also to the anxiety as to whether an actual friendship can encapsulate such values. It is interesting to note that Moxley is not alone among relatively young poets in turning to the memoir genre as a means to meditate on the nature of intimacy, suggesting an intensified need within that generation to negotiate the self in a locatable, shared history over and against compelling forces of disorientation and alienation. It would take Juliana Spahr seven years to write *The Transformation,* and the comparable lengthiness of her and Moxley's memoir-writing is perhaps indicative of the obsessive and difficult nature of such an undertaking. Spahr characterizes her memoir as "barely truthful" and uses a highly playful experimental narrative (with its constant repetition of phrases, shifting pronouns, and lists reminiscent of Gertrude Stein's *The Making of Americans*) to think about the making of self in light of coalition and difference (217).

In contrast, Moxley's *The Middle Room* sits far more within the narrative tradition of Marcel Proust, with Moxley suggesting that she is interested in the "mind's vision of truth" in which experience includes layers of consciousness ("Mysteries"). Dedicated to Helena, Moxley notes that it "began as an elegy [but] ended as an autobiography" (*The Middle Room* 3, hereinafter *Middle*). Moxley further declares:

> This book is not objective history. It is my story, and as such, suffers from the subjective flaws and lapses necessarily present in any single

> person's experience. I apologize if that lens mars any view of the past held dear by those in the company of whom I was lucky enough to pass through this brief moment in time. (*Middle* vii)

At over 600 pages, it traces, *Künstlerroman*-like, Moxley's undergraduate years and the rite of passage toward assuming the vocational role of the "poet" in light of her friendship with Helena. In its initial stages, Moxley's friendship with Helena is viewed in *The Middle Room* through their separation from the larger student body and subsequent recognition as being part of a supportive subgroup. At the University of California in San Diego, Helena, Moxley, and another student, Chuck Cody, form a "lively workshop camaraderie," their identification as a trio giving them a certain standing "born of the perception that [. . .] solidarity [. . .] enclosed and protected our artistic efforts and allowed them to flourish more freely than those of our individualistic comrades" (*Middle* 50–51). This subgroup would extend to include others, which then formed a "collective imagination" that would inform Moxley's "perception of what was possible" (*Middle* 3).

Helena and Moxley's friendship becomes closer during a visit to Helena's house where Helena gives Moxley a copy of Sinclair Lewis's *Main Street* and they jointly recite the Mad Hatter's nonsensical phrase from *Alice in Wonderland*: "Jam yesterday, Jam Tomorrow, but No Jam Today" (*Middle* 53). Their shared identity (particularly as women poets) becomes useful as they are the only two female members of the college magazine (*The Birdcage Review*), and they are able to support one another against the reductive gender dynamics of its editorial group. When Helena fails to attend a meeting, Moxley feels that her own intellectual responses are dismissed as "hysteria" and that her consequence is limited to her sexual availability:

> Helena and I were, after all, strong central members, a fact which masked the more tawdry elements—off-color sexist remarks, accusations of sexual climbing, etc.—but our position notwithstanding, there were still times when I felt dismissed because I was—and I'm sorry to say but there is no better word—fuckable. I also couldn't help but notice that men who had this very quality were considered more, not less, talented. (*Middle* 290)

It is with Helena that she finds recognition, even inspiration as a poet, as they seem to partake in a "conjoined Muse." In a collaboration based on the ubiquitous housewife's manual, *The Joy of Cooking*, "we thought little about what we meant, nor worried whether or not the writing made sense, for inside our 'one mind' every word resonated like strings on an Attic lyre over which were moving the agile fingers of all nine Muses" (*Middle* 187). Their performance of the collaboration is also viewed as merging them into "one soul," Luoma claiming in *Works and Days* that he and Granger "fell in love with both of them" then and there (17). This contrasts with a later collaboration Moxley undertakes with Evans, whom she is then dating: "The 'us against them' melodic complicity that always emerged when I shared the podium with Helena turned with Steve into a sharp 'you against me' pizzicato. It was a different, less assured, alliance" (*Middle* 565).

Moxley and Helena's identity is viewed by Moxley and by others as dyadic, for "within our literary circle, we two (Helena and Jen) [were] inseparable" (*Middle* 233). This dyad is not entirely equal, for Moxley describes their relationship at one point as a kind of sororal mentorship: "Casting her in the role of older sister, I endowed her with superior worldly and literary experience both, and felt completely comforted in knowing that I could turn to her for advice" (*Middle* 134). Ruth Perry and Martine Watson Brownley suggest that women often form intimate relationships with peers rather than more traditional relationships of mentorship, and in the case of Moxley and Helena there is a quite complex, only vaguely acknowledged, negotiation of dominance and submission.

Aristotle defines the complete friend as another or second self, "To perceive a friend [. . .] is necessarily in a manner to perceive oneself, and to know a friend is in a manner to know oneself" (Stern-Gillet 50). Michel de Montaigne also characterizes higher friendship as a form of self-recognition: "Our souls pulled together in such unison, they regarded each other with such ardent affection, and with a like affection revealed themselves to each other to the very depths of our hearts, that not only did I know his soul as well as mine, but I should certainly have trusted myself to him more readily than to myself" (140). Yet to Moxley, Helena is still a mystery, and this generates an aura of power around her: "Though I was beginning to think I understood her, I still knew little about her family or where she was originally from. For all I knew she might have emerged, like Athena, fully grown from the head of some awesome deity" (*Middle* 134). Not only does Helena have a "statuesque" beauty but she is "silently understood to be the best poet in our class." Helena's lack of inhibitions contrasts with Moxley's own self-consciousness: "I was especially in awe of Helena's apparent invulnerability to shame [. . .] She was fiercely independent and, upon discovery of something she did not know, preferred to quietly turn herself into an expert than admit her limitation and ask for help" (*Middle* 135).

A further aspect of Helena that differentiates the two and empowers Helena within the friendship is her "maternal strength" (*Middle* 134). Besides being likened to a goddess of war, Helena is also characterized as a domestic goddess: "There was no question in my mind that she would someday become the original matriarch of a large rural brood." Moxley adds, "She was an intuitive hostess, always preparing for the 'bunches of kids' she would some day cook for" (*Middle* 247). These contradictory versions of female divinity (aggressive and nurturing) are combined when Helena brings Moxley a "magnificent mountain" of birthday cake, which saved Moxley from "my emotional tailspin and moved my mind back to grander things" (*Middle* 163). Helena becomes a Romanticized icon signifying a revolutionary state of solidarity and psychological freedom: "As I bit into the sugary frosting I imagined her as a beautiful masthead, the winged victory of the city bus, her hair blowing wildly in the wind as she holds the blazing cake in front of her like a great flaming beacon of friendship" (*Middle* 163).

Whereas Classical theories of friendship suggest that it is built on unquestioning trust and giving, disruptive feelings emerge when Moxley's and Helena's career paths threaten to diverge. When White and Rae Armantrout invite Helena but not Moxley to the cinema, Moxley feels as if "the invisible 'you're one of us' wand had been gently laid upon Helena's head by these two literary Fairy Godmothers. She was now a 'poet among poets.' I remained one of the crowd, mildly talented but essentially anonymous" (*Middle* 377).

Moxley recognizes that she is "blinded by my envy, as well as my desire to be seen as mature and serious as my friend" (*Middle* 377). Alternatively, Helena continues to support Moxley such that even when she is unable to attend a reading by Moxley, "true to her unblemished record of never forgetting the important events in my life she had phoned earlier that day to wish me best of luck" (*Middle* 564). Contrasting with her friend's unbroken loyalty, Moxley's own negative affective response might be viewed as a form of what Sianne Ngai (borrowing from Søren Kierkegaard) has called an "unhappy self-assertion," an act of individuation that simultaneously demonstrates one's unworthiness to the badge of friendship (181).

Bound up with civic duty and rights, Aristotle's model advocates *responsible* intimacy and is highly gendered. Montaigne summarizes this virtuous friendship accordingly: "Everything actually being in common between them—wills, thoughts, judgements, goods, wives, children, honour, and life—and their relationship being that of one soul in two bodies, according to Aristotle's very apt definition, they can neither lend nor give anything to each other" (141). This complete friendship is a higher form of friendship than those based on utility or shared pleasures. The common love of nonsense, solidarity in poetry classes or editorial meetings, Helena's gifting of books, and Moxley's professional jealousies, all fail Aristotle's delineation of complete friendship. In particular, Moxley's envy might be viewed as evidence of women's incapacity for complete friendship due to an essential lack of control over their emotions. Echoing Aristotle, Montaigne argues that the ordinary capacity of women is inadequate for "that communion and friendship which is the nurse of this sacred bond." He adds, "nor does their soul seem firm enough to endure the strain of so tight and durable a knot" (138). While masculine self-identity is confirmed in such a conceptualization, complete or pure friendship between women and men is impossible, as is friendship between women.

Rather than apologize for the emotional weft of their friendship, Moxley embraces and promotes it. "Between Helena and I certain things were tacitly understood," she says. "Neither guilt nor petty jealousies disrupted our adventures, for our desires were as different as our verses, and the loyalty we felt toward each other as solid as any Soviet bridge; it would carry us over any rubble life dared to strew in our path" (*Middle* 141). In "The Beauty of Friendship," Agnes Heller suggests that friendship flourishes in desire, where there is *freedom and reciprocity* and that this freedom is actualized as a form of "mutual self-abandon" (10). While *The Middle Room* recounts numerous sexual intrigues waged by the two friends, a number of Moxley's poems also suggest heady recklessness. In "During this Revolution," the speaker talks of Helena's friendship as a kind of liquid love that "could cover me like syrup." The poem shifts between the singular pronoun "her" and a collective "our":

It's you and me shorter one,

with a bolder form of naiveté

then, for one tiny booted moment of largesse,
"her"
a vilified craving in night time,

our sweet morning crib notes (*Imagination* 40)

While Helena is characterized as "Dear recondite shooter" and "the strideress" in "During This Revolution," it is Moxley who is "a gun runner" in "Helena & the Regional Boys" (*Imagination* 40–41, 33). In both poems, Moxley presents the two of them as playful outlaws. At the same time, she subverts the masculine discourse of cowboy homosociality, with its unspoken but strong bond between hero and sidekick. With their tender terms of affection, "I'll call her swaggerlee," Helena and Moxley are civic miscreants, "the United Girls of Camp" (*Imagination* 33). This recalls Lauren Berlant and Michael Warner's notion of intimacy as generating queer counterpublics, that is, cultivating nonnormative subjects and fantasies that may be not only contradictory but also conflagratory (322). Based on errant desires, these queer counterpublics contest Aristotle's model of virtuous friendship with its foundation in certainty. They also challenge hierarchies of poetic authority, Moxley noting that Helena and her antics rattled Rothschild's "devotion to the mentor tradition" that was based on the "old-time ideal of an exclusively male circle of poets, in which the machismo of the literary battlefield would not be threatened by the female ego's fondness for flirtation and caprice" (Moxley, *Middle* 127). In "During this Revolution," Moxley likens herself and Helena as "us against the unbothered," as two that make trouble and are as an entity themselves troublesome (*Imagination* 41). "Helena & the Regional Boys" ends with "shame gets a great big mirror all its own," the narrator confessing to desire's pull over radicalism: "I want those boys / like a western crescendo" (*Imagination* 33).

Shame, like the envy Moxley felt at Helena's perceived entrée into the professional poetry world, shakes the confidence of their friendship. Direct conflict between their desires further threatens the friendship. An illicit kiss with Rodefer, for whom Helena then held feelings, makes Moxley realize that she has been turning "against my closest friends." Sexual folly is aligned with career folly, a "fear that these friends will turn against me because I am not adequately smart, because I am not suited for the 'life of the mind'" (Moxley, *Middle* 307–08). Moreover, Moxley's experimentation with lesbianism concerns Helena, who opts for "a cool distance and a newly minted curious look, as though she feared this 'development' the harbinger of awkward futures between us" (*Middle* 315). Intense libidinal desires may reinforce the beauty of friendship but only when they are parallel and narcissistically reflective.

Often Moxley's admiring desire of Helena in *The Middle Room* verges on the erotic, such as her description of Helena at a *Birdcage Review* meeting: "She looked beautiful. Her fair skin glowed with honeyed freckles, and her straw-colored hair, which she always wore straight and parted in the middle, was thick and lustrous" (*Middle* 116). Yet it is roped in and kept under control. Eros and philia are more overtly entwined in Moxley's poetry such as "The Sense Record," where grief for a ghostly friend manifests itself physically, and in a highly sexualized manner:

> I was blood and disease, could drown in her breasts
> flowing blonde between her legs.
> When I crawled back through the grass
> she was waiting, her hair pulled back
> in a thoughtless gesture, her body
> white, round, and supple,
> and I wanting so to possess it. (*Sense Record* 76)

Here, there is desire for possession but also the impossibility of desire *and* possession. There is not the healthy "good" of self-sufficiency that comes from certainty of the other's friendship but "disease" emerging out of loss. Inconsolable grief is equally unquenchable desire. It registers as bodily response, transforming the solid to liquid: "blood," "drown," "flowing." In an interview, Moxley discerns that "the body and mind have their own archive apart from made things" ("Mysteries"). This is further explored in *The Line* where she writes, "The spatial dream-life of complex syntax hides the author's erasure. Having lived through it the flesh knows otherwise" (13). It is in mourning, the "after-word" of friendship, that philia and eros merge.

With the death of the friend, friendship becomes ironically more present, its beauty more openly wounding. As *The Middle Room* records, Helena and Moxley's friendship waned as they each took up with partners who consumed more of their attention. Permanent pairings off would also unravel the "cohesive mythos" of the broader literary group. "The dynamics of our group," relates Moxley, "were [. . .] much altered by the shifting of paired confederates that had taken place over the past year. As much as I used to rely on Helena to be my female ally against the hegemony of Chuck & Co., Steve and I now represented a set" (*Middle* 581). Helena and Bill's reticence could also "make one feel the butt of an ungenerous conspiracy when they were together" (*Middle* 581). Moxley discusses an endpoint to their shared endeavor of poetic self-fashioning: "We knew something had happened and was now over but whether our accomplishments as a group would vanish like raindrops on hot asphalt or metamorphose into some new significance was totally unclear" (*Middle* 471). An "evening's coda" where six of them frolic at the beach is represented in the poem, "Clampdown," where Moxley writes of a shared entropy, a "clock-ticking-down half-decomposed love." Sexual "making it" and poetic "making it" become contiguous as the speaker's attention turns from one to the other: "We must travel away from this noisy surf if ever we hoped to be serious" (Moxley, *Clampdown* 14). A biweekly reading group attempting to resuscitate their bonds is not overly successful. The "clearly dissipated camaraderie" is reinforced through geographical splintering, marked by Moxley and Evans's decision to move to the East Coast (Moxley, *Middle* 582). A return visit to see Helena is "oddly disappointing" as Moxley gets the "impression from my erstwhile collaborator that she had permanently lost her literary ambition, an eventuality I couldn't accept as true." Moxley feels that she is "still playing at a game" that Helena has "grown out of" (*Middle* 622).

The San Diego Literati might be viewed as being what Jeffrey Weeks, Brian Heaphy, and Catherine Donovan have called a "family of choice." Moxley sometimes reverts back to the social contract of marriage in order to explain what is occurring in her relationship with the group:

> Like a career-driven man who assumes that his wife is at home pining for him until the moment that he sees her at a café laughing flirtatiously with an attentive suitor, at once understanding that his preoccupation with work has put his marriage into jeopardy and that he loves his wife very deeply, so too did I realize that my callous departure and family troubles gravely endangered my place among the poets, which, I suddenly realized, was far more important to me than I knew. (*Middle* 358)

What Moxley is doing here is foregrounding familial structures less as organic than as performing particular social narratives. Besides being likened to an older sister, Helena is described as both the "strong-willed farm wife *and* her free-spirited runaway daughter" (Moxley, *Middle* 134). In occupying multiple roles rather than a single script of femininity, Helena is transported beyond the restrictive structures of kinship models for women poets. She can be figured as simultaneously maternal and rebellious, friend and mentor. This, in turn, enables fluidity for Moxley's own poetic constitution.

Just as friendship is framed through a rhetoric of the familial in *The Middle Room,* family is likewise examined through friendship. The grieving for Helena is paralleled by the grieving for another prematurely lost figure in Moxley's life, her mother Josephine (Jo) Crum. Aristotle argues that parental friendship is different from other forms of friendship given the nature of the tie. Jo is a looming figure in Moxley's writing. In "Clampdown," Moxley writes, "She had [. . .] a way with my ego, that eyebrow-raised 'it's for your own good I know you can do better than that' look" to which she is "slowly becoming immune" (*Clampdown* 15). *The Middle Room* outlines the role of Moxley's mother in fostering Moxley's literary ambitions. Jo helps Moxley purchase a lady's desk that becomes talismanic in its glimpsed-at "splendid history" and suggested bright future. Moxley's earliest poem at age twenty is read by her mother who confirms her talent. Jo has literary aspirations herself although they amount to little, and Moxley's literary forays are measured through Jo's brief friendship with the poet Carolyn Forché. Moxley, in some ways, feels responsible for fulfilling her mother's dreams: "Like a child I believed not only that I could become wealthy as a writer of serious literature, but also, and even more implausibly, that in one grand gesture I could alleviate my mother's lifetime's worth of bitter disappointment" (*Middle* 484).

While Helena's subsequent battle with cancer is never raised in *The Middle Room,* Jo's is recorded in light of its effect on her relationship with Moxley. A final trip to Paris sees Moxley and Jo's relationship shift briefly from mother and daughter to friends: "We were stumbling over the cobblestones and giggling like schoolgirls" (*Middle* 485). Around the time Jo starts chemotherapy, Evans reads Robert Duncan's "My mother would be a falconress" to Moxley. The poem seems to encapsulate the invisible emotional ties between her mother and herself: "I dread that she will cast me away, / for I fall, I mis-take, I fail in her mission" (Duncan, *Bending the Bow* 52). Yet the poem also foregrounds the daughter's desire for autonomy and the cruelty required to bring it into effect. For Moxley, Duncan's poem has "an almost frightening resonance" (*Middle* 571). The memoir ends with a journal entry by Moxley: "Lately there has been much general sadness, leaving me floating like a marionette with no puppeteer. It has been two weeks since my mom died" (*Middle* 633). In finishing *The Middle Room* that is the book, the reader follows Moxley's emergence from a complex familial space where she is the guided, sometimes manipulated, "daughter" to a space where she can take up the pen and begin independently.

One of her mother's final letters likens being a poet to "being a drug addict" but refers to the saving grace of friendship: "I only hope you find some like-minded friends, not because you need to show everything you write to this person and that, but because you are likely to feel most comfortable around those with the same [. . .] *madness* [. . .] as it were" (Crum, qtd. in *Middle* 619). Writing is viewed pathologically rather than vocationally but also as something that requires some kind of social bond. Ironically, Jo's words are borne out, for it is Helena and the rest of the San Diego Literati that are able to provide a support network for Moxley in ways that her family cannot. This reflects the shift in the function and valuing of friendships today as being as significant as family, sometimes more so. Certainly the mourning for Helena takes on a quite different inflection from the mourning for Jo, reflecting the very different and complex love Moxley has for friend and mother.

In "The Sense Record," Moxley explores the idea of memory as a "hole" to the dead, which can become a space through which friendship might continue:

> I suppose that I have half-imagined
> my remembrances to be fissures
> through which this place makes known
> the continuance of my absent friends,
> as stars sometime were thought the holes
> through which angelic light came shining. (*Sense Record* 70)

Yet even as "an individual memory complex / stretched across the globe" may attempt to create "vanished-existence maps," it is "destroyed by the nonchalant amnesia / necessary to live" (Moxley, *Sense Record* 71). Moxley acknowledges the impossibility of representing her friendship with Helena or more broadly the San Diego Literati, whether this be through poetic form or through the monument that is *The Middle Room*. Although deploying a discourse of determination through terms like "record," "clampdown," or "insight," what becomes apparent is the elusive nature of and meaning that we give to such affective bonds.

NOTES

1. Key theories on the impossibility of community include Jean-Luc Nancy's *The Inoperative Community* and Maurice Blanchot's *The Unavowable Community*.

2. Evans, "Off the Record."

3. Moxley notes in an interview with Noah Eli Gordon, "The presses I have published with have always been run by friends who do what they do out of love for the art" ("Mysteries").

PART FOUR

Among Friends

TEN | DURIEL E. HARRIS, DAWN LUNDY MARTIN, RONALDO V. WILSON

Black Took Collective

On Intimacy & Origin

Thu, May 31, 2012 at 7:16 PM

Dear Hottest Tooks,
I am sitting in my bed, the sweat from this afternoon's tennis play still drying and the hum of the neighbor's t.v. across the courtyard. I am off to another work event in a little less than a half hour, which might be the perfect time to think of our meeting. It was really in that dining room at Mt. St. Alphonsus in Esopus, NY, that year at Cave Canem—I think we made the announcement that we wanted to call everyone down to the basement for our meeting, a call to challenge forms, the formal, oppositional poetics—we were the oppositional poets, and we wanted answers, less corn bread, kitchen encounters, or more of it all in a way—what was our hunger? I do recall that I was so nervous, sitting up and readying myself to ask the question. It's funny, all these years performing, and I think I feel your bodies next to mine near the ground in that basement, just like we lie around together on stage now. Talk about intimacy. What do you recall of that day? How are you feeling today? Watch any good porn lately? I did. I watched an old Brit man with a long thing—tool, grow into luck and love with a thin brunette—it was so warm and what I need next to this sea. My backhand was pretty awesome today.

Remember this?

From our live writing, *Poetry Off the Page Symposium, Tucson, AZ May 2012.*

> ". . . . Why am I disoriented?
> Where)(oh where, little)
> does the desert begin
> ?

Where do / es disorientation
begin?
again
dessicated DEATH
DESSICATED dance.
if

sound produces forms in water
WHAT? THE F
impact does sound (have) on a body
a body made of water
even the skin

My the faces without the masks are so

Blakn (Blackened: halibut, catfish,
schrimp: bottom feeders

bushy bus(h)y bottom botte body

There's something very curious about the bang. . . ."

Love R-do

Sat, Jun 2, 2012 at 6:01 PM

I remember being very skinny then and looking really cute. You, two, were cute too. We were dripping in it—this individual and collective cuteness. Maybe it was our cuteness and svelteness that convinced people to actually take us up on our invitation and come to meeting in the basement. We were reading Erica Hunt's "Notes for an Oppositional Poetics" and wanted to use it as a launching pad into a conversation about how language can trap us into certain ways of knowing ourselves and the world. These familiar languages, the tropes of blackness, were grating upon us, I think, which was a kind of catalyst for the meeting. Sometimes at Mount Saint Alphonsus they'd feed us fried chicken for lunch and we loved it. This is the cafeteria where you and I met, Ronaldo. This is a moment of love at first sight, that thing people sometimes say doesn't exist. Duri, you and I already knew each other by the time we got to CC. We were in a little short-lived poetry group that will forever go unspoken, its name. What were we writing back then? What types of poems? I wonder how knowing each other has influenced and shaped what we write and how we write it.

Love,
Dawn

Sun, Jun 3, 2012 at 9:50 PM

Took, Darlings:
Ahhhh, Cuteness, I could write about this forever! Two moments come to mind: the first, at a later Cave Canem, Bloomfield Hills, MI, the Cranbrook Schools, which felt different, because Whites trespassed, or We trespassed. I recall reading the group of poems, "Chronophotographe," and seeing Duriel read poems—I remember one of the participants (older) say to her friends (also older)—"See, there's another pretty one," referring to us, the then named "oppositional" poets. I do think that we were given special passage because of our *model-material* looks. I don't think we're too fat now, but we must have been then like perfectly radiant lines, even though we were fried chicken fed, or at least sandwich fed—still perfect.

What were we writing then—I don't recall—I was trying to write about travel? I was so elliptical. I liked to show off how quick I could be with language, and was keen on queer theory, maybe more then than now, but I had this need to move into intricate orders of language. Duri—what were you up to? I just recall you carrying around your DICTIONARY and THESAURUS to the retreat. Dawn you had your Olson. And me, I had DEET and was using I think, CHANEL wash and moisturizer.

I knew I had to keep up with you by not trying to. I could be myself with you. I felt love, and wrote out of the space between love and the questions I wanted to learn to say, but questions I felt growing between our feedings. Lots of people were fucking.

I was leering at construction workers.

I ran a lot. Dawn, you too, ran.

Duri—how did you stay so sharp in all of this excitement?

Love, R-do

Wed, Jun 6, 2012 at 4:18 PM

Dear dears,
I put my feet up & lean back in the window seat of my little house to write what I can recall of our first meetings through the gauze of memory. The phrase reminds me of cheesecloth & a spaceman I crafted from oak tag, permanent marker, burlap, & contact paper when I was about ten years old. To just say, I was ten years old & not waver. To begin with the approximation as a placeholder & to leave it in place to recover whatever else approximately. The directive I follow here. What came before worrying the line at Esopus & the cool basement assembly? Whisperings of an ancient order reestablished, a secret society donning the hoods of fraternité? An awesome crew. Pretty & handsome. Brown & smooth. Succulent. Queers. Stirring the pot. Queries, troublesome theories & play bucking against convention, desire rambling inside all our bodies.

Before the announcement, the idea of it taking shape. Ronaldo so excellent & gorgeously framed. A poem called "Zygotes"? A pair of soft grey capris? A white linen shirt? Dawn let me peruse Myung's *Dura* & a bomb went off in my head. A sudden electricity, a shock through me & flowing. To say, I was bored, finding poetry useless & dull, expected the way the words arranged themselves & I could say, all along, oh yes, right, right, of course. Without surprise or discovery. & Then the challenge of our bodies together. Alright, I admit, I was giddy.

I think Dawn called me before we traveled to Esopus, having seen my name in the mailing as a newbie. & I was relieved. I wouldn't have to perform 'blackness' to move beyond my shyness.

Thinking of these things arouses me: my mind races with ideas for future work, things to do to advance current projects, images of my world brimming with artifacts of my own creation & ours together. My body is alit with sensation.

love,
duri

Wed, Jun 6, 2012 at 10:04 PM

Dearest dear dears,
I am back from my evening class at the window seat with my computer warming my lap. It is cool for late spring here & I turn on the air purifier craving the oxygen increase to give me a lift. I've just had a lightly grilled salmon fillet with asparagus and a premium margarita. Back in the day I would have followed it with coffee. & I may have been migrainous once or twice back then at CC & Gar reminded me to drink lots of water & I did such that by later in the evening when the energy was high I felt better & could stretch & shower & sit with another sexy brown & talk poetry over the tension. Nowhere for the pretties to go with so much water between us.

& With the newly formed BTC I saw/sensed a way out that wasn't a suicide. Ideation had been a room I sat in—a meditation—anchoring my days. This was what I was trying not to write about before BTC, skirting it, even at times by treating the thing 'directly,' distilling it to simplicity. & Then layered upon my dexterity & my dictionary & Super Thesaurus™, vigorous rupture & play bustle. I could name the usual fare for the weight that it was though I still missed the connection the cornbread-&-collards-negro-history-adventures were to represent. Somewhere ditched in the red clay dust I once hated, perhaps. Nooseless and upright. Elder wisdom I imagined the dead had taken with them. How to navigate the waters from under water. I struggled against feeling & longed for someone to protect me from it. Language twisted itself beyond my tongue. An ornate excess. What I worked through with my body not yet visible to me.

At least that's what I say now. How I render it now. It seems true enough. & You, my playmates, reminding me of beauty's different guises.

duriel

Wed, Jun 6, 2012 at 11:21 PM

Having Taken, Dear Took:
A colon. Hmph.

I am reaching back into that past & you know I'm mostly coming up with ellipses.
So long ago.

What I have is a feeling. Our legendary-ness in the air. Palpable & people sweating us.

Staying sharp? At some point then I bought a Concept2 erg/indoor rowing machine. I should use it to work off that tequila.

What now? I am wondering what you're working on and am less interested in then. (Especially since I can't remember it.) A lot worth blocking out & a lot worth celebrating has happened since. & Just now, fresh from an artist residency at Torkwase's latest architectural installation project "Studio South Zero" (SSZ)—running my portable sound studio entirely on solar power in the modular space she designed and assembled in one of the backyard lots of the Dorchester Project on Chicago's south side—I feel supremely excellent about now, & the immediate & long term future.

I am curious about how we talked to each other then. Still getting to know & you two—spending so much more time together. In love is nice. & Who knows what evil ('I'se so wicked') lurks in the nooks of Took. Ask Jemima Blue. & Erica was once my mother & a version of me called Spawn, her son. At one time we were all in New York City, no? Fort Greene & what? Chelsea? Williamsburg? Harlem, US-a?

I think about what I loved so immediately: our laughter and the cadence of our voices, musicking together.

xxdeh

PS what are your favorite nicknames—names others call you/you call yourself/names you call others? That was a question during an improv game tonight, a category, and I said "Squishy"—a nickname I gave a sexy girl once. I might have said, "Squirt," what my father calls me or "Cricket" from my grandfather or "Durii" (Mendi's remix) or "Duri"—softly from BTC. (Awww . . .)

Thu, Jun 7, 2012 at 10:57 AM

Aha! I, too, am back from an evening, here on Long Island's "East End." We did not tonight visit the "black Hampton" as it were, what is called "Sag Harbor" but instead some place on a wooded road in Bridgehampton, for fat shrimp cocktails (belligerently so) and vodka martinis and tuna tar tar salad. Phenomenal. So unlike the fried chicken. I will eat fried chicken for breakfast. Anytime. I'll rub it on my body. Lick off the grease. I'm a whore for it, a whore for you, Duri, who is the only girl or boy who ever met my extended family in the heart of Georgia. O, it was Florida, a backwoodsy thing, and my mother tried to elevate it by taking us all to an afternoon of musical theater, and everyone was bored and you and I were a little tipsy as my aunt snored in the mid afternoon as the players sang their senior song.

I am dreaming of this. I always dream of this. The knock at the door. Persistent knocking. Ha ha. And, also, when we pulled people away from people at Esopus and into a potential, if only for a minute. We knew at the time even that we are not interested in the material that produces reward as its intent. That we are positioning ourselves as outsiders. Art is not a bargain. It may not be "new" when it happens whenever it happens it happens, but art can never be about getting something or somewhere. We knew that. And there we were, saying what if WE are not who we think we are? What if time collapses and then just sinks into a forever w/hole and no one has anything and has to reconcile that?

Potent. A medium. The scent of woodfire burning. We go down a path toward a singing in the forest, we gather ourselves and Duri calls me a "ditch faller" as I trip into a hole. Ronaldo steadies me. We walk. We walk. As work. And we tell each other stories of what we have read by the other.

This skin means nothing to me.

It means something to readers, I think.

DL xx

Thu, Jun 7, 2012 at 11:49 AM

Also, Ronaldo's room smelled of boy. He was horrified that I thought this. Of boy. A pile of sweaty tennis clothes draped over a chair. But, we couldn't stay away from each other. Or, I couldn't stay away from either of you. Late night. 3 or 4 in the morning. Had we already written poems? Or were we writing them? Did we come to each other's rooms to write in each other's presences? I think so. This was the first time I'd understood the power of sitting by another body and writing into the presence of those bodies. We read each others' books from our slim shelves.

Ronaldo calls me Lundy, my middle name. I call him Vergelio. His. We call Duriel, Duri. Cute shortening. Or Ronaldo, R-do. Shortening of the vernacular. Nig, Negrita, Blacks, Tooks. "It was black, black took."[1] Had been thinking of the "idea of blackness," of the constructed body place, of lostness. It's a reversal, maybe meaning black taken. What has been taken, what will be taken back black. "New" forms. I wanted disruption. I wanted to break down the whole collards and cornbread structure and also to fuck late into the night a hot body. Some rooms were vacant. All the rooms were named for saints.

Kisses, Dawn

Thu, Jun 7, 2012 at 12:18 PM

Loves:

Peeking in, my eyes open, heavy, perfect, too, how suicide was averted, and love found—the sun, draping this California I am now living in—my grading marathon done, off to tennis now—to get smelly, *as in* to remain desirable. I will write more and in clearer detail from a beautiful remote place. I need shadows, leaves, and swaying.

Meanwhile, more live writing from our performance at *& Now, UCSD October 2011*:

"Is there something of an interior, an ebonic interior like the bionic woman's circuitry?

Not speaking. Skin, a throat unwound.

Exactly, to be moved
Toward unmaking/unmadenesss
A kind of wrap

CONDeNSAtiON
The mask whitening with each exhalation
And still the mouth unopened.

We're not kidding.

We're working.
I can barely speak.

It's like the dancing again.
The body is like that man on the street—he is a white man walking toward me a black man.
He's afraid. I can tell. In the invisible man, i project something onto him or he onto me. It's difficult to be able to sort it all out.
(I want this all to be about something.)

(Not just an 'investigation.'

This is not a fucking joke.

There's something to it. Trying to get at what was once buried. Who buried it.

Why are you talking about that?

You're not taking this seriously enough.

We put a barrier for a reason.

We decided something—a pushing away.

There's a way of confronting the persistent images.

The fragment—Adorno says—resists totality. Duh.

When you step into it.
You can occupy it perhaps with your whole body.

There's my current preoccupation re: getting worn out.

(This is exactly what I'm talking about.)

Cum buckets have nothing to do with the predominance of images and their resonances. The way they stick around so that some college kids can/will put on some shoe polish.

Brave, really, it's difficult to remove.

I've begun to wonder if this juxtapo is working.

One of them moves."

Love & Shadow & Act(s), R-do

Thu, Jun 7, 2012 at 4:51 PM

R-do's boy stink. Sweaty sports clothes once pristine in their creases offering up the perfume of work. Who can resist the sling of freshly made funk? The evidence of our integrity drawing us together. & Of course we bathed only to funk it up again. Did anyone swim in the Hudson? Having written, writing, conspiring to write. Moving through the cool halls of The Mount at all hours for the purposes of making—poems, conversation, sweat—

Just now a white tailed speckled brown rabbit hops cautiously down the driveway, pauses under the awning, then rips out into the grassy lot. Its large dark eye & its head turned toward me. Its ears swivel as it is joined by another. They hop over one another playfully then hunker down to munch green blades & white flowers by the fence.

When I drive up, their ears swivel but otherwise they do not move.

xo, deh

Thu, Jun 7, 2012 at 7:24 PM

Swiveling Ears. Twitching Cunts and Cock Stems. Quarter System. Semester System. In a big Public University, where does the time to dream go, and to rest? Your letters have been like an oasis for me, dream inducing, in fact.

We communicate in a language outside of manner—we're never too far away from the profane, or the profane surrounds us. I imagined writing to you from the beach, or overlooking the ocean from Campus on my new mini laptop, but alas, I'm in bed with 18 minutes before I have to leave. I'm supposed to write an introduction, but instead I am writing to you. I am thinking of the beds at Mt. St. Alphonsus, and the ways that I was so stoic in how I would force myself not to sleep beneath the covers, to never pull the covers back in order to get poems done.

When did we start talking? When did you begin to enter my dreams? Sometimes when we do stuff like this, writing across emails, or even performing, you come to me in dreams, and we're on panels, or on stage, and we're working, like Dawn says, *sitting by another body, writing into the presence of those bodies.*

Now, in the background, a fan, the bathroom: An insect is there, tested by hot water, and air, and shit stink and it is so fragile in the storm of it all. When we went to Squaw Valley, and rented a house near the houses where their retreat is held—another one of our primary scenes—what were we working out together?

In there, through one another, there was not so much a need for being seen as there became a way to see. Recognition & Nicknames. I love how we propel into the world as a group.

We played darts at our Squaw Valley Retreat. Dawn and I were really competitive. Duri, you did push-ups topless. So Hot. We were skinny, and not old, or older—so what? I know we will always be beautiful. Duri, it moves me to know that you came this way and not that, and Dawn, too, you grounded me in NY. I was never really suicidal, but I was often lost in my own freedom, and so when we work, or talk or think, I feel you both show me the right way, pushing one another into, through, out.

R-do con Dawnsy, Lundy, con Duri, soft, soft in the ———— life.

BTC y Qué?

Fri, Jun 8, 2012 at 3:35 AM

Dear Tooktastics:
I, me. Mein. Amain. Aim I am. Yam.
Moi. Oi. Name. Eat. Am. Kiss.

So, just now thinking of you both, fresh to life, and just wanted to say,

Go—Night Loves.

XO R-do

Sat, Jun 9, 2012 at 2:08 PM

Tooks to the Took to the To:
This is what I fight for, freedom. The Feeders behind me order eggs, and me Ahi Tuna Salad Nicoise & Champagne, even though I want the burger, and the fries, and the eggs, I opt for the leaf and the light and the bread—so before I ordered, a little Indian boy walks by with his Grandmother, and he's staring too, or at least trying to drill a hole through my eyes which he cannot see as I'm in my Aviators, Ray Ban P, and of course I am perhaps the only Brown person he sees that looks like some version of him if he makes it.

He walks by—so cute and short—holding hands tight with Amma, and he turns towards me as he walks away staring back at me still moving forward.

I give him a serious head roll—he cannot see my eyes. They are rolling too. I'm getting Tipsy. He looks so AT me trying to figure it all out, WTF? I'm in full head roll, he turns, he turns, I get more Jiggy. And as he walks away in the distance, he begins to roll his head in imitation. I loved it. Were we Birds? Was I his Mother? I transferred blackness.

I love how we understand performance, like the time Duri, when you confessed a feeling of knowing this is what you wanted in front of a giant audience as you shifted into musical performance, and Dawn, how in the meeting of Big Black Poets in Boston, you talked about the performance implicit in and out of language on the page, the many dimensions of Performance beyond Slam and other Perceived notions of performance. "Why Hate?," you seemed to ask.

&

B-T-C Powers Activate!

Form of a Meta-Cognition!

We are very different, in-running(fights) R-do, Duri in-mind (insects), Dawn in-grounds (bed) a lot. I love how we talk about the work of making art—What are the ways we intersect indirectly—I mean there's the stuff of the work recalling various events, milestones, but there are also places where we intersect in our lives, even so far away, spread across time zones. I love how we are all geographically in three places, three time zones, spanning this US America. Yet around bugs, food, sex of course, we hover, & so are we interested in the field of consumption, fear, the webs around the space of the body? Or most active within the expanse of our imaginations? This by way of the critters, or this through our own creations?

We say we want, somewhere between us, here or there, to write a meta-cognitive statement about what we're presenting. So here it is, like a Trick in the Fields, of a Field hollah that won't tell the reader what to experience, but might place you in our messy bedroom. Sometimes we speak alone. And at other times, on stage, we wear masks, take them off, tweak sounds, some prerecorded, some not. We always write on stage, project our imaginations on wide screens for the audience to read, sure, but writing for us is fluid, the body turned, posed, live-eating chicken wings or on the stage, lying about watching our video-antics, or you may be being recorded? Freestyling. We speak into mics, morph language through machines that we affectionately, at least, sometimes, call our toys. Improv, off the Top, Bottoms, Flipped, Reversed: It's like we become one in all of those places.

It could be anywhere, even here, between any of our entries.

I like that.

You are in our film. A woman who walks through fire not to save, but to catch the pyro, who tries to burn us alive, and so, we write alongside one another. Some bleed. Some do not. Some times. Threads distinct & intermingling. Our improvisational experiments in live performance have succeeded, I believe, in making even more room for our individual soundings in relation. The close listening mandated by improvisatory practice engendering more intimacy—as it is itself an intimacy.

I feel so fortunate to be welcomed into full presence by the idea of us. Early on the urgency I felt was life or death; now it is living well, thriving. I have come to understand, brought into language a glimpse of my attachment to you through being in relation to you, your minds, bodies, my senses of you, in material & virtual space. Learning. Twirling about with the world as our playground!

&

I love how we take care of one another—rub one another's backs, keep each other warm in cold beds at times—we don't fuck, but we are often fucked up together, free. Is BTC a Reality Show? Black Poet Anti-Realness? I love how we do whatever we can to make sure we do what we want. I love how we are always pushing for a space outside of what's comfortable, but we like our comforts at the same time. We just hate reductive, unless we are reducing and making up the facts as we go? I love how we need space, and I love how we make it. We make it by being, knowing that at any moment we can begin filming, or at least, I want to film us being us. I'm selfish, a slave for our rhythms. We need more time, obviously.

I'm on Fourth Street in Berkeley—"Many Rivers to Cross" Jimmy Cliff—I love this song, and as it's playing, and I'm writing to you, it's like having you here. I am surrounded by Whites in button ups, and silks—the Black men who walk by are really hot, Ed Bradley-ish—the promise of some clean long smell, like the funk I cultivate.

Dearests, I will always be a reporter for you, recording, and making for and with you our spectacular music, even while I am on my back or in a seat in leisure, finally.

Love, R-do

Sat, Jun 9, 2012 at 10:34 PM

My loves,
I began this epistle darkly last evening distracted by hunger & killing. In spite of my affinity for Budhha, I find insects intolerable—scurrying, flying & swimming about with their chitinous exoskeletons, jointed legs & compound eyes. I refrain from exterminating them (& spiders) in "free nature" but I cannot cohabit with them, not in the house. Wiki reports that together insects comprise more than half the earth's known living organisms. I read this assertion & reflect that resistance is futile but typing the words I think of Jeff Goldblum's hideous & maniacal Brundlefly & what it means to become a hybrid of self & truly other other. & The beyond: fusion of Brundlefly & Telepod2: cyborg terror.

I wonder if the hatred I hold is born of misunderstanding, if my disgust is akin to xenophobia, a fear of foreignness magnified by the difference of species. Considering this possibility, I acknowledge my rationalization for extermination: all home invading insects (& their pest cohort of spiders & rodents) by nature do harm to human bodies &/or property. Of course, this "fact" is not true. Some of these others are just trying to get along. But they cannot all be caught & released; they hide in the crevices & dark places, multiply in the walls. I have to kill them; it is the logical response.

Sitting with this impulse (& decision), I come upon "inter-being," a term I understand to have originated with Vietnamese Zen monk Thich Nhat Hanh. Inter-being: *everything is in everything else. We experience this reality through mindfulness, through Being in the Here & Now. One life-energy is permeating everything.* The form of the body is illusory.

& So I make hibiscus tea & return to Lundy's notes about skin. How it matters or not to readers, to us. How skin matters to me.

Among the largest of the body's organs, the skin communicates systemic well-being or distress. For me often it is *a throat unwound*, speaking congestion, tension of the unsaid. & The melanin that protects it from damage is, in this country—historically & in this moment—a mark of social death & narratives spun out & permutations, meanings we inherit but choose not to take on. The rupture we hunger for enacted in part by opposition, refusal.

xx duri

Sun, Jun 10, 2012 at 12:58 PM

My sexy Blacks—darklings, browning, taking,

Robins & blue jays today. The blackbirds are gone for now but you are so much with me. Steeping San-Qi flower tea (for circulation), running water in the Brita, setting out blackberries & nectarines for later.

Preparing the morning's fruit snack I wonder where is the wooden watermelon slice we bought at the roadside farm store in MA? Or was it CT? The bites carved out of it suggested tiny greasepaint mouths. The slice itself favored a grin, with its happy & sweet summer-red heart. Black seed teeth. Did it travel with you, R-do, from Holyoke to Santa Cruz? Does it anchor you where it resides?

Grandma Watermelon chuckles. I stall her quip & pause from writing to search.

(Pause)

Glee. Seeking, I have come upon files from the lost past—evidence of our beginnings in printed emails, typed correspondence, and scrawl. This luck while meditating on Dawn Lundy's contemplation of *the constructed body place* & of *what has been taken, what will be taken back black* & R-do's celebration of our delight—*how we need space & make it*—take it—*by being free, knowing at any moment we can begin filming*. My waking mind bustling.

In an email to us [03:24 AM 7/20/99] I write:

> and here's something that i've been playing with . . .
> i think the cloak of understanding as a metaphor is perhaps less complicated than the idea that it is meant to explain . . . but i keep thinking of the cloak of respectability that hides the deviant body, an idea which actually draws me to the construction . . .

> hmmm. might it not be easier to discuss this "perceived" understanding (an idea i've still yet to fully unpack—who's perceiving what? is the understanding perceived by the agents or is this more about the perception of those viewing / receiving the agents? . . .) as a construction that has been naturalized to the extent that it exists and perpetuates itself without question, indeed it resists interrogation because it co-opts the mind, even unto the imagination such that agents subvert their own liberation with self-imposed limits, restraints, etc. it is thus difficult to be free because we cannot truly envision what that freedom would be . . .
>
> okay, the complex underbelly. (complex doesn't really work with underbelly . . . we need something "of the body" how about the "distended flatulent underbelly" (sounds ugly and smelly and uncomfortable . . . they probably wouldn't be all that interested in seeing it, would they? i don't want to see it.)
>
> maybe we should consider some other part of the body, i.e. the face? in that sense we'd be confronting the entity squarely as equals. still, there is something very intriguing about the underbelly: it is vulnerable and it is at the very core of the being.
>
> i guess part of what will influence my thinking is the relationship between us and the body that the cloak hides. is the body primarily ours? or is the body much larger than us (being partially ours and primarily that of the world outside of us . . .)?

Reading the recovered portions of this email I am curious. What was I writing toward? Who are the "they" we were writing to interest?

In the same manila folder, an envelope dated July 09, 1999 sent to Chicago from Dawn's house in Northampton & addressed to me in Dawn's hand from "It Was Black, Black Took Editorial Collective." I nearly swoon. Yes, yes . . . There had been a Call . . .

In another email to us later that day [Tuesday, July 20, 1999 5:40:59 PM] forwarding a message re: the critical role of mission statements, I write:

> do you think Black Took should live longer than the anthology (tentatively titled Os Sacrum, just cause i like it . . .)? what about title ideas . . . ? what theoretical gumdrop do you want to turn on its head?

& Now a Ptown letter from Ronaldo dated October 26, 1999 mentioning disassembled notes for the collective statement, research stuff, manuscripts & Comp Exams passed!
It ends with a little ditty:

> Black lack is whack
> said the rebel racked
> in busy Surinam

Aha! Dance dance evolution! An earlier Black Took peaks out from the disheveled stack, nodding its little nappy head.

XxooxX
Durii

Sun, Jun 10, 2012 at 2:02 PM

Black Negroes of the 21st Century!

. . . My north my south my east my west
my working week and my Sunday rest . . .

Who's gonna deliver us from evil now. Hunh? No one, that's who.

A few nights ago I was invited to a queer salon in Manhattan. Jorie Graham was the featured poet, and the whole night was fabulous and untroubled and took place in a sweet Manhattan apartment. I made some new white gay boyfriends. And, Jorie Graham, poetry royalty, was purely brilliant and spoke whole essays to answer questions, as if she were reading her own mind. I've never seen anything quite like it. So this is not about the salon but what occurred to me at the salon, not for the first time and certainly not for the last. There's never any bad behavior. It's like everyone save one or two is at a job interview. R-do tells me a tale of a batterer getting physically removed from David Buuck's house. I wish they'd taken him out in the street and kicked him. Maybe they did? One can hope.

I's happy! I's happy.

Everything's been let loose from its core!

Duriel's and Ronaldo's and my faux gendered bodies (we are close to being the same gender, don't you think?) and R. Erica watching over us. Ronaldo and I go out to a bar and pretend that we're married to each other and a couple of swingers. We are latched onto. What does the couple next to us experience in their desire? I feel sorry for them. Another day, later, someplace else, we tell the waiter at a Doubletree Hotel that we are married, that we have a brood at home. She believes us. We did give birth once to a child after all. She is a child of love. Love child. Born into the pages of a book, the web world of a listserv and circulated there quite happily until she was forced to confront her own being. Is it a boy or a girl people asked constantly. Why should we decide that, we respond. Questions caked in presumption. They leap out into the stratosphere wreaking all sorts of havoc. Outside in. O, my souls—my playmates—we have produced beings that lap lap so perfectly.

O, what would I have ever done without you—all of you, gender-free child included?

Love, Dawn

Sun, Jun 10, 2012 at 3:45 PM

Tooks!
So much has transpired in just these last few days, and I wonder if our being in touch with one another in such close proximities to the question of intimacy has triggered a kind of flash-renaissance in all of us, or flash dancing, or better yet fame. Leroy. Debbie Allen.

I performed with the poet Ariana Reines at David Buuck's house in Oakland, which was packed to the rafters.

Here are some highlights that I'll fill out as I can. Just in from a 6 mile run in the bay where I made my daily freestyle, and highlights of this too as they become clear in some way that makes the un-sense. Dawn, by the way, are you in the air headed to Naropa? And Duri, I'm glad you are taking in the time and space. I like the immediate repose you're in, the looking from out of your porch.

Duri—And you must be swimming in freedom (insects be[ware] under [there!])—I think this is the internal rhyme of it all, that BTC is all a resounding sonic gesture to freedom—I dunno,

back to the party in Snippets:

Ariana read in the backyard, using a lamp as a mic, and she promised to never, again, read from the book she read from. She spoke of body parts and fragments, fields and desire, the accumulation of one field that collapsed on another, sense layering. She said she should pee on the recording mic in the grass in front of her. She had on pink pants. I stood up in front near her to sway like I like, to dance with words—I was lost in her loss, and she was gaining and gaining, and then she got a request to read her Baraka poem, and I realized that she's doing something around cultivation of the animal, the body, our other, and the vanity and play in between these realms is perhaps what keeps us attentive, and attenuated to her poetry.

There was a break between our readings. An alcohol run. Some muscular White man in a big fro hit another between sets, I think, an Asian man, in the back of the head. A fight? Well almost, the words "logic" I heard and other faux-invectives: "He is an abuser!" "He is Violent—He's an Offender"—"Are you asking me to leave?" "He's not welcome in these spaces!"

Turns out David and some others man-grabbed him after he refused to leave, well after he was asked nicely to do so. David must be a great top. One can tell. A house party! A Salon! Anyhow, I helped to hold the White fro-guy at bay before he went really crazy, yelling and all this, and finally he was thrown out. But not before his fingers clutched to the door-frame. I felt his hard stomach and tried to soothe him, but Khary Polk, who was also there, pointed out that I made sure my new Mac Air was safe before I went over to help.

Some were shaken up. I was sad. I was excited.

I read inside David's living room. I started by playing a video of the PBS *Mister Rogers Neighborhood* Remix that's gone viral on YouTube, "Garden of Your Mind"—and I relaxed in his auto-tuned voice, like we do before our BTC throw downs, and then played this new off the dome rap of mine I did at the Peet's Cafe on 4th street in Berkeley, talking with, through, and around white people (and many browns here and there, some free, some not). A black daddy was sharing my table. I whispered, next to him, about space, propriety, speaking in/about the various zones of desire, where one chooses to sit, where one knows they can sit, or not, how some babies are free to run, others clutched to the body in sacks, some flirt, others, props. I let it fly for 14 minutes. I played this "song-poem" intermittently with my newly bought lap top and portable speakers, but mostly I went off the top, letting it all go from directly inside my head.

Note: I am moving totally towards freestyle as a vehicle, away from the written word, for now, or the written word as in the freestyle. I will not edit like the good slave, but the bad ass I want to see untaxed.

I rapped about the relationship between the peri-performative and the performance, the word and whatever else I felt—there was a J. L. Austin moment. There was a moment around tennis. I knew it was being recorded. I knew that a poet had to stand up in the face of the violence of the night, to break the fuck out of violence that had its fingers clinging to some of us.

Here's a question:

If you were almost hit by a daddy on a bike, White, he in yellow and in thin muscle, and you said "Hey Hey Hey" in a low voice like he said "Hey Hey Hey," then your voice got slightly higher as you said, "Shut the fuck up!" after being accused of being in the way (in a nonexistent bike lane, a lane runners and bikers share), and the White daddy then asked for help, specifically "about when to go left or right?" Would you say anything back? I let that bitch azz biker turn around and talk to himself—he rode next to me, totally ignored, and for awhile he kept asking and asking, and then finally, he sigh, resigned, "anyway, I guess it's my problem . . ." I relaxed my eye lids, and kept running, still in meditation:

As Duri Says:

"i keep thinking of the cloak of respectability that hides the deviant body, an idea which actually draws me to the construction . . .

hmmm. might it not be easier to discuss this 'perceived' understanding (an idea i've still yet to fully unpack—who's perceiving what? is the understanding perceived by the agents or is this more about the perception of those viewing / receiving the agents? . . .) as a construction that has been naturalized to the extent that it exists and perpetuates itself without question, indeed it resists interrogation because it co-opts the mind, even unto the imagination such that agents subvert their own liberation with self-imposed limits, restraints, etc. it is thus *difficult* to be free because we cannot truly envision what that freedom would be . . ."

I think *difficult* (emphasis ours) is right—we do this, go for the hard way, the highway I always run next to, the highway next to the bay, the flow in my line between the two. I try in my own way with us to push through the run, "open it up," I say as I sprint, open and pushing, and balanced, and running and running—

I was thinking about *Surinam* this morning, the way we ambush

the Plan(tation), Im,pro,se:

I was thinking how this year with you

We: Is a Centering.

Line.

& Lines with you,

worth brea[h]ta[king]

for strides.

Love, R-do

Sun, Jun 10, 2012 at 6:00 PM

Loves of Life,
I've always been interested in how our individual ideas both intersect and diverge from each others'—in terms of aesthetics, ideology, approaches to form and language, and the so-called "content" of the work. Fissures of collectivity. Divergences productive, perhaps, of chance recognitions. After our last performance in Tucson, we were on a panel together where we were asked a series of questions about the body and writing. I've been thinking about these questions since that moment and am composing a series of four short lectures on the matter for my talk this week at Naropa. I'm wondering about the seemingly inherent presumption that privileging the body as an entity to be known is the ideal thing, or that the body produces writing, or that there is a specialness to that potential production.

I have a student who called the body a "flesh sack."

The body itself is produced by by by—

It is also function. I almost wrote fucktion. That too.

The body is no more stable a place than this skin I'm in.

Where does the I reside?

Lots of people like to talk about the past and memory. I have no memory though the past haunts me. Dark cloisters and dark hands. When I try to remember I only imagine.

I am not deluded. I know that there is a physical form, flesh, tendons, bones, arteries, blood, water, organs, etc. and that the physical form shits, fucks, bleeds, etc. It experiences things in the world, too, the projection of a gender or a race onto it. I have cut off all my hair because it's summer. A woman asked me what country I'm from in the JFK Airport. "Here," I say. I ask her what country she's from; she, too, says, "Here," but then "via Sri Lanka." I cannot tell her race. Several men cut me in the line at the gate, squeezing by, bumping their oversized carry-ons against my legs.

When the three of us encountered each other in the same place, at Cave Canem, for the first time, there was much talk of it being a "safe space," a space where we no longer had to experience certain projections of self in the aloneness of being the only black body in the writing sphere. The notion of safety. The cruz. What's familiar and not familiar. What challenges and what reminds one of an imagined mother's bosom. A black mother, busty and singing and rocking.

My loves, I love how we can produce with and against each other without this kind of safety but within a kind of fraught safety. We're allowed to annoy each other. We're allowed to disagree. We're allowed to cuddle each other in bed. I have woken more than once with my arm around you, R-do, in bed—remember your firm palate in Fort Greene? We slept there many nights. Neither of us got hard-ons. And, you, Duriel, who is always so freshly scrubbed and clean compared to me. I'm like a dirty boy who's been playing in the woods all day. I know exactly what your face and hair products smell like. One is never completely safe. I like this. I live in this. Court it.

Big smooches, D

Mon, Jun 11, 2012 at 10:06 AM

Travelers,
I fell deeply into sleep before I could complete and send this message last night. Now it is morning & I miss you boys. Your shoulders, hands & hips. Your sexy calves. Your pheromone stink. It's 6am in Cali. Have you been running, R-do, already this morning? In Boulder it's 7 or so. What adventures do you retrace sleeping in, dirty Lundy boy?

. . .

Faves,
Just in from the fab party. Plenty of actors, food, drinks & crying. Stories of transformation. Expressions of gratitude for the opportunity to exercise & develop our instruments & make art through the encounter & move beyond fear to possibility. & Wisecracks. Rapid fire mixed in. Plus a few uncanny immigration detention center stories. Canada anyone? (Reminding me of slowing it down approaching the border crossing cue

at Ogdensburg, NY en route to Chicago, New York, Los Angeles . . . via Ottawa, fleeing North Country isolation, trying not to tip the officers off to my intention to haul ass on the 416 to make it through security, make my plane. *Where will you park your car & how long will you be gone? I use BizPark at the airport, sir. & I'll be gone not long enough.* If I didn't get out, I knew I would die in Canton. Somewhere off US-11 or Riverside Drive/County Road 27. Under the bridge just beyond the cluster of trees where the river splits. *Take me to the river . . . drop me in the water . . . push me in the water . . .*)

I love Al Green & the Talking Heads. What an amazing band that would be.

I promised myself I would return home to search the archives for nuggets.

(Pause.)

I find a few things: a series of emails documenting a back & forth about "poetics" on the CC listserv; a cfp from Catherine McKinley; two issues of "Success Tips for Black Writers;" & a lengthy missive about hip hop & literary blackface with an excellent anecdote including a fave rediscovered term "nigganiggaz" from Mendi.

I will begin this epistle once again attempting to use my new vocabulary word correctly in a long & detailed sentence.

Ahem . . .

Faves,
Cruising down Main Street (Blo-No) on my way home from the fab party sporting a simply styled gele head wrap, white kurti & navy blue sari wrap pants in my little black car with the windows down blasting Joni Mitchell's "Tenth World" (*Don Juan's Reckless Daughter,* 1977), I see no nigganiggaz dancing in the street, nary a one; there's no one dancing in the street—in spite of the call of Tenth World's afrocuban drums (*Baila mi rumba, Baila, mira mama, Baila mi rumba . . .*).

Would I recognize the nigganiggaz should they appear? Would the nigganiggaz recognize me?

The fleeting urge to coon journal, to record my racial(ized) experiences in authentic BTC fashion, slips by me & out of doors. I think the urge is like a memory trace, the hint of sensory perception & I am suddenly aware of the house's quiet humming of electric things. My computer's fan sings with the fridge, the AC, the air purifier, the sleep sound generator. Their white noise chorus muffles distraction. Until I am hungry & begin to fidget.

(Pause)

A quick protein fix.

"Back on the block 'til the cops say, 'Freeze.'" Nearly typed "back on the black," which could be, too.

Dawn writes:

> What's familiar and not familiar. What challenges and what reminds one of an imagined mother's bosom. A black mother, busty and singing and rocking.

Is she a nigganigga (a compound double nigga), a nigga (single shot), or a simple nigga? Or is she a nigra, Negress, Nubian, or Negro? A Black? A "bittle lack"? A colored wet nurse? I don't know her beyond her periodic appearance in my psyche as a mammy made-up thing, an interloper from some other imagination, & always at a distance. I've never touched her or interrogated her directly. Does she know me? Is this a test?

The familiar. A support? Or a hidden (or open) threat? Reference determines value. Both/&. One's demons kept close.

Some degree of safety is a need. To be constantly vigilant, to live in crisis mode is trauma. I've had my fill of that mode of being, have released it to historical actuality & other losses I cannot recover. As I have also released the absolute, epistemological crisis, #9 (extracted some 4 ½ years ago), my imaginary terrier Rusty & the idyllic fantasy of childhood, red meat & dairy, roller coasters, Ebony™ & Jet™, high heels & the compulsion to control.

Ha! That's a lie (or two)—wishful thinking. We see each other clearly, those last two & I, though most times I look the other way. I find it helpful to immerse myself in the possibility of the adventure & showing love to my ankles often go barefoot in the house. Still, I cannot bring myself to part with the Vince Camutos I bought at Nordstrom's during our Pomona shopping spree last fall. Though a 9-hour day in those fab wedge-heeled boots mandated 6 weeks of PT and a fresh pair of Sauconys. This awareness, itself, is a new adventure in physical form.

I do not like pain. But to be completely safe is to exist & make without question, discovery, or possibility. It is a certain death before death. & Where's the pleasure in that?

. . .

All tidied up. Late morning comes knocking & the temp's rising quickly in the corn. Thank fossil fuels for AC. The studio awaits my return, the return of the cyborg sound body. I will extend myself into the hum. For there are tracks to be laid & drops to be made. Argh! The landline's weekday ringing has begun.

. . .

Dear BTC,

I want this, us together. Not sure I can cuddle you without getting a hard-on, though. But I promise, I won't let it show.

Yours,
Duri

NOTE

1. From the "Objects" section of Gertrude Stein's *Tender Buttons* (Stein 476).

BIBLIOGRAPHY

Adorno, Theodor W. *Notes to Literature*. Vol. 1. Trans. Shierry Weber Nicholsen. New York: Columbia UP, 1991. Print.

Agamben, Giorgio. *Nudities*. Trans. David Kishik and Stefan Pedatella. Stanford, CA: Stanford UP, 2011. Print.

Alighieri, Dante. *Dante's Inferno*. Trans. John D. Sinclair. Oxford, NY: Oxford UP, 1961. Print.

Allen, Donald. Donald Allen Collection, MSS 0003, Archive for New Poetry. Mandeville Special Collections Library. U of California, San Diego.

———, ed. *The New American Poetry: 1945–1960*. New York: Grove Press, 1960. Print.

Almond, Steve, and Julianna Baggott. *Which Brings Me to You: A Novel in Confessions*. Chapel Hill, NC: Algonquin Books, 2006. Print.

Andrews, Bruce. "Code Words." Rev. of *Image-Music-Text*, by Roland Barthes. *L=A=N=G=U=A=G=E* 6 (December 1978). Print.

———. "*L=A=N=G=U=A=G=E*." *The Little Magazine in America: A Contemporary History*. Ed. Ian Morris and Joanne Diaz. Evanston, IL: Triquarterly, forthcoming 2012. Print.

———, Charles Bernstein, Ray DiPalma, Steve McCaffery, and Ron Silliman. *Legend*. New York: L=A=N=G=U=A=G=E/Segue, 1980. Print.

Arendt, Hannah. *The Human Condition*. 2nd ed. Chicago: U of Chicago P, 1998. Print.

———. "On Men in Dark Times: Thoughts about Lessing." In *Men in Dark Times*. Trans. Clara and Richard Winston. New York: Harcourt, Brace & World, 1968. 3–32. Print.

Armantrout, Rae. *Collected Prose*. San Diego: Singing Horse Press, 2007. Print.

———. "Interview with Rae Armantrout." Conducted by Sam Feldman. *Chicago Weekly Blog*. 28 January 2010. Web. <http://blog.chicagoweekly.net/2010/01/28/interview-with-rae-armantrout/>. 7 February 2011.

———. "An Interview with Rae Armantrout." Conducted by Lynn Keller. *Contemporary Literature* 50.2 (2009): 219–39. Print.

———. *Veil: New and Selected Poems*. Middletown, CT: Wesleyan UP, 2001. Print.

———. "Why Don't Women Do Language-Oriented Writing?" *L=A=N=G=U=A=G=E* 1 (February 1978). Print.

———, and Ron Silliman. "Engines." In Silliman, *The Alphabet*. 37–41.

———, Steve Benson, Carla Harryman, Lyn Hejinian, Tom Mandel, Ted Pearson, Bob Perelman, Kit Robinson, Ron Silliman, and Barrett Watten. *The*

Grand Piano: An Experiment in Collective Autobiography, San Francisco 1975–1980. Ten volumes. Detroit: Mode A, 2006–2010. Print.

Ashbery, John. "Writers and Issues: Frank O'Hara's Question." In *Selected Prose*. Ed. Eugene Richie. Ann Arbor: U of Michigan P, 2004. 81–83. Print.

Ashton, Susanna. *Collaborators in Literary America, 1870–1920*. New York: Palgrave MacMillan, 2003. Print.

Augustine, Jane. Rev. of *Collected Works* by Lorine Niedecker. *Jacket* 21 (2003): n.p. Web. <http://jacketmagazine.com/21/aug-penb.html> 25 May 2012.

Badhwar, Neera Kapur, ed. *Friendship: A Philosophical Reader*. Ithaca, NY: Cornell UP, 1993. Print.

Bagioli, Mario. "Rights or Rewards? Changing Frameworks of Scientific Authorship." In Bagioli and Galison 253–80.

———, and Peter Galison, eds. *Scientific Authorship: Credit and Intellectual Property in Science*. London: Routledge, 2003. Print.

Barg, Barbara. [untitled]. *L=A=N=G=U=A=G=E* 9/10 (October 1979). Print.

Barthes, Roland. "La mort de l'auteur." *Manteia* V (1968). Reprinted in *Image-Music-Text*. Ed. and trans. Stephen Heath. London: Fontana/Collins, 1977. 142–48. Print.

Bartram, William. *Travels*. Ed. Mark Van Doren. New York: Dover Publications, 1955. Print.

Benjamin, Walter. *Illuminations: Essays and Reflections*. Ed. Hannah Arendt. New York: Schocken, 1969. Print.

Berlant, Lauren, and Michael Warner. "Sex in Public." In *Intimacy*. Ed. Lauren Berlant. Chicago: U of Chicago P, 2000. 547–66. Print.

Bernstein, Charles. "Community and the Individual Talent." *Diacritics* 27.3/4 (Summer/Winter 1996): 176–95. Print.

———. "The Conspiracy of 'Us.'" *L=A=N=G=U=A=G=E* 8 (June 1979). Print.

———. *Content's Dream: Essays 1975–1984*. Los Angeles: Sun & Moon Press, 1986. Print.

———. "The Expanded Field of *L=A=N=G=U=A=G=E*." *Routledge Companion to Experimental Literature*. Ed. Joe Bray, Alison Gibbons, and Brian McHale. New York: Routledge, 2012. 281–97. Print.

———. "From A to Z." Rev. of *From A to Z*, by Johanna Drucker. *L=A=N=G=U=A=G=E* 1 (February 1978). Print.

———. "Hearing 'Here': Robert Creeley's Poetics of Duration." In *Content's Dream: Essays 1975–1984*. Los Angeles: Sun & Moon, 1986. 292–304. Print.

Berrigan, Ted. "Bean Spasms." In Waldman and Warsh 38–43.

———. *The Sonnets*. New York: Penguin, 2000. Print.

———, and Ron Padgett. "Waterloo Sunset." In Waldman and Warsh 109.

Blanchot, Maurice. *The Unavowable Community*. Trans. Pierre Joris. Barrytown, NY: Station Hill Press, 1988. Print.

Bloch, Ernest. *The Utopian Function of Art and Literature: Selected Essays*. Trans. Jack Zipes and Frank Mecklenburg. Cambridge, MA: MIT P, 1988. Print.

Bockris, Victor. *Beat Punks*. Cambridge, MA: Da Capo Press, 2000. Print.

Bök, Christian. "Introduction to 'Flarf-arf-arf.'" Bachelor Machines. *Insubordinate Automata*. 22 May 2010. Web. <http://bachelormachines.netfirms.com/bachelormachines.org/InsubordinateAutomata/=94.> 11 June 2012.

Bond, Michael. "The Moon on Black Cherries." In Weishaus 9.

Boon, Carl J. "Parataxis and Possibility: Ron Silliman's *Alphabet*." Diss. Ohio State U, 2007. Print.

Brainard, Joe. *Bolinas Journal*. Bolinas, CA: Big Sky, 1971. Print.

Breslin, Glenna. "Lorine Niedecker: The Poet in Her Homeplace." In Willis, *Radical Vernacular* 189–206.

Brinnin, John. *Dylan Thomas in America*. London: J. M. Dent & Sons, 1957. Print.

Butera, Karina. "The Presentation of Gendered Selves in Everyday Friendship." Diss. Deakin U, 2008. Print.

Caddel, Richard. "Consider: Lorine Niedecker and Her Environment." In Penberthy, *Lorine Niedecker: Woman and Poet*. 281–86.

Cantwell, Robert. *Bluegrass Breakdown: The Making of the Old Southern Sound*. Urbana and Chicago: U of Illinois P, 1984. Print.

Cavell, Stanley. *The Claim of Reason: Wittgenstein, Skepticism, Morality, and Tragedy*. New York: Oxford UP, 1979. Print.

Cazé, Antoine. Conference Presentation. Modern Language Association, Los Angeles, January 2011.

Chadwick, Whitney, and Isabelle de Courtivron, eds. *Significant Others: Creativity and Intimate Partnership*. London: Thames & Hudson, 1993. Print.

Chambers, Deborah. *New Social Ties: Contemporary Connections in a Fragmented Society*. New York: Palgrave Macmillan, 2006. Print.

Chiasson, Dan. "Entangled: The Poetry of Rae Armantrout." *New Yorker*. 17 May 2010: 110–12. Print.

Cixous, Hélène, and Catherine Clement. *The Newly Born Woman*. Trans. Betsy Wing. Minneapolis: U of Minnesota P, 1986. Print.

Clare, John. *The Later Poems of John Clare 1837–1864*. Vol. 1. Ed. Eric Robertson and David Powell. Oxford, UK: Clarendon Press, 1984. Print.

Clark, Tom. "From 'Neil Young.'" In Waldman and Warsh 287–92. Print.

Clarke, Cheryl. *After Mecca: Women Poets and the Black Arts Movement*. New Brunswick, NJ: Rutgers UP, 2005. Print.

Cohen, Rachel. *A Chance Meeting: Intertwined Lives of American Writers and Artists, 1854–1967*. New York: Random House, 2004. Print.

Cooper, Dennis. "Brigid Polk's 'Scars.'" *DC's*. n.p. 23 October 2007. Web.

<http://denniscooper-theweaklings.blogspot.com/2007/10/brigid-polks-scars.html>. 24 August 2010.

Corman, Cid. "With Lorine: A Memorial 1903–1970." *Truck* 16 (1975): 57–90. Print.

Coupe, Laurence. *Beat Sound, Beat Vision: The Beat Spirit and Popular Song.* Manchester, UK: Manchester UP, 2007. Print.

Crane, Hart. *The Complete Poems and Selected Letters and Prose.* New York: Liverwright Publishing Corp., 1966. Print.

Creeley, Robert. *As We Sit.* Los Angeles: Black Sparrow, 1974. Print.

———. *The Collected Poems of Robert Creeley.* Berkeley: U of California P, 1982. Print.

———. *Contexts of Poetry: Interviews 1961–1971.* Bolinas, CA: Four Seasons Foundation, 1973. Print.

———. "The Innocence." In *The New American Poetry.* Ed. Donald Allen. New York: Grove Press, 1960. 77. Print.

———. *Tales Out of School: Selected Interviews.* Ann Arbor: U of Michigan P, 1993. Print.

———. *Thirty Things.* Monoprints by Bobbie Creeley. Los Angeles: Black Sparrow, 1974. Print.

Curry, Renée R. *White Women Writing White: H. D., Elizabeth Bishop, Sylvia Plath, and Whiteness.* Westport, CT: Greenwood Press, 2000. Print.

Damon, Maria. *The Dark End of the Street: Margins in American Vanguard Poetry.* Minneapolis: U of Minnesota P, 1993. Print.

———. "Electronic Poetics Assay: Diaspora, Silliness and—Gender?" In *Postliterary America: From Bagel Shop Jazz to Micropoetries.* Iowa City: U of Iowa P, 2011. 203–27. Print.

Dana, Robert. *Against the Grain: Interviews with Maverick American Publishers.* Iowa City: U of Iowa P, 1986. Print.

Davenport, Guy, and Jonathan Williams. *A Garden Carried in a Pocket: Letters 1964–1968.* Ed. Thomas Meyer. Haverford, PA: Green Shade, 2004. Print.

Davidson, Michael. "Compulsory Homosociality: Charles Olson, Jack Spicer, and the Gender of Poetics." In *Cruising the Performative.* Ed. Sue-Ellen Case, Philip Brett, and Susan Leigh Foster. Bloomington: Indiana UP, 1995. 197–216. Print.

———. *Guys Like Us: Citing Masculinity in Cold War Poetics.* Chicago: U of Chicago P, 2004. Print.

———. *The San Francisco Renaissance: Poetics and Community at Mid-century.* Cambridge, UK: Cambridge UP, 1989. Print.

———, Lyn Hejinian, Ron Silliman, and Barrett Watten. *Leningrad.* San Francisco: Mercury House, 1991. Print.

Davies, Alan. Rev. of *Theory of Emotion,* by Diane Ward. *L=A=N=G=U=A=G=E* 11 (January 1980). Print.

Davis, Jordan. Email to Flarf@googlegroups.com. 4 April 2009.

Degentesh, Katie. [Flarfette Jones/Flarfety Flarf Flarf]. "The Popsicle." *Flarflist*. Summer 2002. Web. 11 June 2012.

Delanty, Gerard. *Community*. New York: Routledge, 2003. Print.

Derrida, Jacques. *The Politics of Friendship*. Trans. George Collins. London: Verso, 1997. Print.

Dewey, Anne. *Beyond Maximus: The Construction of Public Voice in Black Mountain Poetry*. Stanford, CA: Stanford UP, 2007. Print.

———. "Gendered Muses and the Representation of Social Space in Robert Duncan's Poetry." *Contemporary Literature* 50.2 (2009): 299–331. Print.

Dorris, Michael, and Louise Erdrich. *The Crown of Columbus: A Novel*. New York: HarperCollins, 1991. Print.

Drucker, Johanna. "Women & Language." *Poetics Journal* 4 (May 1984): 56–68. Print.

Duhamel, Denise, Maureen Seaton, and David Trinidad, eds. *Saints of Hysteria: A Half-Century of Collaborative American Poetry*. Berkeley: Soft Skull Press, 2007. Print.

Duncan, Robert. *Bending the Bow*. New York: New Directions, 1968. Print.

———. "Introduction." In *Duncan's Introductions at the Poetry Center, San Francisco State University*. Ed. Robert J. Bertholf. *Chicago Review* 45.2 (1999): 74–120. Print.

———. "The Sweetness and Greatness of Dante's Divine Comedy" (1965). In *Fictive Certainties*. New York: New Directions, 1985. 142–61. Print.

DuPlessis, Rachel Blau. "Anne Waldman: Standing Corporeally in One's Time." In Kane, *Don't Ever Get Famous*. 173–94.

———. *Blue Studios: Poetry and Its Cultural Work*. Tuscaloosa: U of Alabama P, 2006. Print.

———. "Lorine Niedecker, the Anonymous: Gender, Class, Genre and Resistances." In Penberthy, *Lorine Niedecker: Woman and Poet*. 113–38.

———. "Manifests." *Diacritics* 26.3–4 (1996): 31–53. Print.

———. *The Pink Guitar: Writing as Feminist Practice*. London: Routledge, 1990. Print.

DuPlessis, Rachel Blau, and Peter Quartermain, eds. *The Objectivist Nexus: Essays in Cultural Poetics*. Tuscaloosa: U of Alabama P, 1999. Print.

Eiseley, Loren. *Darwin's Century: Evolution and the Men Who Discovered It*. New York: Anchor Books, 1961. Print.

Eliot, T. S. *Notes Towards the Definition of Culture*. London: Faber and Faber, 1962. Print.

———. *T. S. Eliot: Collected Poems, 1909–1962*. New York: Harcourt Brace Jovanovich. 1983. Print.

Ellingham, Louis, and Kevin Killian. *Poet Be Like God: Jack Spicer and the San Francisco Renaissance*. Hanover, NH: UP of New England, 1998. Print.

Epstein, Andrew. *Beautiful Enemies: Friendship and Postwar American Poetry.* New York: Oxford UP, 2006. Print.

———. "'There Is No Content Here, Only Dailiness': Poetry as Critique of Everyday Life in Ron Silliman's *Ketjak.*" *Contemporary Literature* 51.4 (2011): 736–76. Print.

Evans, Steve. "The American Avant-Garde after 1989: Notes Towards a History." In *Assembling Alternatives: Reading Postmodern Poetries Transnationally.* Ed. Romana Huk. Middletown, CT: Wesleyan UP, 2003. 86–113. Print.

———. "Off the Record: Remarks on Coteries, Infrastructure, and Gossip." *Naropa SWP.* 2010. Web. <http://www.thirdfactory.net/media/Steve-Evans_Coterie-Infrastructure-Gossip.mp3>. 1 November 2011.

Faas, Ekbert. *Towards a New American Poetics: Essays and Interviews.* Santa Barbara: Black Sparrow Press, 1978. Print.

Falk, Jane. "Finger Pointing at the Moon: Zen and the Poetry of Philip Whalen." In *The Emergence of Buddhist American Literature.* Ed. John Whalen-Bridge and Gary Storhoff. Albany: SUNY Press, 2009. 103–22. Print.

Finlay, Ian Hamilton. *Detached Sentences on Friendship.* n.p. Illus. Kathleen Lindsley. Lanarkshire, Scotland: Wild Hawthorn Press, 1991. Print.

Foster, Edward Halsey. *Understanding the Black Mountain Poets.* Columbia: U of South Carolina P, 1995. Print.

Foucault, Michel. "Friendship as a Way of Life." In *The Essential Works of Michel Foucault 1954–1984.* Vol. I. *Ethics: Subjectivity and Truth.* Ed. Paul Rabinow. Trans. Robert Hurley et al. New York: New Press, 1994. 135–56. Print.

———. "What Is an Author?" In *Textual Strategies: Perspectives in Post-Structuralist Criticism.* Ed. Josué V. Harari. Ithaca, NY: Cornell UP, 1979. 141–60. Print.

Franklin, Benjamin. *The Works of Benjamin Franklin; with Notes and a Life of the Author.* Vol. 6. Ed. Jared Sparks. Boston: Tappan and Whittemore, 1856. Print.

Fraser, Kathleen. "Overheard." *Poetics Journal* 4 (May 1984): 98–105. Print.

———. *Translating the Unspeakable: Poetry and the Innovative Necessity.* Tuscaloosa: U of Alabama P, 2000. Print.

Friedman, Ed. Rev. of *Hog Wild,* by Susie Timmons. *L=A=N=G=U=A=G=E* 11 (January 1980). Print.

Friedman, Marilyn. "Feminism and Modern Friendship: Dislocating the Community." In Badhwar 285–302.

Frost, Elisabeth. *The Feminist Avant-Garde in American Poetry.* Iowa City: U of Iowa P, 2003. Print.

Galison, Peter. "The Collective Author." In Bagioli and Galison 329–49.

Gardner, Drew. "Chicks Dig War." In *Petroleum Hat*. New York: Roof Books, 2005. 20–23. Print.

———. "Message to Flarf Listserv." *Flarflist*. 4 November 2009. Web.

Garrity, Jane, and Tirza True Latimer. "Queer Cross-Gender Collaboration." In *Cambridge Companion to Gay and Lesbian Writing*. Ed. Hugh Stevens. Cambridge, UK: Cambridge UP, 2010. 185–201. Print.

Gelpi, Albert, and Robert J. Bertholf. *Robert Duncan and Denise Levertov: The Poetry of Politics, the Politics of Poetry*. Stanford, CA: Stanford UP, 2006. Print.

Golding, Alan. *From Outlaw to Classic: Canons in American Poetry*. Madison: U of Wisconsin P, 1995. Print.

Gray, Timothy. *Gary Snyder and the Pacific Rim: Creating Countercultural Community*. Iowa City: U of Iowa P, 2006. Print.

Green, Penny. "Patti Smith." *Interview* (October 1973): 20–25. Print.

Grenier, Robert. Rev. of *Writing Is an Aid to Memory*, by Lyn Hejinian. *L=A=N=G=U=A=G=E* 8 (June 1979). Print.

Hair, Ross. "'Hemi-demi-semi Barbaric Yawps': Jonathan Williams and Black Mountain." *Journal of Black Mountain College Studies* 3 (2012): n.p. Web. <http://www.blackmountainstudiesjournal.org/wp/?page_id=893> 25 May 2012.

Hampson, Robert, and Will Montgomery, eds. *Frank O'Hara Now: New Essays on the New York Poet*. Liverpool, UK: Liverpool UP, 2010. Print.

Harryman, Carla. *The Middle*. San Francisco: Gaz Press, 1983. Print.

Harvey, David. *Spaces of Global Capitalism: Towards a Theory of Uneven Geographical Development*. London: Verso, 2006. Print.

Heath, Stephen. "Difference." *Screen* 19.3 (Autumn 1978): 51–112. Print.

Hejinian, Lyn. In "Excerpts from Sight." *Poetry from Sojourner: A Feminist Anthology*. Ed. Ruth Lepson with Lynne Yamaguchi. Champaign: U of Illinois P, 2004. 88–91. Print.

———. *The Language of Inquiry*. Berkeley: U of California P, 2000. Print.

———, and Leslie Scalapino. *Sight*. Washington, DC: Edge Books, 1999. Print.

Heller, Agnes. "The Beauty of Friendship." *South Atlantic Quarterly* 97.1 (1998): 5–22. Print.

Herd, David. "Collaboration and the Avant-Garde." *Critical Review* 35 (1995): 36–63. Print.

Highfill, Mitch. "Blogs Make Me Horny." *Flarflist*. 5–8 October 2007. Web. 11 June 2012.

Hinderlither, Beth, et al., eds. *Communities of Sense: Rethinking Aesthetics and Politics*. Durham, NC: Duke UP, 2009. Print.

Hinton, Laura, and Cynthia Hogue. "Introduction." In *We Who Love to Be*

Astonished: Experimental Women's Writing and Performance Poetics. Tuscaloosa: U of Alabama P, 2002. 1–12. Print.

Holloway, Julia Bolton. "Introduction: Life of the Author." In *Il Tesoretto,* by Brunetto Latini. Ed. and trans. Julia Bolton Holloway. New York: Garland Publishing, 1981. Print.

Hooks, Bell. *Feminist Theory: From Margin to Center.* (1984). 2nd ed. Boston: South End Press Classics, 2000. Print.

Howe, Susan. "Howe on Owen." Rev. of *Hearts in Space,* by Maureen Owen. *L=A=N=G=U=A=G=E* 13 (December 1980). Print.

———. "The Pacifica Interview." *L=A=N=G=U=A=G=E* Supplement No. 3 "The Politics of Poetry: A Supplement" (October 1981). Print.

Hunt, Erica. "Notes for an Oppositional Poetics." In *The Politics of Poetic Form: Poetry and Public Policy.* Ed. Charles Bernstein. New York: Roof, 1990. 197–212. Print.

Hutcheon, Linda, and Michael Hutcheon. "A Convenience of Marriage: Collaboration and Interdisciplinarity." *PMLA* 116.5 (2001): 1364–76. Print.

Irmscher, Christopher. *The Poetics of Natural History: From John Bartram to William James.* New Brunswick, NJ: Rutgers UP, 1999. Print.

Izenberg, Oren. "Language Poetry and Collective Life." *Critical Inquiry* 30 (2003): 132–59. Print.

Jenison, Ruth. "Waking into Ideology: Lorine Niedecker's Experiments in the Syntax of Consciousness." In Willis, *Radical Vernacular* 131–50.

Johnson, Joyce. *Minor Characters: A Beat Memoir.* New York: Penguin, 1999. Print.

Kane, Daniel. *All Poets Welcome: The Lower East Side Poetry Scene in the 1960s.* Berkeley: U of California P, 2003. Print.

———. "*Angel Hair* Magazine, the Second Generation New York School, and the Poetics of Sociability." *Contemporary Literature* 45.2 (2004): 331–67. Print.

———. "'Nor Did I Socialize with Their People': Patti Smith, Rock Heroics, and the Poetics of Sociability." *Popular Music* 31.1 (2012): 105–23. Print.

———, ed. *Don't Ever Get Famous: Essays on New York School Writing after the New York School.* Champaign, IL: Dalkey Archive Press, 2006. Print.

Kaplan, Carey, and Ellen Cronan Rose. "Strange Bedfellows: Feminist Collaboration." *Signs* 18.3 (1993): 547–61. Print.

Kaplan, Michael. *Friendship Fictions: The Rhetoric of Citizenship and the Liberal Imaginary.* Tuscaloosa: U of Alabama P, 2010. Print.

Karell, Linda. *Writing Together, Writing Apart: Collaboration in Western American Literature.* Lincoln: U of Nebraska P, 2002. Print.

Kay, Richard. "The Sin(s) of Brunetto Latini." *Dante Studies* 112 (1994): 19–31. Print.

Keller, Lynn. "'Just one of / the girls:— / normal in the extreme':

Experimentalists-To-Be Starting Out in the 1960s." *Differences: Journal of Feminist Cultural Studies* 12.2 (2001): 47–69. Print.

———. *Thinking Poetry: Readings in Contemporary Women's Exploratory Poetics*. Iowa City: U of Iowa P, 2011. Print.

Kelley, Mike. *Foul Perfection: Essays and Criticism*. Cambridge, MA: MIT P, 2003. Print.

Kinnahan, Linda. *Lyric Interventions: Feminism, Experimental Poetry, and Contemporary Discourse*. Iowa City: U of Iowa P, 2004. Print.

Koestenbaum, Wayne. *Double Talk: The Erotics of Male Literary Collaboration*. New York: Routledge, 1989. Print.

Kyger, Joanne. *About Now: Collected Works*. Orono, ME: National Poetry Foundation, 2007. Print.

———. *All This Every Day*. Berkeley: Big Sky, 1975. Print.

———. "Congratulatory Poetics." Interview. *Convivio* (1983): 109–20. Print.

———. "A Conversation with Joanne Kyger." Interview by Lawrence Nahem. *Occident* (vol. viii, new series, 1974): 142–57. Print.

———. Letter to Linda Russo. 20 March 2012.

———. Papers. Mandeville Special Collections Library. University of California, San Diego.

———. *Places to Go*. Los Angeles: Black Sparrow, 1970. Print.

———. *Strange Big Moon: The Japan and India Journal: 1960–1964*. Berkeley, CA: North Atlantic, 2000. Print.

Laird, Holly A. "'A Hand Spills from the Book's Threshold': Coauthorship's Readers." *PMLA* 116.2 (2001): 344–53. Print.

———. *Women Co-Authors*. Urbana: U of Illinois P, 2000. Print.

Lamm, Kimberly. "The Question of Race in the American Avant-Garde." Rev. of *Race and the Avant-Garde: Experimental Asian American Poetry Since 1965*, by Timothy Yu. *Contemporary Literature* 50.4 (2009): 831–39. *Project Muse*. Web. 2 April 2012.

Leibowitz, Herbert. Introduction. *Blues & Roots/Rue & Bluets: A Garland for the Southern Appalachians*, by Jonathan Williams. 2nd ed. Durham, NC: Duke UP, 1985. n.p. Print.

Levertov, Denise. "Some Notes on Organic Form." In *New and Selected Essays*. New York: New Directions Press, 1992. 67–73. Print.

Lewis, C. S. "Friendship—The Least Necessary Love." In Badhwar 39–47.

London, Bette Lynn. *Writing Double: Women's Literary Partnerships*. Cornell, NY: Cornell UP, 1999. Print.

Lundquist, Sara. "Another Poet among Painters: Barbara Guest with Grace Hartigan and Mary Abbott." In *The Scene of My Selves: New Work on the New York School Poets*. Ed. Terence Diggory and Stephen Paul Miller. Orono, ME: National Poetry Foundation, 2001. 245–64. Print.

Lunsford, Angela, and Lisa Ede. *Singular Texts/Plural Authors: Perspectives on Collaborative Writing*. Carbondale: Southern Illinois UP, 1990. Print.

Luoma, Bill. *Works & Days*. West Stockbridge, MA: Figures/Hard Press, 1998. Print.

Mac Low, Jackson. "Letter to the Editor." *L=A=N=G=U=A=G=E* 8 (June 1979). Print.

———. "Museletter." *L=A=N=G=U=A=G=E* 2 (April 1978). Print.

Mandel, Ernest. *Late Capitalism*. Second Edition. London: Verso, 1998. Print.

Mayer, Bernadette. "Experiments." In *The L=A=N=G=U=A=G=E Book*. Ed. Bruce Andrews and Charles Bernstein. Carbondale: Southern Illinois UP, 1984. 80–83. Print.

McCarthy, Tom. "Patti: Poet as Macho Woman." *Village Voice* (7 February 1974): 42. Print.

Meltzer, David. "Songs of David Dog the Lion." In Weishaus. n.p.

Merleau-Ponty, Maurice. *The Primacy of Perception*. Trans. James M. Edie. Evanston, IL: Northwestern UP, 1964. Print.

Mesmer, Sharon. Telephone conversation with Maria Damon. 7 September 2010.

Meyer, Thomas. "JW Gent & Epicurean." *Jacket* 39 (Late 2009). Web. <http://jacketmagazine.com/38/jwb12-meyer-thomas.shtml>. 10 May 2012.

Middleton, Peter. "The British Niedecker." In Willis, *Radical Vernacular* 247–70.

———. "Lorine Niedecker's 'Folk Base' and Her Challenge to the American Avant-Garde." In DuPlessis and Quartermain 160–88.

Montaigne, Michel de. "Of Friendship." *The Complete Essays of Montaigne*. Trans. Donald M. Frame. Stanford, CA: Stanford UP, 1976. 135–44. Print.

Moxley, Jennifer. *Clampdown*. Chicago: Flood Editions, 2009. Print.

———. "Fragments of a Broken Poetics." *Chicago Review* 55.2 (Spring 2010): 17–27. Print.

———. *Imagination Verses*. New York: Tender Buttons, 1996. Print.

———. *The Line*. Sausalito, CA: Post-Apollo Press, 2007. Print.

———. *The Middle Room*. Berkeley: Subpress, 2007. Print.

———. "Mysteries." Interview with Noah Eli Gordon. *Jacket* 7 (Early 2009). Web. <http://jacketmagazine.com/37/iv-moxley-ivb-gordon.shtml>. 9 June 2012.

———. "Pillow Talk: A Short History of a Small Magazine." *Arras: New Media Poetry and Poetics*, n.d. Web. <http://www.arras.net/impercipient_intro_paragraphs_htm>. 1 October 2010.

———. *The Sense Record and Other Poems*. Washington, DC: Edge Books, 2002. Print.

Nancy, Jean-Luc. *The Inoperative Community*. Trans. Peter Connor et al. Minneapolis: U of Minnesota P, 1991. Print.

Nelson, Maggie. *Women, the New York School, and Other True Abstractions*. Iowa City: U of Iowa P, 2007. Print.

Nero, Bob. "Remembering Lorine." *Truck* 16 (Summer 1975): 136–40. Print.
Ngai, Sianne. "Jealous Schoolgirls, Single White Females, and Other Bad Examples: Rethinking Gender and Envy." *Camera Obscura: A Journal of Feminism, Culture, and Media* 47.2 (2001): 177–229. Print.
Niedecker, Lorine. *"Between Your House and Mine": The Letters of Lorine Niedecker to Cid Corman, 1960 to 1970*. Ed. Lisa Pater Faranda. Durham, NC: Duke UP, 1986. Print.
———. *Collected Works*. Ed. Jenny Penberthy. Berkeley, Los Angeles, and London: U of California P, 2002. Print.
———. "Letters." *Truck* 16 (Summer 1975): 41–54. Print.
———. "Local Letters." In Penberthy, *Lorine Niedecker: Woman and Poet* 87–107.
———. *Tenderness & Gristle: The Collected Poems (1936–1966)*. Penland, NC: Jargon Society, 1969. Print.
Nielsen, Aldon Lynn. *Black Chant: Languages of African American Postmodernism*. Cambridge, UK: Cambridge UP, 1997. Print.
Nietzsche, Friedrich. *Human All Too Human, A Book for Free Spirits*. Trans. R. J. Hollingdale. Cambridge, UK: Cambridge UP, 1986. Print.
Non/Narrative. Poetics Journal 5 (May 1985). Print.
Notley, Alice. *Doctor Williams' Heiresses: A Lecture Delivered at 80 Langton Street, San Francisco, Feb. 12, 1980*. Berkeley: Tuumba Press, 1980. Print.
Obenzinger, Hilton Manfred. "Obenzinger.com." *Poetics List*. 3 March 1999. Web. <http://listserv.buffalo.edu/cgi-bin/wa?A1=ind9903&L=POETICS>. 30 August 2012.
O'Hara, Frank. *The Collected Poems of Frank O'Hara*. Ed. Donald Allen. Berkeley: U of California P, 1995. Print.
———. "Personism: A Manifesto." *The Selected Poems of Frank O'Hara*. Ed. Mark Ford. New York: Alfred A. Knopf, 2008. 247–49. Print.
Owen, Maureen. Rev. of *Entrance to the City*, by Rachel Bijou. *L=A=N=G=U=A=G=E* 11 (January 1980). Print.
Oxford English Dictionary. 2nd ed. 1989. "eccentric, adj." *OED Online*. Oxford University Press. 5 May 2011. Web. <http://www.oed.com>.
Padgett, Ron, and David Shapiro. *An Anthology of New York Poets*. New York: Vintage, 1970. Print.
Patterson, Tom. "O for a Muse of Fire: The Iconoclasm of Jonathan Williams and The Jargon Society." *Afterimage* 23 (1996): 8–12. Print.
Peattie, Donald Culross. *Flowering Earth*. Bloomington and Indianapolis: Indiana UP, 1991. Print.
Penberthy, Jenny. *Lorine Niedecker and the Correspondence with Zukofsky, 1931–1970*. Cambridge, UK: Cambridge UP, 1993. Print.
———, ed. *Lorine Niedecker: Woman and Poet*. Orono, ME: National Poetry Foundation, 1996. Print.

Penley, Constance, and Janet Bergstrom. "The Avant-Garde: Histories and Theories." *Screen* 19.3 (Autumn 1978): 113–27. Print.

Perelman, Bob. "'Fucking / me across the decades like we / poets like': Embodied Poetic Transmission." In Kane, *Don't Ever Get Famous* 195–214.

———. *The Marginalization of Poetry: Language Writing and Literary History*. Princeton, NJ: Princeton UP, 1996. Print.

———. "My Avant-Garde Card." *New Literary History* 41 (2010): 875–94. Print.

Perlman, John. "Letter to the Editor." *L=A=N=G=U=A=G=E* 2 (April 1978). Print.

Perloff, Marjorie. *The Dance of the Intellect: Studies in the Poetry of the Pound Tradition*. Cambridge, UK: Cambridge UP, 1985. Print.

Perry, Ruth, and Martine Watson Brownley, eds. *Mothering the Mind: Twelve Studies of Writers and Their Silent Partners*. New York: Holmes and Meier, 1984. Print.

Peters, Margot. *Lorine Niedecker: A Poet's Life*. Madison: U of Wisconsin P, 2011. Print.

Polk, Brigid. *Scars*. Boston: Telegraph Books, 1972. Print.

Quartermain, Peter. "Take Oil/and Hum: Niedecker/Bunting." In Willis, *Radical Vernacular* 271–83.

Raffa, Guy. *The Complete Danteworlds: A Reader's Guide to the Divine Comedy*. Chicago: U of Chicago P, 2009. Print.

Ramsby, Howard II. *The Black Arts Enterprise and the Production of African American Poetry*. Ann Arbor: U of Michigan P, 2011. Print.

Rancière, Jacques. *Aesthetics and Its Discontents*. Trans. Steven Corcoran. Cambridge, UK: Polity Press, 2009. Print.

———. *Dissensus: On Politics and Aesthetics*. Trans. Steven Corcoran. London: Continuum, 2010. Print.

———. *The Politics of Aesthetics*. Trans. Gabriel Rockhill. London: Continuuum, 2004. Print.

Reed, Brian. "'Footprints of a Wild Ballet': The *Poem-Paintings* of Frank O'Hara and Norman Bluhm." In Hampson and Montgomery 211–28.

Rich, Adrienne. "Compulsory Heterosexuality and Lesbian Existence." In *Blood, Bread, and Poetry: Selected Essays, 1979–1985*. New York: W. W. Norton and Co., 1986. 23–75. Print.

Rifkin, Libbie. *Career Moves: Olson, Creeley, Zukofsky, Berrigan, and the American Avant-Garde*. Tuscaloosa: U of Alabama P, 2000. Print.

———. "'My Little World Goes On St. Mark's Place': Anne Waldman, Bernadette Mayer and the Gender of an Avant-Garde Institution." *Jacket* 7 (1999). Web. <jacketmagazine.com/07/rifkin07.html>. 17 May 2011.

———. "Reconsidering the Company of Love: Creeley between Olson and Levertov." In *Form, Power, and Person in Robert Creeley's Life and Work*. Ed.

Stephen Fredman and Steve McCaffery. Iowa City: U of Iowa P, 2010. 143–58. Print.

———. "That We Can Somehow Add Each to Each Other?:" George Oppen Between Denise Levertov and Rachel Blau DuPlessis." *Contemporary Literature* 51.4 (2010): 703–35. Print.

Russo, Linda. "Dealing in Parts and Particulars: Joanne Kyger's Early Epic Poetics." In *Girls Who Wore Black: Women Writing the Beat Generation*. Ed. Nancy Grace and Ronna Johnson. New Brunswick, NJ: Rutgers UP, 2002. 178–204. Print.

———. "Poetics of Adjacency: *0–9* and the Conceptual Writing of Bernadette Mayer and Hannah Weiner." In Kane, *Don't Ever Get Famous* 122–50.

Said, Edward W. *Beginnings: Intention & Method*. London: Granta, 1975. Print.

Saroyan, Aram. *Complete Minimal Poems*. New York: Ugly Duckling Presse, 2007. Print.

Scalapino, Leslie. "Experience/'On' Sight." Hejinian and Scalapino, n.p.

———, and Ron Silliman. "What/Person: From an Exchange." *Poetics Journal* 9 (1991): 51–68. Print.

Schjeldahl, Peter. "Poetry: A Job Description." *L=A=N=G=U=A=G=E* 13 (December 1980). Print.

Schuyler, James. "The Morning of the Poem." In *Collected Poems*. New York: Farrar Straus Giroux, 1993. 259–303. Print.

Seaton, Peter. "Texte." *L=A=N=G=U=A=G=E* 11 (January 1980). Print.

Sewell, Lisa. "Introduction." In *American Poets in the 21st Century: The New Poetics*. Ed. Claudia Rankine and Lisa Sewell. Middletown, CT: Wesleyan UP, 2007. 1–15. Print.

Shanley, Mary Lyndon. "Marital Slavery and Friendship: John Stuart Mill's *The Subjection of Women*." In Badhwar 267–84.

Shaw, Lytle. *Frank O'Hara: The Poetics of Coterie*. Iowa City: U of Iowa P, 2006. Print.

———. "On Coterie: Frank O'Hara." *Jacket* 10 (October 1999). Web. <http://www.jacketmagazine.com/10/shaw-on-ohara.html>. 24 August 2010.

Sher, Gail. "An Exorcism of Representational Language." Rev. of *Red Light with Blue Sky*, by Beau Beausoleil. *L=A=N=G=U=A=G=E* 11 (January 1980). Print.

Sherry, James. Rev. of "Letters" in *Tottels* 17, by Lynne Dreyer. *L=A=N=G=U=A=G=E* 11 (January 1980). Print.

Silliman, Ron. *The Alphabet*. Tuscaloosa: U of Alabama P, 2008. Print.

———. "Benjamin Obscura." *L=A=N=G=U=A=G=E* 6 (December 1978). Print.

———. Email to Linda Russo, 28 April 1998, posted on the *Electronic Poetry*

Center. Web. <http://epc.buffalo.edu/authors/kyger/silliman.html>. 3 May 2012.

———. "If by writing we mean literature (if by literature we mean poetry) (*if* . . .)) . . ." *L=A=N=G=U=A=G=E* 9/10 (October 1979). Print.

———. "An Interview with Ron Silliman." Conducted by Tom Beckett. *Difficulties* 2:2 (1985): 34–46. Print.

———. Interview. Conducted by Gary Sullivan. n.d. Web. <http://home.jps.net/~nada/silliman.htm>. 7 February 2011.

———. *The New Sentence*. New York: Roof Books, 1987. Print.

———. "Particulars: in re Mac Low." *L=A=N=G=U=A=G=E* 9/10 (October 1979). Print.

———. *Silliman's Blog*. 24 February 2003. Web. <http://ronsilliman.blogspot.com/2003_02_23_archive.html>. 7 February 2011.

———, ed. *In the American Tree: Language, Realism, Poetry*. Orono, ME: National Poetry Foundation, 1986; 2nd ed., 2002. Print.

Simpson, Megan. *Poetic Epistemologies: Gender and Knowing in Women's Language-Oriented Writing*. Albany: State U of New York P, 2000. Print.

Skinner, Jonathan. "Particular Attention: Lorine Niedecker's Natural Histories." In Willis, *Radical Vernacular* 41–59.

Smethurst, James. *The Black Arts Movement: Literary Nationalism in the 1960s and 1970s*. Chapel Hill: U of North Carolina P, 2005. Print.

Smith, Hazel. *Hyperscapes in the Poetry of Frank O'Hara: Difference/Homosexuality/Topography*. Liverpool: Liverpool UP, 2000. Print.

Smith, Patti. Foreword. In *An Accidental Autobiography: The Selected Letters of Gregory Corso*. Ed. Bill Morgan. New York: New Directions, 2003. xi-xii. Print.

———. *Horses*. Arista Records, 1975. Vinyl recording.

———. *Just Kids*. New York: Ecco, 2010. Print.

———. Letter to Anne Waldman. n.d. Series 1 Box 5 Folder 13. Angel Hair Papers, Fales Special Collections Library, New York U.

———. Letter to Anne Waldman and Michael Brownstein. n.d. Box 15. Anne Waldman Papers, Special Collections Library, U of Michigan.

———. Letter to Anne Waldman. 24 May. Box 15. Anne Waldman Papers, Special Collections Library, U of Michigan.

———. *Patti Smith at the Poetry Project*. Rec. 10 February 1971. CD.

———. "Piss Factory." *Hey Joe / Piss Factory*. Mer Records, 1974. Vinyl recording.

———. *Seventh Heaven*. Boston: Telegraph Books, 1972. Print.

Smith, Patti, and Victor Bockris. "The Poetry of Performance: An interview with Patti Smith." *Carry Out* (1972): 2–17. Print.

Snyder, Gary. Papers. Contemporary Literature Collection. Simon Fraser University. Vancouver, British Columbia.

———. *Riprap & Cold Mountain Poems*. San Francisco: Four Seasons Foundation, 1969. Print.

Spahr, Juliana. *Swoonrocket*. 27 November 2006. Web. <http://swoonrocket.blogspot.com/2006_11_01_archive.html>. 15 April 2012.

———. *The Transformation*. Berkeley: Atelos, 2007. Print.

Stein, Gertrude. *Selected Writings of Gertrude Stein*. Ed. Carl Van Vechten. New York: Vintage Books, 1990. Print.

Stern-Gillet, Suzanne. *Aristotle's Philosophy of Friendship*. Albany: State U of New York P, 1995. Print.

Stillinger, Jack. *Multiple Authorship and the Myth of Solitary Genius*. New York: Oxford UP, 1991. Print.

Stone, Marjorie, and Judith Thompson, eds. *Literary Couplings: Writing Couples, Collaborators, and the Construction of Authorship*. Madison: U of Wisconsin P, 2006. Print.

Sullivan, Gary. "Fast-posting Flarfy." *Flarflist*. 1 October 2001. Web. 10 August 2012.

———. "The Flarf Files." Michael Magee. *Electronic Poetry Center*. State U of New York at Buffalo. 3 August 2011. Web. <http://epc.buffalo.edu/authors/bernstein/syllabi/readings/flarf.html>.

———. Interview with Rodney Koeneke. *Newer Metaphysicals*/Mipoesias. 2008. Web. <http://mipoesias.com/ INTERVIEWS2008/>. 10 August 2012.

———. "The Last Couple of Days." Response to Barrett Watten. *Poetics List*. Wayne State U. 14 September 2001.

———. *The New Life* (comic strip). *Rain Taxi Review of Books* 10.4 (2005/2006). Web. <http://raintaxi.com/online/2005winter/> 10 August 2012.

Taggart, John. "Letter to the Editor." *L=A=N=G=U=A=G=E* 2 (April 1978). Print.

———. Rev. of *A Still Life*, by Thomas A. Clark. *L=A=N=G=U=A=G=E* 11 (January, 1980). Print.

Thomas, Lorenzo. "An Afro-American Word Sculptor." Rev. of *O Africa Where I Baked My Bread* and *Grandsire*, by Lance Jeffers. *L=A=N=G=U=A=G=E* 11 (January 1980). Print.

Thoreau, Henry David. *Walden*. Ed. Stephen Fender. Oxford, NY: Oxford UP, 1997. Print.

Thorpe, John. *The Cargo Cult*. Bolinas, CA: Big Sky, 1972. Print.

Vermont, Charlie. "Vertical Portrait of Joanne Kyger." *Jacket* 11 (April 2000). Web. <http://jacketmagazine.com/11/kyger-vermont.html>. 12 June 2012.

Vickery, Ann. *Leaving Lines of Gender: A Feminist Genealogy of Language Writing*. Middletown, CT: Wesleyan UP, 2000. Print.

Waldman, Anne. *Another World: A Second Anthology of Works from the St. Mark's Poetry Project*. Indianapolis: Bobbs-Merrill, 1971. Print.

———. Email to Daniel Kane. 19 February 2012.

———. Foreword. *Strange Big Moon: The Japan and India Journals, 1960–1964*, by Joanne Kyger. ii–x. Print.

———, and Lewis Warsh, eds. *Angel Hair Sleeps with a Boy in My Head: The Angel Hair Anthology*. New York: Granary Books, 2001. Print.

Ward, Geoff. *Statutes of Liberty: The New York School of Poets*. 2nd ed. New York: Palgrave, 2001. Print.

Warsh, Lewis. *Part of My History*. Toronto: Coach House, 1972. Print.

———, and Tom Clark. "Chicago." In Waldman and Warsh 275–77.

Watten, Barrett. "After Radical Particularity: Language Writing and the Untruth of the Whole." Conference Presentation. Université de Bretagne Occidental, Brest, France, May 2011.

———. *The Constructivist Moment: From Material Text to Cultural Poetics*. Middletown, CT: Wesleyan UP, 2003. Print.

———. "First Response: *The Grand Piano*." Web. <www.english.wayne.edu/fac_pages/ewatten/posts/post31.html>. 16 January 2013.

———. "How *The Grand Piano* Is Being Written." Web. <www.english.wayne.edu/fac_pages/ewatten/posts/post34.html>. 16 January 2013.

———. "Language Writing and the Mediation of Modernity." Conference Presentation. Modernist Studies Association, Vanderbilt University, November 2008.

———. "Presentism and Periodization in Language Writing, Conceptual Art, and Conceptual Writing." *Journal of Narrative Theory* 41, no. 1, special issue on *Non/Narrative*, ed. Carla Harryman (Spring 2011): 125–61. Print.

———. "The Secret History of the Equal Sign: *L=A=N=G=U=A=G=E* between Discourse and Text." *Poetics Today* 20.4 (1999): 581–627. Print.

Weeks, Jeffrey, Brian Heaphy and Catherine Donovan. *Same Sex Intimacies: Families of Choice and Other Life Experiments*. London: Routledge, 2001. Print.

Weil, Simone. *Waiting on God*. Trans. Emma Craufurd. New York: Putnam, 1951. Print.

Weishaus, Joel, ed. *On the Mesa: An Anthology of Bolinas Writing*. San Francisco: City Lights, 1971. Print.

Welch, Lew. *I Remain: The Letters of Lew Welch and the Correspondence of His Friends*. Ed. Donald Allen. Bolinas, CA: Grey Fox, 1980. Print.

Weller, Barry. "The Epic as Pastoral: Milton, Marvell, and the Plurality of Genre." *New Literary History* 30.1 (1999): 143–57. Print.

Whalen, Philip. Papers. Reed College. Portland, Oregon.

———. *Scenes of Life at the Capital.* Bolinas, CA: Grey Fox, 1971. Print.

Williams, Bernard. *Truth and Truthfulness: An Essay in Genealogy.* Princeton, NJ: Princeton UP, 2002. Print.

Williams, Jonathan. *Blackbird Dust: Essays, Poems, and Photographs.* New York: Turtle Point Press, 2000. Print.

———. *Blues & Roots / Rue & Bluets: A Garland for the Southern Appalachians.* n.p. Photographs by Nicolas Dean. New York: Grossman Publishers, 1971. Print.

———. *An Ear in Bartram's Tree: Selected Poems, 1957–1967.* New York: New Directions, 1972. Print.

———. Interview with David Annwn. In *Prospect into Breath: Interviews with North and South Writers.* Ed. Peterjon Skelt. Twickenham, Middlesex, and Wakefield, UK: North and South, 1991. 45–58. Print.

———. *Jubilant Thicket: New and Selected Poems.* Port Townsend, WA: Copper Canyon Press, 2005. Print.

———. *The Magpie's Bagpipe: Selected Essays.* San Francisco: North Point Press, 1982. Print.

———. *A Palpable Elysium: Portraits of Genius and Solitude.* Jaffrey, NH: David R. Godine, 2002. Print.

Williams, Raymond. *Marxism and Literature.* Oxford, NY: Oxford UP, 1977. Print.

Willis, Elizabeth. "Possessing Possession: Lorine Niedecker, Folk, and the Allegory of Making." *XCP: Cross-Cultural Poetics* 9 (2001): 97–106. Print.

———, ed. *Radical Vernacular: Lorine Niedecker and the Poetics of Place.* Iowa City: U of Iowa P, 2008. Print.

Women Writers Union. "From Women Writers Union: Statement of Purpose." *L=A=N=G=U=A=G=E* 13 (December 1980). Print.

Yu, Timothy. *Race and the Avant-Garde: Experimental and Asian American Poetry Since 1965.* Stanford, CA: Stanford UP, 2009. Print.

Zukofsky, Louis. *A Test of Poetry.* New York: CZ Publications, 1980. Print.

CONTRIBUTORS

BLACK TOOK COLLECTIVE was cofounded in 1999 by Duriel E. Harris, Dawn Lundy Martin, and Ronaldo V. Wilson at Cave Canem, a retreat for African American Poets. They are a group of Black post-theorists who perform and write in hybrid experimental forms, embracing radical poetics and cutting-edge critical theory about race, gender, and sexuality.

MARIA DAMON teaches poetry and poetics at the University of Minnesota. She is the author of *The Dark End of the Street: Margins in American Vanguard Poetry* and *Postliterary America: From Bagel Shop Jazz to Micropoetries*, and coeditor (with Ira Livingston) of *Poetry and Cultural Studies: A Reader.*

ANDREW EPSTEIN is an associate professor at Florida State University. He is the author of *Beautiful Enemies: Friendship and Postwar American Poetry*, and his essays have recently appeared in *Contemporary Literature*, *Wallace Stevens Journal*, *Jacket 2*, and other journals.

ROSS HAIR is a lecturer in the School of American Studies at the University of East Anglia, UK, and the author of *Ronald Johnson's Modernist Collage Poetry*.

DURIEL E. HARRIS is the author of *Drag*, *Amnesiac: Poems*, and *Speleology*, a collaboration with video artist Scott Rankin. Current projects include the AMNESIAC media art project and "Thingification," a solo play in one act. She is an associate professor of English and teaches creative writing, literature, and poetics at Illinois State University.

DANIEL KANE is reader in English and American literature at the University of Sussex in Brighton, England. His publications include *We Saw the Light: Conversations between the New American Cinema and Poetry* and *All Poets Welcome: The Lower East Side Poetry Scene in the 1960s.*

DAWN LUNDY MARTIN is the author of *Discipline*, *A Gathering of Matter / A Matter of Gathering*, and two chapbooks, *Candy* and *The Mourning Hour.* She is an assistant professor of English at the University of Pittsburgh.

PETER MIDDLETON is the author of *Distant Reading*, as well as other books and essays on poetry and modern literature, and is currently finishing a book on

American poetry and science in the Cold War. His poetry is collected in *Aftermath*. He is a professor of English at the University of Southampton, UK.

LINDA RUSSO is the author of *Mirth*, a book of poems. Her essays on contemporary American poets have appeared in *Don't Ever Get Famous: Essays on New York Writing after the New York School*, in *Jacket* magazine, and as the preface to Joanne Kyger's *About Now: Collected Poems*. She teaches at Washington State University.

LYTLE SHAW is associate professor of English at New York University. His books include *Cable Factory 20*, *Frank O'Hara: The Poetics of Coterie*, and the forthcoming *Fieldworks: From Place to Site in Postwar Poetics*.

ANN VICKERY is a senior lecturer in Literary Studies at Deakin University. She is the author of *Leaving Lines of Gender: A Feminist Genealogy of Language Writing*, *Stressing the Modern: Cultural Politics in Australian Women's Poetry* and coauthor with Maryanne Dever and Sally Newman of *The Intimate Archive: Journeys through Private Papers*. She also coedited *Manifesting Australian Literary Feminisms: Nexus and Faultlines* with Margaret Henderson.

BARRETT WATTEN is coauthor of *The Grand Piano: An Experiment in Collective Autobiography*, author of *The Constructivist Moment: From Material Text to Cultural Poetics*, and coeditor of *Diasporic Avant-Gardes: Experimental Poetics and Cultural Displacement* and *A Guide to Poetics Journal: Writing in the Expanded Field, 1982–1998*. His volumes of poetry include *Frame (1971–1990)*, *Bad History*, and *Progress/Under Erasure*. He teaches at Wayne State University.

RONALDO V. WILSON is the author of *Narrative of the Life of the Brown Boy and the White Man* and *Poems of the Black Object*. Wilson is a visiting assistant professor of poetry, fiction, and literature in the Literature Department of the University of California, Santa Cruz. His latest book is *Farther Traveler: Poetry, Prose, Other*.

INDEX

CONTEMPORARY NORTH AMERICAN POETRY SERIES

Industrial Poetics: Demo Tracks for a Mobile Culture
By Joe Amato

What Are Poets For? An Anthropology of Contemporary Poetry and Poetics
By Gerald L. Bruns

Reading Duncan Reading: Robert Duncan and the Poetics of Derivation
Edited by Stephen Collis and Graham Lyons

Postliterary America: From Bagel Shop Jazz to Micropoetries
By Maria Damon

Among Friends: Engendering the Social Site of Poetry
Edited by Anne Dewey and Libbie Rifkin

Purple Passages: Pound, Eliot, Zukofsky, Olson, Creeley, and the Ends of Patriarchal Poetry
By Rachel Blau DuPlessis

On Mount Vision: Forms of the Sacred in Contemporary American Poetry
By Norman Finkelstein

Form, Power, and Person in Robert Creeley's Life and Work
Edited by Stephen Fredman and Steven McCaffery

Redstart: An Ecological Poetics
By Forrest Gander and John Kinsella

Jorie Graham: Essays on the Poetry
Edited by Thomas Gardner
University of Wisconsin Press, 2005

Gary Snyder and the Pacific Rim: Creating Countercultural Community
By Timothy Gray

Urban Pastoral: Natural Currents in the New York School
By Timothy Gray

Racial Things, Racial Forms: Objecthood in Avant-Garde Asian American Poetry
By Joseph Jonghyun Jeon

We Saw the Light: Conversations between the New American Cinema and Poetry
By Daniel Kane

History, Memory, and the Literary Left: Modern American Poetry, 1935–1968
By John Lowney

Paracritical Hinge:
Essays, Talks, Notes, Interviews
By Nathaniel Mackey
University of Wisconsin Press, 2004

Behind the Lines:
War Resistance Poetry on the American Homefront
By Philip Metres

Hold-Outs:
The Los Angeles Poetry Renaissance, 1948–1992
By Bill Mohr

Frank O'Hara:
The Poetics of Coterie
By Lytle Shaw

Renegade Poetics:
Black Aesthetics and Formal Innovation in African American Poetry
By Evie Shockley

Radical Vernacular:
Lorine Niedecker and the Poetics of Place
Edited by Elizabeth Willis